CW01066520

THE OBLIGATION TO OBEY IN LEGAL THEORY

For my Parents

The Obligation to Obey in Legal Theory

HILAIRE McCOUBREY
Professor in Law and Director of Postgraduate Affairs
University of Hull, Law School

Dartmouth
Aldershot • Brookfield USA • Singapore • Sydney

Published by
Dartmouth Publishing Company Limited
Gower House
Croft Road
Aldershot
Hants GU11 3HR
England

Dartmouth Publishing Company
Old Post Road
Brookfield
Vermont 05036
USA

British Library Cataloguing in Publication Data
McCoubrey, H. (Hilaire), 1953-
  The obligation to obey in legal theory
  1.Obedience (Law) 2.Law - Philosophy
  I.Title
  340.1

Library of Congress Cataloging-in-Publication Data
McCoubrey, H., 1953-
  The obligation to obey in legal theory / Hilaire McCoubrey.
      p.   cm.
  "This book derives from a thesis ... degree of Ph.D. ... 1990 ...
  University of Nottingham"--Acknowledgements.
  Includes bibliographical references and index.
  ISBN 1-85521-825-9
  1. Obedience (Law) I. Title.
  K258.M39 1996
  340'.1--dc20   96-8163
                                                                  CIP

ISBN 1 85521 825 9
Printed in Great Britain by
Antony Rowe Ltd, Chippenham, Wiltshire

Contents

Foreword   *vi*
Acknowledgements   *viii*

1   Obligation as a Key to Jurisprudence   1

2   Positivist Models of Legal Obligation   15

3   Moral Analyses of Obedience to Law   50

4   Obligation in Post-Positivist Theories   92

5   Sceptical Analyses   129

6   Superior Orders and Obligations   161

7   Validity and Obligation   184

8   A Theory of Legal Obligation   201

Select Bibliography   *220*
Index   *225*

Foreword

The obligatory character of law is immediately apparent, no statute or court 'suggests' action in its context of application, but the basis for and even the reality of the 'obligation' imposed by law is the subject of a wide range of seemingly incompatible theoretical appreciations. Claimed bases for legal obligation range from the potential or actual application of coercive force, through varying appreciations of formal authority to undilute moral claims. Such divergences have led to a number of jurisprudential controversies and 'debates', including that between the positivist and naturalist positions. The former arguing broadly for the formal identification of law within a given system and in earlier forms emphasizing the role of coercion, the latter arguing for the application of moral criteria as an important element of the identification of obligation. This is not the only controversy existing in the area but it is both prominent and one of long pedigree. In recent years the unwisdom of seemingly absolute distinctions has been recognized and one of the tendencies of modern legal theory has been to seek a convergence of, *inter alia*, moral and formalist analysis in a new synthesis. Another tendency has been to deny, on a variety of grounds, the very existence of legal obligation, treating it, e.g., as either an artefact of class repression or as a misrepresentation arising from an obfuscatory conventional form of legal discourse.

The broad contention which is advanced in this book is that much of the seeming inconsistency in the theoretical treatment of legal obligation derives from a misperception of conventional linguistic usage. Conventional legal discourse treats 'obligation' as an implicitly quasi-moral and unitary phenomenon. In conformity with the later linguistic philosophy of Wittgenstein, it is here contended that legal obligation must be admitted to involve multiple linguistic usages, including at least three different types of 'obligation' which may be associated with provision of positive law. It is then argued that the proper understanding of the obligation to obey in the context of any given positive legal proposition rests upon the interaction of these factors and not upon criteria relation to any singular definition of such obligation. Thus, a perfectly obligatory (complete) law will carry both formal and moral obligations in favour of compliance and will in appropriate cases potentially be backed by measures of enforcement. In practice most legal provisions will not be so 'complete' and the degree and quality of the obligation which they impose will turn upon the mode and extent of the interaction referred to. There is no convergence between these factors, they are indeed distinctively different one from another in both their nature and effects. It is for this reason that their interaction is of foundational importance in theoretical analysis. Recognition of this would dispose of many conventional 'debates', such as that between naturalism and positivism, since the 'contending' theories are not asking the same questions about the same phenomenon and are, therefore, not offering the same 'answers'.

It is emphatically not the intention behind this book to claim that *all* jurisprudential controversy upon legal obligation can be resolved in the light of an emphasis upon interaction between different 'obligations', still less is it sought to advance some new substantive theory of 'obligation'. The aim is rather to advance of contextual analysis of the obligation(s) to obey which, by showing a number of existing controversies to be founded upon misconceptions, may provide a means whereby a more fruitful analysis of a complex central legal phenomenon may be advanced. The recognition of the complexity of the phenomenon, or rather phenomena, of legal obligation is an important step in this process, which may also lead to a more fruitful development of general jurisprudence.

H. McCoubrey
University of Hull
September 1996

Acknowledgements

This book derives from a thesis submitted for the degree of Ph.D, awarded in 1990, as a staff candidate at the University of Nottingham. The work is in bulk the same, apart from alterations of style and presentation necessary for the conversion of a thesis into a monograph and the taking into account of a number of changes and developments relevant to the subject which have arisen in the intervening period. My thanks are due in particular to Professor D.J. Harris of the Department of Law at the University of Nottingham, who acted as adviser during the preparation of the thesis. Neither he nor anyone else has, however, any responsibility for the arguments which are advanced or the conclusions which are reached herein. These are exclusively the responsibility of the author who now presents this work.

1 Obligation as a Key to Jurisprudence

The science, or art, of jurisprudence in its many aspects may be considered an endeavour to understand the nature, origins, functioning and limitations of the phenomenon of law, whether broadly or narrowly conceived. In whatever way this task is approached, an important consideration will necessarily be the identification of the basic characteristics of the legal enterprise. Amongst the most immediately apparent of these is the essentially non-optional nature of legal provision. Upon the obligatory or 'obliging' appearance of law there is general agreement across the broad spectrum of legal theories, but there is little, if any, consensus upon the nature, or even the 'reality', of the obligation seemingly imposed by legal norms. The starting point was simply stated by H.L.A.Hart in his comment that,

> Where there is law, there human conduct is made in some sense non-optional or obligatory.[1]

The same essential point is made by Karl Olivecrona, thus,

> the word 'law' ... commands respect. ... State Officials ... feel obligated to apply the rules of law ... . When [it] ... become[s] known to the general public, the law will influence their conduct. The new law causes a change in ideas about what one should do and should not do ...[2]

Superficially such statements seem to amount almost to truisms. The whole appearance of positivist legal provision is one of mandatory imperation. Thus, for example, the opening words of an English or Scottish statute, 'Be it enacted by the Queen's Most Excellent Majesty [etc.] ... as follows' is unequivocally the language of imperation and, indeed, of implicit compulsion. Similarly, the judgments rendered by courts are not couched as suggestions but are presented in the form of orders or directions. This seemingly

1

obligatory character of law is, however, much less plain upon closer scrutiny.

The essential difficulty is indicated by the appearance in the quoted statement by H.L.A. Hart of the words 'in some sense'. Both the nature of the 'obligation' to obey law and the means of its attachment are open to widely varying and even *prima* facie incompatible interpretations.   J.W. Harris sets out a basic dilemma in this area as follows,

> For one to be able to affirm that a *prima facie* moral duty to obey English Law exists, one must be satisfied that, whatever comes out of ... English law ..., there are reasons (stateable in advance) why it is morally right to comply [with its demands] ... .[3]

The potential conflict between formal and moral analyses which this statement implies informs a fundamental debate upon the nature of the obligation to obey law.   Harris goes on to identify five commonly encountered claimed bases for a *prima facie* obligation to obey law.   These are (i) that 'law' is by its nature inherently binding, (ii) that gratitude for the benefits conferred by state and country carries with it an obligation to obey, (iii) a duty derived from an implied promise to comply with law founded upon some version of a 'social contract', (iv) a principle of 'fairness', found most clearly in the justice theory advanced by John Rawls, and (v) promotion of the public good, broadly a 'utilitarian' argument reducible ultimately to the proposition that a society with law is preferable to one without and thus that compliance serves the common good.

These arguments and variants upon them are indeed commonly to be found advanced by legal theorists.   Many involve some form of express or implied 'consent' to be bound by laws and this element is summed up by Paul Harris in his remark that,

> [T]he only moral obligations individuals have are those they have taken themselves in some way or another - in other words, ... all moral obligations are voluntarily self-assumed.[4]

It is possible to argue such a position in the context of a liberal political society but the conclusion is by no means unavoidable in consideration of a *prima facie* obligation to obey positive law.   Indeed, it must in fairness be noticed that in relation to this issue Paul Harris himself goes on, very significantly in the present context, to make the additional comment that

[A] general *prima facie* obligation to obey the law can be grounded in a feature of what it is to be a moral person at all, and this provides a basis of a conditional obligation to which all moral persons must be committed.[5]

It is certainly the case that a 'consent' theory presents major difficulties in the context of an obligation to obey law, not least because in the case of most citizens the consent will be highly notional and evidenced more by lack of active dissent than by any overt act of approval. The absence of active consent leads some theorists to deny that there can be any meaningful obligation to obey law or, as for M.B.E. Smith, to argue that any obligation which there may be must be trivial in nature.[6] None the less, legal discourse is replete with the language of 'obligation' at various levels and its practical operation depends to a considerable extent upon the presumption of there being such an obligation. The centrality of apparent or supposed obligation in the operation of law imparts a special importance to the question of its nature or reality as a matter of legal theory. Within the broad spectrum of legal theories the question of the obligation to obey has been approached, directly and indirectly, in a variety of ways. Such diversity of opinion may in itself generate some scepticism as to the reality of the supposed obligation to obey law, although diversity may equally reflect more the context in which given arguments were advanced, a point made admirably by Roger Cotterrell.[7] If scepticism upon this matter is ultimately justified, not only would much legal discourse necessarily be held to be founded upon an illusion, but much of the practical operation of law would seem to be founded upon false premises.

An examination of the use of the language of 'obligation' in practical and theoretical legal discourse reveals in fact a considerable diversity of intention. This may suggest a confusion tending to confirm a sceptical conclusion as to the reality and significance of an obligation to obey, or it may suggest that the apparent 'obligatory' characteristic of law is the product of the interaction of distinct, if often convergent, factors which should not be treated as if it were a unitary phenomenon.

Of the available models of an obligation to obey law, the simplest involves a direct equation between the apparent obligatory character of law and the potential for institutional coercion of those subject to it. This approach is especially associated with the early model of analytical positivism advanced by Jeremy Bentham and John Austin. Indeed, at the root of his theory, Jeremy Bentham himself set out the basic definition of 'law' as being

> an assemblage of signs declarative of a volition [of] the sovereign ... concerning the conduct to be observed ... such volition trusting for its accomplishment to the expectation of certain events ... the prospect of which it is intended should act as a motive upon those whose conduct is in question.[8]

This is conventionally, if rather over-simply, summarized as 'the command of a sovereign backed by a sanction'. The compulsive element in this formula is represented by the 'sanction' embodied in the idea of a motivation for compliance founded upon the expectation of consequences. Bentham, unlike Austin, did concede the possibility that such sanctions might be positive rather than negative in nature in some circumstances. It is also significant that he did not suggest that sanctions represent the only, or even necessarily the most important, motivation for compliance with law. Bentham's concept of 'sovereignty' was founded upon a factual 'habit of obedience', the origin of which was left open and which might clearly involve factors other than potential or actual coercion. Even so, within their defined 'province of jurisprudence', the early positivists treated actual or potential 'sanctions' as the definitive feature of the obligatory character of law.

The vision of law as essentially a *potestas coactiva* has by no means been limited to early positivist theory. Such diverse theorists as St. Augustine of Hippo and the classical Marxists have also, in different ways, treated law as broadly an expression of institutional coercion. In St. Augustine's case law was dismissed, even at its most virtuous, as a coercive restraint upon the perversely and obdurately sinful, without much relevance for those inclined to proper conduct. For the classical Marxist, in contrast, law is an instrument of class domination, especially associated with the 'bourgeois' phase of social development, and is ultimately a means by which the ruling class maintains its position as against subordinate classes.

Despite its consonance with at least some of the observable facts of a legal order, the equation of the obligatory characteristic of positive law with coercive force is ultimately problematic. It is not, of course, a perception unique to classical positivism. It can be argued, as, for example, a classical Marxist might, that any other supposed basis for an obligation to obey law is merely a cloak covering the basic reality of coercive force at the heart of positive law. Somewhat related, but distinct, ideas can also be found amongst critical legal scholars. All this said and without in any way denying the association of law with a potential for coercive imposition, it may also be suggested that law is treated in practice as having a normativity beyond mere compulsion.   The practical conduct of most societies suggests that social reaction to legal provisions may certainly be seen to go beyond the direct effects of anticipated enforcement.   Bentham and Austin themselves implicitly admitted this through their reference to a 'habit of obedience', even whilst excluding the details of its basis and origin from their 'province of jurisprudence'.

The revision of positivist legal theory   undertaken by H.L.A. Hart a century after Austin's work originated in a perception that of the inadequacies of an imperative and coercive model of law.   Hart drew a distinction between the concepts of 'being obliged', i.e. compelled, and being 'under obligation', i.e. recognizing a sense of duty.[9]   According to Hart it is the latter rather than the former which is distinctively associated with positive law.   This is presented as an 'internal' model of law, in contrast with the 'external', sanctions based, model advanced by Bentham and Austin. Hartian obligation then rests upon the assumption made by participants in a legal order of the 'rightness' of its provision.   The key factor in this model is one of recognition.   Once a provision is recognized as meeting the criteria for identification adopted in a society, operating through a union of primary or secondary rules, it will be accepted within system as imposing an obligation in cases to which it is applicable.   It is implied that acceptance of the 'rightness' of law as a critical reflective standard will be an attribute of a political society as a whole, but it is clear that Hart considered the detailed operation of recognition as primarily a matter for officials and lawyers.

This tendency to emphasize the role of the official mind is manifested in a more extreme form in the 'pure theory' advanced by Hans Kelsen[10] in which law is treated as a hierarchy of norms, resting ultimately upon a *grundnorm*, addressed exclusively to officials.   Inevitably, 'obligation' as such plays little or no role in the Kelsenian analysis, being treated as one of the 'impure' elements purged from a model intended as a blueprint for legal systems in general.

The positivist models of legal theory, and most especially that which was advanced by H.L.A. Hart, have an obvious attraction when seen from the viewpoint of the legal practitioner since it largely reflects their experience of the law and its practice.   The practical identification of applicable legal norms and prediction of the operation of formal, intra-systemic, 'obligations' on behalf of their clients comprises much of the work of the legal profession. A similar point may be made in the case of the judiciary.   It can be said that their task is to determine intra-systemic 'obligation' in cases actually reaching the point of litigation.[11] For this reason positivist and neo-positivist thinking has enjoyed a century or so of predominance in Anglo-American law schools.   This has perhaps been most extreme in England, tempered in Scotland by the civilian affinities of the national legal tradition and in the United States both by the implications of the constitutional tradition and the influence of 'Realist' thought.   A generally 'positivistic' outlook and a sometimes extreme emphasis upon intra-systemic analysis remains, however, the staple of Anglo-American legal thought.   There are, however, good reasons to doubt the sufficiency of such analyses.

The self-sufficient concepts of early legal positivism were originally devised by Bentham in reaction against the prevalent and much debased pseudo-naturalist thinking of the late 18th century, as manifested, e.g., in the Introduction to Blackstone's *Commentaries*.   Naturalist theories in their true form are characterized by the inclusion of moral or ethical as well as formal factors in the criteria of legal identification.   Thus, in the 13th century St. Thomas Aquinas defined 'law' as,

> rationis ordinatio ad bonum commune ab eo qui curam communitatis habet, promulgata[12]

meaning, a rational ordinance promulgated for the good of the community by, in effect, a 'sovereign'.[13]   Here there may be seen the formal elements of sovereign enactment and promulgation, but also the additional 'moral' requirements of rationality and intent for the public good.   Upon such a view the 'obligation' imposed by positive law derives at least in part from a moral evaluation of its content and effect, rather than merely from either apprehension of sanctions or formal recognition of intra-systemic 'authority'. The great preponderance of internal naturalist debate has, not surprisingly, been upon the question of the nature and derivation of the moral authority of law.   Bentham and Austin dismissed such argument from the 'province of jurisprudence' upon the basis that the morality of a law does not impinge upon the 'facts' pertinent to its practical identification and application.   In H.L.A. Hart's analysis the idea of 'authority' re-emerges in the positivist canon, but in a narrowly intra-systemic form.   Positivists tend scornfully to dismiss St. Augustine's proposition that 'lex iniusta non est lex',[14]   i.e. an unjust law is no law.   In interpreting this classic and important, but sadly much misunderstood, naturalist statement it has not uncommonly been argued that the seeming contention that 'legal' norms must *ex hypothesi* be 'just' is not only incorrect as a matter of observation but a violation of the basic dichotomy between descriptive and normative, 'is' and 'ought', propositions advanced by David Hume.[15]   The broader contention that the naturalist argument falls foul of the Humean dichotomy has been strongly denied, e.g., by Finnis[16] and this general position will be supported in following chapters.   The attack upon the particular proposition advanced by St. Augustine may also be contended to have been ill-founded.   In an exploration of the moral nature of law to contend that an immoral law fails to meet the criteria under consideration and is therefore in some degree defective is hardly surprising.   It would by no means follow from this, however, that such a purported legal norm could not be recognized and applied by courts and other secular institutions in accordance with 'positivist' criteria of identification.

This leads to a most important consideration which may be set out in the form of a proposition that the questions asked about 'law' by a legal practitioner and a moral philosopher or ethicist may in part overlap but are not essentially the same.   The former is concerned with formal issues relating ultimately to the answers likely to be given to certain questions by a court, whereas the latter is concerned with the moral and/or communitarian nature of law as a social and political phenomenon.   That a morally oriented 'naturalist' theory reaches different conclusions from a formally oriented 'positivist' theory need occasion no great surprise since answers are being given to essentially different questions.   If this is accepted, the two approaches may be seen not necessarily to be in conflict since such a condition could only arise if differing answers were being given to the same or similar questions.   Equally, and obviously, 'positivist' and 'naturalist' approaches are not the only forms of enquiry which may be addressed to the phenomena of law and the obligation to obey.   For other approaches also, the nature of the question being asked is a matter of fundamental significance in assessing the implications of the theory concerned.

In modern jurisprudential thought there has emerged, from a number of points of view, a clear unease with the conventionally accepted emphasis upon positivistic formalism which is found in much legal discourse and analysis.   There are a number of long established traditions which deny the existence of any genuine obligation to obey positive law.   Reference has been made above to the classical Marxist concept of law as no more than an oppressive *potestas coactiva* which is used simply as a mechanism for the maintenance of the interests and domination of a ruling class.   In such theory an obligation to obey is no more than a terminological artifice which serves the end of disguising and sustaining the underlying 'reality' of economic power relationships.   A basic aspect of this analysis is denunciation of 'legal fetishism', meaning the treatment of law as an autonomous phenomenon rather than as an element of the social 'superstructure' built upon an underlying base of economic relations.   This strict Marxist model is open to question on a number of grounds, not least its own 'economic fetishism', and it was substantially modified in the former Soviet Union as it has also been in the People's Republic of China.   The principle of non-autonomy is nonetheless important.   The tendency of conventional western jurisprudence to treat law as if it were an autonomous phenomenon has been one of the least satisfactory products of the positivist ascendancy.   Ultimately derived from the Benthamite and Austinian notion of a limited 'province of jurisprudence', the autonomous model of law has, almost by default, been allowed to imply that all the questions to be asked about law may be addressed within the parameters of the positivist canon.   Neither Bentham nor Austin actually made such a claim but it has, wrongly, been taken as a consequence of their approach.   Denial of the autonomy of law is not a solely Marxist proposition, but the emphasis given to the point is one of the signal services rendered to jurisprudence by the Marxist analysis.

A somewhat similar scepticism may be seen in the much more recently developing 'deconstructive' analyses advanced by the Critical Legal Studies movement.   Here conventional legal discourse, including the language of legal obligation, is treated as a largely obfuscatory technical mode of communication which, again, serves to conceal the real nature of the socio-political agenda being served by legal norms.

The 'scepticism'[17] of the Marxist and Critical approaches may be seen as general in nature.   Rather more specific 'scepticisms' of different significance for the study of the obligation to obey law are found in the American and Scandinavian Realist movements.   The two approaches are 'sceptical' in very different ways.   American Realism is centred largely upon the 'practical' concerns of legal practitioners but in a purportedly more fundamental fashion than are the conventional positivist analyses.   It originated in the proposition of Oliver Wendell Holmes that the starting points of jurisprudential analysis should be the viewpoint of the 'bad man' and the actual behaviour of courts, rather than the conventional focus upon formal legal rules.[18]   In this type of analysis any concepts of an obligation to obey law become of peripheral importance at most. Scandinavian Realism has quite different implications which are more central to substantive argument upon the nature of a perceived obligation to obey law. This school of thought arose in the first place from the work of Axel Hagerstrom at the turn of the 19th and 20th centuries[19] and concentrates upon the psychological 'reality' of legal phenomena. That law operates as a system of ideas to at least as great an extent as it does as one of factual implementation is hardly a controversial proposition, indeed it partly underlies the analysis of H.L.A. Hart. Scandinavian Realism, however, places a much greater emphasis upon the psychological dimension and claims it to be a key to jurisprudence which avoids the pitfall of an 'imperative fallacy' to which most conventional jurisprudence is alleged to be prey. Such a claim on behalf of a particular emphasis of interest seems manifestly excessive, but to discount the extent of the claim is not to deny the genuine significance of the analysis. Once a purely factual model of an obligation to obey has been rejected, as it must surely be, 'obligation' becomes of necessity a matter of ideas. Within this, extremely broad, model the attachment of a sense of normativity to legal concepts upon the psychological level is a matter of obvious significance. This issue is most particularly addressed in the work of Karl Olivecrona.[20] As with other analyses, however, Olivecrona's work cannot usefully be taken out of context. To reduce 'obligation' almost to the level of Pavlovian conditioning ignores the importance of the substance of the ideas themselves and their inter-relationship, the latter being argued to be of fundamental significance.

Quite apart from the development of the various theoretical approaches which might be labelled 'sceptical' there has developed over the course of the second half of the 20th century a more general unease with many aspects of the conventional positivist analyses. This unease originated in part from the revelation in 1945 of the full extent of the abuse of legal formalism in the Third Reich, in the context of which a number of problems arose in relation to the extent and nature of the obligation to obey law both immdiately and in the post-war period.[21] The central problem for the present purpose is that of the extent to which a self-sufficient 'professional' analysis rests upon implicit, but possibly false, assumptions, *inter alia*, about the quality of the obligations undertaken or imposed. The Third Reich presented an example of this problem.[22] This is not a blanket explanation for modern trends in the theory of legal obligation, it may, however, be symptomatic of the essential character of the basic concerns underpinning some of these trends.

An early post-war manifestation of such concern may be seen in the 'procedural natural law' advanced by Lon L. Fuller.[23]   Although proceeding beyond the remit of strict 'positivism' it may be questioned whether Fuller's work should strictly be termed 'naturalist', being, perhaps, more an important contribution to neo-positivist thought.[24]   The conventional positivist model of law has also been fundamentally questioned in the work of R.M. Dworkin.[25]   His 'Rights Thesis' denies the 'rules' model of law and admits morally principled adjudication in 'hard cases' which does not require naked 'judicial legislation' of the type anathematized by Bentham.   Again, however, the moral and other 'standards' introduced by Dworkin seem largely to refer to the formalized intra-systemic morality of the legal order itself.   In addition to these developments there has also been a marked modern revival in mainstream 'naturalist' thinking, in which the work of J.M. Finnis, deriving to a significant extent from a Thomist base, is prominent.[26]

Such a brief survey of legal theories impinging upon the issue of the obligation to obey law indicates the widely diverse opinions which have been advanced upon the subject.   The appearance of seemingly conflicting theoretical perceptions leads to the assumption, commonplace in the general development of legal theory, that some or all of these theories must, at best, be misdirected if not, indeed, simply erroneous.   A satisfactory modern theoretical analysis of the obligation to obey law must clearly either resolve the apparent inconsistencies found in existing theory or dismiss large parts of the present body of opinion as untenable.   In the present argument the former approach is in large part preferred over the latter.

It is a principal contention of the discussion which follows that the apparent conflict between naturalist, positivist, realist, critical and other perceptions in this area is very largely an illusion founded upon a false assumption that the obligation to obey law is a unitary phenomenon susceptible to a single 'correct' analysis.   The genesis of such an illusion in the context of conventional legal discourse is easy to comprehend.   The causes of this misdirection of argument and debate include conventional assumptions and methodological errors found in much past and current theorising.   The primary concern of legal scholarship with questions of obligation is inevitably focused upon formal intra-systemic obligations, which is to say those which are generated within and recognized by the institutions of an established legal order.   These are, quite properly, the central concerns in this area of the practising legal profession.   It is hardly surprising in this context that there should be a voluminous literature upon obligations generated in such formal categories as contract, tort, succession and so on, which is founded upon the assumption of the 'authority', in a Hartian sense, of positive legal provision.   To this, in principle, little exception may reasonably be taken.   As a matter of practical concern the intra-systemic obligations formally arising at law are self-evidently of great importance.   Misdirection creeps in only when this formalist or 'professional' level of discussion is taken to be the necessarily dominant or even the only valid form of analysis.   In essence this is a form of the erroneous perception of law as an autonomous phenomenon or, as a Marxist would put it, of 'legal fetishism'.   Law may be taken by the legal practitioner as a 'given' proposition capable of analysis within the closed world of its own terms, but it must always be remembered that this is a specialized and limited viewpoint which may be convenient for its own particular purposes but which is not ultimately either complete or adequate.

Law cannot, in its generation, interpretation or application truly be divorced from its social context.   On the contrary, from the political and social   influences upon the legislative process to the exercise of judicial discretions in the determination of cases, law is a structure of formalized norms related to the society in which it operates not through any simple or singular linkage but through a complex and varied web of relationships.   Its obligatory characteristic is clearly an important aspect of the face presented by positive law to the society in which it operates and it seems reasonable to suggest that this is not a unitary phenomenon, but as much the product of a complex interaction of factors as the general relation of law to society.   Such a view concords with modern linguistic philosophy.   The later linguistic philosophy of Wittgenstein emphasizes the usage of terms in a 'games' model of language, in contrast with his earlier model of logical atomism which emphasized the individual 'meaning' of terms.[27]   Applying this approach to a term such as 'obligation' in its legal context(s), it becomes clear that a number of 'meanings' may be associated with it according to the context of usage and that the term may be considered a 'bracket' for a diverse group of phenomena.   If this is the case, it becomes possible at once both to resolve many of the apparent conflicts in the theoretical appreciations of an obligation to obey law and to set out a framework for the development of a modern theory of legal obligations purged from false conflict.   It will be argued that there is no single 'obligation to obey' provisions of positive law. It will be suggested, instead, that such a perceived obligation to comply with legal prescription is, in reality, ultimately the product of an uneasy interaction between at least three different factors.   Of these, the formalist intra-systemic concept of legal obligation is merely the most superficially apparent as a consequence of its inevitable predominance in the established forms of conventional legal discourse.   The very use of a normative terminology in this context, however, betrays an origin in analogy with a much broader sense of 'obligation'.   The 'internal' assumption of the 'rightness' of positive law as a critical reflective standard emphasized by H.L.A. Hart and which underlies much technical legal discourse cannot ultimately be treated as a self-sustaining phenomenon.   The 'internal' assumption of legal rectitude is open to critical appraisal by reference to the moral-purposive nature of the legal enterprise and, in certain extreme cases, it may be concluded that these assumptions were founded upon false premises.   Such a conclusion would not fall foul of the Humean dichotomy between descriptive and normative propositions.   A law may be formally correct but defective in its moral quality and here there will arise not a question of the existence or otherwise of some absolute 'obligation to obey' but, rather, one as to which of several obligatory factors will predominate in the given situation.   It is also the case, as Bentham and Austin correctly observed, that legal provision is commonly associated with the potential for coercion and this too is a factor to be weighed in the balance.

Many divergences in the theoretical treatment of an obligation to obey positive law may be argued to represent differences in focus of concern rather than dispute upon the nature of a single phenomenon.   It cannot, however, be argued that all conflict between theoretical appreciations can be rendered illusory.   There is much scope for genuine dispute where divergent views are actually being advanced in relation to the same phenomenon.   In the light of all these considerations the need in modern theory is not for any new concept of the obligation to obey as such, there being already an embarrassing plenitude of such theories.   The need is much more for an analytical context in which the relationships and interaction of the distinct factors which jointly constitute the totality of the apparent obligatory characteristic of law may usefully be examined.

The argument in the following chapters will be devoted primarily to the pursuit of that end.   The appropriate methodology readily suggests itself. The principal categories of relevant theory will be examined and placed in an appropriate use context.   Examination of these various usage-contexts will then provide the foundation for the establishment of an adequate theoretical framework for analysis of the relationship which exists between the factors contributing to the apparent obligatory characteristic of positive law. From this there may be derived an understanding of the nature of the obligation(s) to obey law and their limitations.

Beyond this a much greater claim may be advanced. The value of brief 'definitions' of 'law' may very properly be questioned in view of the complexity of the subject matter. Nonetheless, the attachment of normativity to certain patterns of conduct, or, in H.L.A. Hart's phrase, the rendering of conduct 'in some sense non-optional or obligatory'[28] is of central importance in the working of positive law and, thus, in its understanding. A modern theoretical understanding of the obligatory characteristic of positive law would clearly not 'define' law, still less a 'province of jurisprudence,. It might, however, fairly be represented as a significant aspect of a viable model of law and, thus, at least a key, if not indeed the key, to many of the most important and intractable problems of jurisprudence.

Notes

1   H.L.A. Hart, *The Concept of Law*, 2 ed., with postscript ed. by P.A. Bulloch and J. Raz (Clarendon, Oxford, 1994), p.82.
2   K. Olivecrona, *Law as Fact*, 2 ed. (Stevens, 1971), p.89.
3   J.W. Harris, *Legal Philosophies* (Butterworths, 1980) p.210.
4   P. Harris, 'The Moral Obligation to Obey the Law' in Harris, ed., *On Political Obligation* (Routledge, 1990), p.151 at p.153.
5   Ibid., at p.160.
6   M.B.E. Smith, 'Is there a *prima facie* Obligation to Obey the Law?' (1973) 82 *Yale Law Journal*, p.950.
7   R. Cotterrell, *The Politics of Jurisprudence - A Critical Introduction to Legal Philosophy* (Butterworths, 1989), passim.
8   J. Bentham, *Of Laws in General* (1782), ed., H.L.A. Hart (University of London, Athlone Press, 1970), p.1.
9   See H.L.A. Hart, op.cit., Chapter V.
10 See H. Kelsen, *General Theory of Law and State*, trans. Anders Wedberg (Cambridge, 1949).
11 The civil example is given, but criminal cases may also be seen as a determination of obligations, specifically of breaches of obligation, as between an individual and the state.
12 St. Thomas Aquinas, *Summa Theologica*, 1a2ae. 90,4.
13 The Thomist concept was framed in wider terms than those of political sovereignty and included the Laws of God which Austin also termed

'laws properly so called'.   The narrower concept of political sovereignty is to be found as a focus of Aquinas' attention e.g. in *De Regimins Principum*.

14   St. Augustine of Hippo, *De Libero Arbitrio*, I.V,33.

15   D. Hume, *A Treatise of Human Nature* (1740), Bk.III, Ch.1, para.36.

16   See J. Finnis, *Natural Law and Natural Rights* (Clarendon, Oxford, 1980), pp.33-48.

17   For justification of the use of this term see Chapter 5.

18   See O.W. Holmes, 'The Path of the Law' (1897) 10 *Harvard Law Review*, 457.

19   See A. Hagerstrom, *Inquiries into the Nature of Law and Morals*, ed. K. Olivecrona, trans., C.D. Broad (Almqvist and Wiksel, 1953).

20   See K. Olivecrona, op.cit.

21   See Chapter 7.

22   Ibid.

23   See Lon L. Fuller, *The Morality of Law*, revised edn.   (Yale, 1964).

24   For discussion see Chapter 4.

25   See, in particular, R.M. Dworkin, *Taking Rights Seriously* (Duckworth, 1977).

26   See J. Finnis, op.cit.

27   A discussion of the development of this theory will be found in A. Kenny, *Wittgenstein* (Allen Lane, Penguin, 1973).

28   See note 1.

2 Positivist Models of Legal Obligation

Analytical positivism has for much of the past one hundred and fifty years been the dominant analysis in conventional Anglo-American jurisprudence. Its attraction, certainly for the legal practitioner, seems to lie in its apparently 'common sense' observation of the 'fact' of law. The essentially social realist methodology of positivist legal thought is founded upon an attempt to analyse law upon a basis of objective 'scientific' observation freed from *a priori* assumptions and value judgments.

The non-optional character of legal provisions is basic to positivist legal theory. The leading modern positivist, H.L.A. Hart, put the point clearly in his statement that,

> where there is law, ... human conduct is made in some sense non-optional or obligatory.[1]

The 'sense' in which this is the case has, however, been variously interpreted within the positivist tradition.

The Command Theory: Bentham and Austin

The objective of the founders of the School, Jeremy Bentham (1748-1832) and John Austin (1790-1859), was to advance a 'scientific' jurisprudence freed from the subjective quasi-naturalism which infected the conventional jurisprudence of their day. Bentham's argument was in part inspired by the confusion which he found in Blackstone's uncritical account of the British constitution in the Introduction to his *Commentaries*, with its random appeals to 'natural rights' in support of particular provisions and practices.[2] His theory was not, however, founded only upon academic inspirations. It was also informed by a very strong political motivation. Bentham felt a powerful

15

revulsion from the violence of the French Revolution, which he saw as having ideological roots in the ideas of 'natural rights' advanced by, amongst others, Rousseau, imparted a vitriolic quality to much of his anti-naturalist rhetoric which did not, in retrospect, necessarily well serve his cause. He objected as a result to any idea that there might be 'rights' external to positive law which could transcend the formal claims generated by and within an established legal order. The nature of his objection is made manifest in his statement that,

> the natural tendency of [naturalist] ... doctrine is to impel a man, by the force of conscience, to rise up in arms against any law whatever that he happens not to like.[3]

H.L.A. Hart analysed this as an objection to the 'criterionless' nature of claims to 'natural rights', commenting that,

> The criterionless character of alleged natural rights means that appeals to them in political argument must either result in unsettleable controversy or ... will create a gap which men are ... prone to fill by identifying as natural rights whatever 'political caprice' they have to gratify ... .[4]

Bentham himself remarked also that,

> Rights are the fruit of the law alone; there are no rights without law - no rights contrary to law - no rights anterior to law.[5]

It can be argued that Bentham's perception of the natural tendency of naturalist thought was to a large extent erroneous,[6] but the consequence for his theory was in any event an attempt to explain compliance with positive law without reference to morality or to any other evaluative criteria.

Notwithstanding his iconoclastic rhetoric, Bentham's legal theory was not actually a clean break from earlier traditions. It may reasonably be argued to represent the culmination of a process of secularization which had commenced with the fading of the medieval 'world' view represented by writers such as St. Thomas Aquinas. The course of this process can be seen in the social contractarian theories which were advanced in the 17th and 18th centuries. They traced the obligation to obey positive law to a hypothetical 'social contract' involving surrender of anarchic and/or insecure 'natural rights' to one or another form of political authority, rather than to any inherent moral claim possessed by governments. Bentham's immediate inspiration did not, however, come directly from that tradition but from the secular philosophy of David Hume. In particular it came from Hume's celebrated dictum that,

> nothing can be more unphilosophical than those systems which assert that, virtue is the same with what is natural, and vice with what is unnatural. ...[T]he character of natural and unnatural can ... [never], in any sense, mark the boundaries of vice and virtue.[7]

From this was derived a basic distinction between descriptive and normative, 'is' and 'ought', propositions. Bentham carried this distinction into jurisprudence by dividing the subject matter into two quite distinct areas which he termed 'expositorial' and 'censorial'. He explained the division in the following terms,

> To the province of the Expositor it belongs to explain to us what .... the law is: to that of the Censor, to observe to us what he thinks it ought to be. The former, therefore, is principally occupied in stating, or in inquiring after facts: the latter in discussing reasons.[8]

Bentham's debt to Hume extended far beyond the basic distinction between expositorial and censorial jurisprudence. Hume, like Bentham, rejected the idea of 'natural' virtues and rights and, therefore, sought to set up in their place a criterion of *usefulness* as a basis for the assessment of the quality of actions or provisions. This has clear links with the *utilitarian* censorial jurisprudence advanced by Bentham and also relates directly to his concept of the 'obligation' to obey law. Hume analysed obedience to government precisely in terms of usefulness. J. Harrison succinctly sums up his position.

> our natural obligation to obey government arises directly from the fact that government is to man's interest, this obligation ceases when it is not.[9]

Hume thus denied that governments have any inherent claim to be obeyed, whether founded upon a promissory 'contractual' basis or upon any other basis. Despite this, it may be considered unlikely that social contractarians such as Thomas Hobbes or John Locke would have taken any strong exception to Harrtson's formulation of Hume's position. Social contractarian theorists founded their basic promissory model of government precisely upon a pragmatic end of 'security' in one or another form and in most, although not quite all, of their theories a duty to obey would be terminated in case of failure to meet that end. This, for example. was the rationale advanced in favour of the English 'Glorious Revolution' of 1688-1689 which toppled James II in favour of William III and Mary II. Stripped of its social contractarian rhetoric this does not seem very far removed from Hume's criterion of 'usefulness'. Bentham was, however, distanced from Hume in so far as he excluded consideration of the fundamental reasons for obedience from both his expository and censorial jurisprudence, concentrating instead upon the proximate causes of obedience.

For the avoidance of superfluous recitation it may be said in brief that Bentham advanced a *Command* model of law in which the primary concepts were those of sovereign imperation and associated sanctions. Bentham's concept of sovereignty did not involve any 'right' to rule but merely observation of the fact of obedience. Thus, he advanced a definition of a sovereign as

> any person or assemblage of persons to whose will a whole political community are (no matter on what account) supposed to be in a disposition to pay obedience: and in preference to the will of any other persons.[10]

Austin considered that to this there should be added a 'negative' mark of sovereignty, that the sovereign should not be in a habit of obedience to any other person or body.[11] In the light of Bentham's arguments upon limitations of sovereignty[12] this addition may be thought to have been unnecessary. Bentham himself went on to define a 'law' as,

> an assemblage of signs declarative of a volition conceived or adopted by the sovereign in a State, concerning the conduct to be observed in a certain case by a certain person or class of persons, who ... are or are supposed to be subject to his power: such volition trusting for its accomplishment to the expectation of certain events which it is intended such declaration should upon occasion be a means of bringing to pass, and the prospect of which it is intended should act as a motive upon those whose conduct is in question.[13]

This was not advanced as a model of any particular positive legal provision, but, rather, as a conceptual 'complete law' the elements of which might be found scattered amongst a number of formal provisions, with indeed several common elements amongst them. In this formulation the element of sovereign command is represented as a political fact, the incentive to compliance is then found in the attached 'volition'.

Bentham expressed this division in terms of a *Directive Part*, defined as an expression of will as to conduct, stated to be the *Principal Law*, and a *Prediction* threatening or promising the consequences which are held to motivate compliance.   The Prediction is then divided into two types of 'subsidiary laws', the *Proximate Subsidiary Law*, prescribing the penalty or reward which is the 'sanction', and *Remote Subsidiary Laws*, providing for the procedures necessary for the implementation of the 'complete law'. These latter in particular afford an example of elements which may be common to many principal laws and perhaps, as in the case of provisions for the maintenance of courts of law, to all of them.   The anatomy of a Benthamite 'complete law' may then be set out as follows:

The Direction		The Prediction
The Principal Law expressing sovereign will as to conduct	+	Proximate Subsidiary Law setting out the sanction
		Remote Subsidiary Laws providing for Processes of Implementation

Of these elements, it is the proximate subsidiary law which supplies the cause of obedience.   The essence of the idea is the attachment to a sovereign volition of a simple causal motivation to compliance in the form of anticipation of defined consequences flowing from disobedience, or in some cases from obedience.   This was founded upon the same simple assumption which underlay Bentham's utilitarianism.   That is to say,

> Nature has placed mankind under the governance of two sovereign masters, pain and pleasure.[14]

Bentham's explanation for compliance with law was founded upon the simple aversion of human beings from pain and their attraction to gain or pleasure.

In Bentham's usage 'pain' and 'pleasure' may be taken as near-synonymous with detriment and benefit, although the cruder implications of physical discomfort and enjoyment clearly come within the scheme.   The 'sanctions' through which these twin motivations were said to be applied were divided by Bentham into four categories,

> the physical, the political, the moral and the religious: and inasmuch as the pleasures and pains belonging to each of them are capable of giving a binding force to any law or rule of conduct, they may all of them be termed 'sanctions'.[15]

This is on first sight a somewhat startling statement, importing as it appears to, the very moral and ethical elements which Bentham was at such pains to exclude from his expositorial jurisprudence.   However, neither Bentham nor Austin sought to deny that law may be affected by matters falling outside the limits of their jurisprudence and, quite clearly, moral considerations might well serve as a motivation to compliance with law.   To that extent, therefore, such factors might be considered 'sanctions' but, in Bentham's analysis, they could never be considered to be definitive of it in distinction from any other kind of normative structure.   For the purposes of his expositorial jurisprudence Bentham was primarily concerned with the 'political' sanctions.   The physical sanction, in the sense of a simple use of force, may arise in conjunction with any of the other three.   Bentham assigned the moral and religious sanctions to a category of 'auxiliary sanctions', by which he meant that they might impinge upon the functioning of law but could not form any part of its basic nature.   The 'political' sanction, in contrast, is so termed because it is applied by or through sovereign agency and is deliberately attached to statements of sovereign volition as a means of securing compliance therewith.

Understood in these terms, the motivation for compliance with positive law becomes simply,

> the expectation of so many lots of pain and pleasure, as connected in a particular manner in the way of causality with the actions with reference to which they are termed motives ... in the shape of pleasure ... they may be termed alluring motives: ... in the shape of pain coercive.[16]

The most significant term in Bentham's analysis upon this point is 'causality'.   Thus the motivation for compliance with positive law in this model rests not upon any idea of 'right' on the part of the legislator or of 'duty' on the part of the subject, but in a simple causal connection between action and anticipated consequence.

This is, however, a more subtle analysis of sanctions than that later advanced by Austin, in particular because it is prepared to admit sanctions which are other than coercive or penal. Austin was not prepared to make such a concession but tried to force all motivational 'sanctions' into a coercive mould. Thus, he thought it necessary to explain compliance with such essentially facilitative provisions as the Wills Act 1837 by reference to a 'sanction of nullity', meaning that compliance is secured through fear of failure to attain a desired objective which is, in some sense, apprehension of a 'penalty'. Bentham clearly regarded the negative or penal sanction as the typical case but was prepared to recognize an 'alluring' or promissory 'sanction' holding out attainment of a desired objective as the reward for compliance. Laws supported only by 'alluring' sanctions in this way were termed by Bentham *praemiary* in nature. This analysis is not necessarily perfect but it may be argued at least better to match the actual operation of provisions such as the Wills Act 1837 than the stricter logic of 'sanctions' insisted upon by Austin. Bentham's account is, however, none the less subject to clear limitations, most of which can be argued to result directly from the parameters which he himself set to his jurisprudence.

Bentham treated the idea of an obligation to obey law in principle as a fiction and, in parallel with his general approach to legal theory, sought to account for compliance with law in terms limited to apparent social fact. He therefore considered that to say that a person is under an 'obligation' in respect of his or her conduct is to say no more than that in the event of failure to observe the prescribed conduct in the given situation 'pain' (or loss of 'pleasure') may be anticipated. Specifically 'legal' obligation is then distinguished from other forms only by the fact that the anticipated consequence of inappropriate behaviour will arise from action by agents of the sovereign. Thus, as H.L.A. Hart remarks,

> The central element ... is a starkly simple idea: it is nothing but the likelihood of suffering in the event of doing or failing to do an action. What differentiates legal obligation from other forms is that the sanction or suffering which is relevant is suffering at the hands of officials chosen to administer it according to law.[17]

This comment, upon Bentham rather than Austin, underemphasizes the possibility of positive or promissory 'sanctions' but is otherwise a succinct statement of the early positivist analysis of the nature of legal obligation. Hart argues[18] that Bentham's theory of obligation is in fact 'mixed', containing both an imperative and a probabilistic element, both action by sovereign agency and anticipation of such action.   Both of these elements and their combination in this manner are open to question.

Defects of the Command Theory

H.L.A. Hart points out in *The Concept of Law* that to force or coerce someone into acting in a given way, or even to induce action through a promise of reward, is by no means the same as placing that person under an 'obligation' to act in that way.   When a person is said to be placed 'under an obligation' to do something it is implied that he or she would in some sense act 'wrongly' in doing otherwise.   No such implication is carried by forcing a course of conduct upon someone, indeed not uncommonly the coercion may have been applied to compel action perceived by the actor as 'wrong'.   In his own development of positivist theory Hart sought to distinguish between compulsion and obligation to act as between categories of 'being obliged' and being 'under obligation'.   The adequacy of this distinction may be open to some question but it is one which Bentham and Austin hardly made at all.   In his endeavour to reduce the functioning of law to 'scientifically' observable social fact Bentham was driven to an analysis of obligation which, at whatever apparent remove, is ultimately reliant upon the related facts of power and obedience.   Amongst the consequences of this is the inability of the theory to take account of a feeling of 'obligation' as a factor in securing compliance with law.   This is not in itself very remarkable since the consideration of normativity inevitably raises moral and ethical issues which Bentham was expressly concerned to exclude form his consideration of law. Endeavours by later positivists, such as H.L.A. Hart, to produce a better differentiated theory of obligation have also encountered difficulties partly because the limitations imposed by the positivist approach preclude a fully adequate discussion of the wider argument. Even if the undifferentiated imperative aspect of concept of obligation which Bentham sets out in his positivist model and, indeed, even the general form of his theory of sovereignty could be accepted, there remains the probabilistic element of his theory. If it is in fact unlikely that a wrongdoer will suffer in consequence of his or her non-compliance with law, does it then follow that the 'obligation' in question is thereby weakened or even vitiated? This would be a curious conclusion, since it would entail the bizarre consequence that the more ingenious an offender might be in evading the law, the less would be his or her obligation to obey it. It is true that a law which is widely ignored will lose credibility and may ultimately fall into practical, if not, in English theory, into technical, desuetude. This fits perfectly into the framework of Bentham's theory of sovereignty as a diminution and eventual vitiation of the habit of obedience, but it does not relate directly to the issue of the obligation to obey an extant and functioning law. Hart is markedly critical of this aspect of Bentham's theory, remarking that,

> the relevant connection between disobedience and punitive sanctions is not the likelihood of the latter, given the former, but that the courts should recognise disobedience as a reason according to law for its punishment.[19]

Hart argues that the probabilistic element in ideas of obligation relates not to the meaning of the concept but to the 'force' of statements made about it.[20] He gives as a parallel the statement that 'there is a bull in the field', which may be a simple answer to a question or a warning depending upon the 'force' of the utterance.[21] Hart concedes, however, that Bentham's position might be defended upon the basis that his definition does not conform with the common usage of 'obligation', connoting in some sense an idea of 'oughtness', but was used in a technical utilitarian context focusing attention upon the social fact.

It has been argued by P.M.S. Hacker[22] that as well as the 'mixed, imperative/probabilistic' theory, hints of other forms of obligation theory can be found in Bentham's work. H.L.A. Hart was dismissive of this claim, and argued that Hacker's examples must be considered, at most, to be special cases of limited application. Whether or not this is view is accepted, the mixed imperative/probabilistic theory does appear to represent Bentham's primary concept of obligation. It must ultimately be conceded that it is difficult to maintain a theory which is founded upon the premise that ideas of power and probability of consequence jointly form an adequate basis for a concept of the obligation to obey positive law. It may in this regard be argued in particular that the association of these factors is not able to provide a full explanation of the apparent normativity of legal provisions. This is not a phenomenon capable of the direct observation which Bentham sought but it clearly plays a part in the reaction of those subject to laws. Whether such normativity is a moral phenomenon as Naturalists would argue[23] or, in one way or another, a manipulative artefact as Marxist, Realist and deconstructive Critical theorists would suggest,[24] it is in its way a 'fact', even if one of which Benthamite positivism is inherently incapable of taking account.

The Self-Limitation of Classical Positivism

At this point it becomes important to recognize the self-set limitations of analytical positivism. Both Bentham and Austin excluded moral and ethical factors from their criteria of legal identification and thus also from their analysis of motivations to compliance with law. Thus, a person might obey law for reasons of moral sympathy with its content but might also for the same reason comply with the dictates of religion, rendering such a motivation not *uniquely* identificatory of law. In Bentham's analysis the political sanction is especially attached to legal demands and is therefore an identifying characteristic of specifically 'legal' obligation. Viewed in terms of the later linguistic philosophy of Wittgenstein, emphasizing usage rather than essential 'meaning', the nature of Bentham and Austin's enterprise becomes both clearer and more readily capable of acceptance. In fact Bentham's argument was not really addressed to the nature of 'obligation' in any normally recognizable sense. His focus was specifically upon motivation to compliance in a narrow context not unrelated to Oliver W. Holmes' emphasis upon the attitude of the 'bad man' in legal analysis.[25] The defects of this view, in terms of undifferentiated imperation and the probabilistic factor, as well as more general moral and ethical argument, become manifest only when the discussion of formal impulsion to compliance is sought to be expanded into wider debate upon 'obligation'. It may be noted that Austin included the Will of God as the first amongst his category of 'laws properly so called',[26] even whilst he effectively excluded it from his limited 'province of jurisprudence'. This seems to recognize the existence of a variety of factors relating to 'law' to be found outside the very narrowly defined 'province of jurisprudence' which Austin addressed.

Indeed, Bentham's own 'expositorial' analysis was intended only as a preliminary work of definition in preparation for a 'censorial' analysis defining a 'scientific' basis for 'good' law making. Unfortunately neither Bentham nor Austin appear to have given very satisfactory answers to the wider problems of 'obligation' once they ventured beyond the narrow context of their sanctions-based model of motivation for compliance - whatever the value of that model within its original and proper setting.

The Relevance of the Principle of Utility

Bentham's 'censorial' jurisprudence was founded upon the principle of utility, of which he stated that,

> An action ... may be said to be conformable to the principle of utility ... when the tendency it has to augment the happiness of the community is greater than any which it has to diminish [it].[27]

This is commonly represented as a principle of 'the greatest happiness of the greatest number', although Bentham himself disapproved of this as an over-simplification.[28] Since most actions contain elements of both pain and pleasure, the practical operation of the principle clearly requires some mechanism for the determination of the balance as between 'pain' and 'pleasure' in the tendency of any given action. Bentham sought to provide such a mechanism in the felicific calculus.

Bentham was inevitably, in social realist context of his theory, concerned with the material consequences of actions and he tried to assess these upon an almost mathematical basis. He was centrally concerned with acts which are 'mischievous' in tendency, categorizing such 'mischief' as either primary or secondary in character.[29] He gave robbery as an example.[30] The primary mischief is obvious. The secondary mischief takes two forms. First the fear of others that they might also be robbed and second the effect of a successful robbery in reducing the deterrent fear of capture upon other potential robbers. Both the primary and the secondary mischiefs which may be attendant upon an action must then be weighed in the balance against all the benefits which to be gained in order to calculate its overall tendency.

If such a calculus is accepted its implications are obvious.   In a case where the sum of the mischief outweighs the sum of benefit the action is held, upon the felicific calculus,   to be rightly penalized.   It is here that a significant paradox arises.   In Bentham's analysis compliance with rules made for the aversion of mischief is to be secured through the actual or threatened application of, primarily negative, sanctions.   Punishment itself is, however, when viewed in isolation, plainly itself a 'mischief' which must therefore be accounted a negative factor in the felicific calculus.   The evil of punishment is then tolerable only when it is balanced by a countervailing benefit.   Bentham admitted this as a difficulty, commenting that,

> all punishment in itself is evil.   Upon the principle of utility, if it ought at all to be admitted, it ought only to be admitted in so far as it promises to exclude some greater evil.[31]

The 'greater evil' concerned was conceived as any significant detriment to the community.   Bentham, however, considered the community itself to be a fictional designation for the mass of individuals comprising it and thus capable of being injured only through injury to some or all of its individual members.   Thus he stated that,

> If the whole assemblage of any number of individuals be considered as constituting an imaginary compound body, ... any act that is detrimental to any one or more of those members is, as to so much of its effects, detrimental to the state.[32]

The community is thus argued to act rightly in punishing actions which are detrimental to the interests of all or any of its members.   The application of motivations to compliance rests then upon conclusions derived from the application of the felicific calculus.   This model can, however, only be considered to be an extremely mechanistic framework of reference.   It attempts to reduce the analysis of highly complex social interactions to a precisely calculated formula, but in so doing it excludes a great many factors which are in practice relevant to the assessment of 'sanctions' and the question of compliance more generally.   The end result is a theoretical appreciation which purports to proceed upon a basis of 'scientifically' observed 'fact' but which actually excludes much of practical significance in the actual operation of law.   The consequences of this basic defect become very obvious in some of the applications of the theory.

Constitutional Limits upon Obligation in Classical Positivism

The defects of over-simplification in the classical positivist analysis can be seen very plainly in its treatment of limitations placed upon the capacity of a sovereign to 'command'. Bentham did not seek to deny the obvious point that a political sovereign may be subject to a variety of political, ethical or moral constraints in his, her or its exercise of power. He felt it necessary, however, to exclude such matters from his formal expository analysis. He did, nonetheless, include within its ambit the apparent formal limitations which may be set upon sovereign action.

Bentham and Austin differed in their views of formal limitations upon sovereign power. Bentham considered them to be anomalous and undesirable but still potentially within his sphere of jurisprudence. Austin, in contrast, relegated such constraints, along with public international law, to an extra-jurisprudential realm of 'positive morality'. H.L.A. Hart remarked that,

> Bentham ... [held] that to fetter the supreme legislator by laws limiting its competence was never wise ... . But legal limitations on a supreme legislature were not for Bentham, as they were for Austin, inconceivable.[33]

The principal difficulty posed by the concept of a legally limited sovereign in a command theory of law lies in the notion that a sovereign might successfully 'command' its own future action or that of its successors. Austin expressed the point clearly, thus,

> in spite of the laws which sovereigns have imposed on themselves, or [their] ... successors ..., the position that sovereign power is incapable of legal limitation will hold universally or without exception.
>
> As it regards the successors to the sovereign ... a law of this kind amounts, at the most to a rule of positive morality. As ... regards its immediate author, it is merely a law by metaphor. ... [W]e cannot speak of a law set by a man to himself, though a man may adopt a principle and ... observe it. ... [Such laws] are merely principles or maxims ... [adopted] as guides or ... [commanded] as guides to ... successors in sovereign power. [34]

Even so, Bentham admitted two principal forms of limitation upon the exercise of supreme legislative power, one by reference to a limited disposition of subjects to obedience and the second by reference to a species of 'transcendent' law in the form of a self-denying ordinance on the part of the sovereign.

The development of these ideas seems somewhat confused, which is perhaps indicative of the difficulty experienced in forcing the concept of limited sovereignty into the mould of command theory. Bentham appears to have believed that sovereignty as such could only be limited by what he termed an 'express convention'[35] embodying an agreement that legislative power should in some sense be limited. One case would be the submission upon terms of one government to another or the joining of several states together in a federal union. Bentham appears to have been willing to concede some juridical status to such express conventions and even the possibility of judicial review of legislative action upon this basis.[36] He did not, however, permit the possible juridical status of such limiting agreements to cloud the concept of 'sovereignty' as a social fact rather than a matter of 'rights'. He treated such express conventions, therefore, not as limitations in their own right but rather as curtailments of the disposition to obedience. As Hart commented,

> The express convention ... seems to be important in Bentham's view only as a signal showing the extent of the subjects' disposition to obey; [37]

In addition to such inter-state conventions, Bentham was also willing to concede in principle the possibility of a limitation upon the disposition to obedience within a unitary state.[38] He gave as examples the fact that the Jews were willing to obey Antiochus except for eating his pork and that the Huguenot protestants were willing to obey Louis XIV in everything except attendance at Mass. These, however, seem to be instances of political resistance rather than agreed formal limitations upon sovereign power.

Bentham did, nonetheless, concede that some qualification of the disposition to obedience might be enshrined in law.[39] He did not, however, proceed beyond this to concede that sovereignty and its scope might actually, from a positivist viewpoint, be a phenomenon defined by law. Having conceived of sovereignty in terms of an essentially unqualified disposition to obedience, Bentham could only treat limitations upon the disposition to obey as anomalous exceptions to the 'normal' pattern and thus was unable adequately to account for constitutionally limited sovereignty. Significantly J. Raz comments here critically upon the supposedly 'factual' and objective analysis of legal 'sovereignty' advanced by Bentham that,

It seems that Bentham never made up his mind on the question of the distinction between legal limitations and de facto limitations of sovereignty. .... [H]e tries to explain legal phenomena by direct reference to social facts in a way which we cannot but judge to be confused.[40]

A similar point was made by Hart, giving the example of a situation in which the people as a whole approve of the violation of a formally stated limitation upon sovereignty, e.g., in the persecution of an unpopular minority.[41] What a sovereign in practice *can* do may well not be at one with what is *constitutionally permissible* and it seems dangerously misleading to seek to equate the two. As Raz and Hart imply, the attempted 'realism' of Bentham's analysis at this point falls foul of the actual complexity of legal and constitutional practice.

Separately from the issue of limitations upon sovereignty through a reduced disposition to obey, Bentham considered the idea of a limitation upon legislative competence through a self-denying ordinance on the part of the sovereign.[42] He described provisions of this kind as laws *in principem*, i.e. directed to the sovereign, as distinct from laws *in populum* directed to subjects. Laws *in principem* do not, however, fit any more easily into an imperative theory than do express conventions limiting legislative competence. A sovereign entity can clearly form a will in respect of its own future action, but whether it can do so bindingly and, if so, what would be the supporting sanction are matters of great difficulty within a Benthamite analysis. Still more so is the question of how a law *in principem* is to be made binding upon future sovereigns. Bentham seems to have considered such laws to operate as a form of *pacta regalia* to the effect that legislative competence should be subject to certain limitations and that, in consequence, the subjects should enjoy certain 'privileges'.

Bentham considered that laws *in principem* are supported only by 'auxiliary sanctions' such as popular opinion and moral or political pressures. He did admit that in some courts might apply sanctions *stricto sensu* in support of such laws, but the matter was left vague.[43] In such a case Bentham felt that sovereignty would be divided between the 'sovereign' popularly so called and the courts. He disapproved of judicial review of legislation, considering it to be a usurpation of a sovereign function, but, unlike Austin, he did admit the possibility. He remarked of it,

A Parliament, let it be supposed ... pays too little regard to ... the interests of the people. Be it so. The people ... have at least, some share in choosing

> it.   Give to the Judges a power of annulling its acts and you transfer a
> portion of the supreme power ... to a set of men in the choice of whom [the
> people] ... have not the least imaginable share ... .[44]

Bentham was, however, careful to admit that a power of judicial review of
legislation could not reasonably be equated with the capacity of sovereign
imperation per se.   Thus he added that,

> There is a wide difference between a positive and a negative part in
> legislation.   ... The power of repealing a law even for reasons given is a great
> power: too great indeed for Judges: but still very distinguishable from and
> much inferior to that of making one.[45]

Here too, as with the idea of limitations upon sovereign action through a
limited disposition to obedience, Bentham seems not adequately to distinguish
between legal definition and apparent social fact.   In particular, his model
took no account of internalized values in legal, including constitutional,
administration.   The exclusion of intra-systemic values has been a major
cause of criticism of classical positivist 'command' theory, both within and
beyond the realm of positivist legal theory.   The idea is, in different ways, at
the root of H.L.A. Hart's attempt to introduce a concept of 'authority' into
positivist analysis and Dworkin's anti-positivistic model of 'principled'
adjudication in 'hard cases'.

Bentham's analysis encounters especial difficulty in the context of
constitutional limitations upon future sovereigns.   The continuity of laws
notwithstanding changes in sovereign identity is in general a stumbling block
in any unqualified 'command' theory, but nowhere more so than in the case
of laws *in principem*.   That a sovereign entity should be able to bind the will
of its successors would be almost impossible in Bentham's understanding of
sovereignty and his conclusion that so far as future sovereigns are concerned,
such 'laws' can only have an exhortatory effect as recommendations was
inevitable.   A sovereign might, of course, be impelled into observance, and
perpetuation, of such 'laws' by extra-jurisprudential factors such as public
opinion, but could not, upon Bentham's analysis, be 'obliged' so to do in a
legal sense.   In concentrating upon practical legislative capacity, however,
Bentham   failed   fully to consider the possibility of an attempt by a
government to legislate in a manner which might, upon some principled
analysis, be considered actually to be *ultra vires* (beyond the powers) within
the   terms   of   the   constitutional   structure   of   the   country   concerned.

Bentham did touch upon the possibility in discussing judicial review of legislation, but his disapproval of this idea prevented his reaching any very satisfactory conclusions.

Summation of the Classical Positivist Position

The classical positivist accounts of the causes of compliance with law can clearly be argued to be subject to significant flaws. A direct causal connection between sanctions and compliance with particular legal provisions, once a general but undefined disposition to obedience exists, can only afford a very strained account of the obligation to obey law because of its exclusion of factors not amenable to 'factual' observation. The argument returns at this point to issues of context and linguistic usage. The context of classical positivist theory was clearly stated by Austin at the outset of his lectures upon jurisprudence,

> The principal purpose ... of [these] lectures, is to distinguish positive laws [the appropriate matter of jurisprudence] from ... objects with which they are connected by ... resemblance and analogy [and] the common name of 'laws'; and with which they are often blended and confounded.[46]

This, in some ways strikingly 'modern', attempt to obviate contextual confusion can be argued itself to have fallen into precisely such confusion. The formal intra-systemic concerns of classical positivism are necessarily narrowly focused, but the founders of the school did not admit the possibility of other concerns within their 'province of jurisprudence'. It is from the belief that positivism can supply a self-contained and complete account of legal phenomena that the potential for confusion arises.

As Morrison implies in his account of Austin's work,[47] an analysis of law founded upon factual appearance is jeopardized when it leaves no room for consideration of the point that law consists not only, or even primarily, of law-fact in the sense of the making and application of rules, but also of ideas about and perceptions of fact which have in practice a vastly significant impact upon the nature of the 'facts' themselves. The imposition of limitations upon the range of phenomena permitted to be observed may, in short, severely distort interpretation of the facts which are purportedly to be considered. Morrison comments, very pertinently in this context, that,

> Austin ... considered ... that when we talk law we are ... talking fact ... . Yet there are complexities involved in explaining just what facts we are picturing when we reason legally, and Austin made matters too simple for himself.[48]

It may strongly be argued that law as 'fact' rests upon law as concept and, indeed, that in the ultimate analysis law consists of ideas of which law-fact is no more than the outward manifestation. Any attempt to analyse law and legal phenomena by reference to observable fact alone is, thus, necessarily incomplete.

Bentham's analysis of the obligation to obey law in terms of a simple causality can be accepted only within very narrow terms of reference, since it is intrinsically incapable of taking into account any concept of normativity as such and the understanding of this element is ultimately basic to the understanding of the obligation to obey. It must, however, be remembered that in his 'expositorial' jurisprudence Bentham was concerned only with the presently observable facts of obedience. In his discussion of the 'habit of obedience' in this context he was careful to avoid issues of its origin and continuance. The defect of his argument lies not in the, declared, narrowness of its objectives but in its claim to supersede other theories which had different and more broadly defined intentions. Austin supplies the clearest example of the failure of classical positivist legal theory through simple over-extension. In a famously iconoclastic statement he asserted that,

> Now, to say that human laws which conflict with divine law are not binding, that is to say are not laws, is to talk stark nonsense. The most pernicious laws ... have been and are continually enforced as laws by judicial tribunals. Suppose an act innocuous, or even positively beneficial, be prohibited by the sovereign under penalty of death; if I commit this act, I shall be tried and condemned, and if I object to the sentence, that it is contrary to the law of God, who has commanded that human lawgivers shall not prohibit acts which have no evil consequences, the Court of Justice will demonstrate the inconclusiveness of my reasoning by hanging me up, in pursuance of the law of which I have impugned the validity.[49]

Within the, carefully limited, context of Bentham and Austin's own classical analytical positivism this proposition is, undeniably to a large extent true. Ronald Dworkin strongly emphasises the importance of internalized moralities in his 'rights thesis'[50] but in doing so he is actually referring to those intra-systemic criteria which were so strongly criticised by John

Austin.[51]   In general it is clearly the case that 'pernicious laws are continually enforced by judicial tribunals' and the classical naturalists did not seek to deny this.   Indeed, St. Augustine of Hippo pointed out that the Christian martyrs were judicially condemned, albeit unjustly.[52]   What is a truism in the process of narrow intra-systemic discourse of classical positivism becomes, however, itself 'nonsense' when transferred into the broader context of moral or ethical discourse.   The all too evident fact that people may be condemned according to positive law, irrespective of 'justice', does not entail the conclusion that extra-systemic arguments upon justice are therefore rendered baseless, which Austin did not necessarily claim.   Nor does it imply that extra-systemic arguments upon the obligation to obey may not be weighed in the balance against formal intra-systemic duties, notwithstanding coercive imposition of the latter.

Once these essential contextual distinctions are accepted it becomes clear that the arguments of analytical positivism in its original form(s) did not relate directly to the 'obligation' to obey at all.   The principal concern of early positivism was with the formal identification of legal rules and the attachment to them of intra-systemic motivations for compliance.   Such a model impinges upon 'obligation' only very indirectly, with an emphasis more upon the external application of 'sanctions' than upon normativity as such.   The model in its own context is not necessarily perfect, but it is far more tenable than it appears when extended into extra-systemic issues for the consideration of which it is singularly ill-adapted.

The 20th Century Revision of Positivism: H.L.A. Hart

The limitations of, in particular, Austin's account of the obligation to obey law supplied a major motivation for the principal 20th century restatement of positivist legal theory, by H.L.A. Hart in *The Concept of Law*.[53]   Hart's basic objection to the command model of law as stated by Austin[54] lay in the inadequacy of coercion as an explanation for compliance with law.   Bentham or Austin did not in fact advance sanctions as an exclusive mode of securing compliance with law, but merely as a principal diagnostic feature of 'legal' norms.   The emphasis which is in practice adopted by their theory must, nonetheless, be concluded ultimately to give an inadequate account of the general nature of the broad motivations to compliance with positive law.

Hart made this point through the example of a gunman coercing a bank clerk to hand over money in the course of a robbery, in contrast with the legal demands made by governments.[55] Hart argued that these two categories can by no means be equated one with the other. In the first place, the power of the gunman over the bank clerk is limited to the face-to-face confrontation and the clerk's actions will not be directed by his wishes outside that circumstance. Hart pointed out that this cannot be a sufficient model for law, not least because of the social and economic impossibility to maintain such a system of constant coercive supervision over all citizens. It might be argued that in some totalitarian states systems of informers approach such a model, but even then the supervision is hardly so detailed, effective and immediate as that of the gunman. Hart adduced in evidence for his criticism the fact that even criminal statutes, the most overtly coercive form of law, are phrased in general terms as to the prescribed, or proscribed, conduct and also in terms of the persons addressed.[56] This is self-evidently the case. Hart proceeded therefore to distinguish between two forms of pressure upon individual conduct, advancing categories of *being obliged* and *being under obligation*.[57] The former is straightforwardly coercive as in the gunman example, or - to express it otherwise - as in the proposition 'I obliged the person to apologize'. The latter is normative and involves some sense of duty, as in the proposition 'the person felt an obligation to make amends'. It was Hart's contention that the motivation to obey law is founded more upon the latter than the former. Thus, the bank clerk who discovers more money in the cash drawer after the departure of the robber will, presumably, feel no obligation to pursue him in order to hand it over. On the other hand, a taxpayer who inadvertently omits to declare some element of his or her income for tax assessment would recognize some obligation to declare the outstanding sum and make the further tax payment due. In this sense the demands of the gunman and the Inland Revenue are different in type, even though both superficially share the characteristic of potential coercive enforcement. The latter, in short, are made with recognized authority and have an efficacy far transcending the immediate expectation of the application of coercive force.

Criminal statutes in most jurisdictions are almost invariably phrased generally and addressed to the broad mass of people, or at least to that mass of the population who might find themselves in the situation to which the statute in question has been directed. Nevertheless, their ultimate impact can in reality only be upon the individuals by whom 'the community' is comprised. At the level of its actual operation the direction can only take the form, e.g, that 'you (personally) shall not steal (this thing)'. The implication that classical positivist expositorial legal theory at this level either denies the generality of laws or demands constant individual coercion is a *reductio ad absurdem* which seriously misrepresents the arguments of both Bentham and Austin and has no obvious effect in advancing that of Hart.

The Basis of Legal Authority in Hart's Theory

The issue of authority addressed by Hart goes to the foundation of the habit of obedience, a matter not unrealized but deliberately left aside by Bentham in his analysis of consequences rather than causes. Hart's response to this problem is interesting, if founded upon a somewhat unfortunately structured argument. He approached the issue through the medium of a hypothetical legal anthropology. The starting point is Rex I, a King established by force in the first place but having in the course of time come to be obeyed habitually by the bulk of the population. In short, the crudest possible type of Benthamite or Austinian sovereign, in effect an enthroned gunman. Such a situation, according to Hart, has the makings of a legal order but no more. He comments that in such a community,

> unity is constituted by the fact that its members obey the same person, even though they have no view as to the rightness of doing so.[58]

If upon the death or (rather unlikely) the abdication of Rex I he is succeeded by (e.g.) his eldest son Rex II, Hart argued that the major leap to a genuinely 'legal' order would have been made. Rex II has not taken power by force but has claimed it by virtue of some sort of 'right'. There has appeared a *rule of succession*, in this case monarchic primogeniture, which is the cause of the observed fact of obedience but not one with it. The distinction made by Hart is that whereas the subjects of Rex I accepted his power as a matter of fact, with the accession of Rex II they have come to obey with some sense of constitutional propriety (of 'rightness') in so doing. Force may not be absent from the scheme but legitimacy is now a prime consideration.

Hart elaborated this point by drawing three fundamental distinctions between rule-based behaviour and that which is merely habitual. Firstly a 'habit' consists of no more than convergent behaviour with no sense of inherent 'rightness', whereas a 'rule' is characterized by stigmatization of deviation as in some sense 'wrong'. Secondly, deviation from the conduct enjoined by a rule is seen as in itself meriting criticism without reference to any external effect. Finally, and effectively in summation of the previous two points, Hart argued that rules are distinguished from habits by the existence of an *internal aspect*.

Hart's 'internal aspect' of law bears directly upon the question of the obligation to obey and merits scrutiny in some detail. A habit is merely an observable fact, such as that people often do wear raincoats in wet weather. There is no sense of normativity about such conduct and it has, therefore, only an *external* observational aspect. A rule, in contrast, is characterized by association with a sense of 'rightness' in compliance and, conversely, of 'wrongness' in deviation. It becomes not merely a conventional practice but a *critical reflective standard* which is, for those involved in the system from which it springs, in some sense 'obligatory'. It is this sense of 'obligation' which Hart argued to be a distinguishing mark of law.[59] The function of the *internal aspect* in Hart's theory is thus to fill in the blank left by Austin, and also Bentham, as to the cause of the habit of obedience which lay at the root of their conception of sovereignty.

The Place of the Rule of Recognition

That the operation of law as a critical reflective standard is important could hardly be denied. It is not, however, a distinguishing feature of rules of law in comparison with any other normative standards. It might be argued to be a yet stronger feature of, for example, rules of morality. Hart did not deny this, nor did he claim that the species of obligation involved in his *internal* aspect arises independently of the law itself. Instead we return to his hypothetical legal anthropology and the 'legal' order generated by the accession of Rex II through the operation of a rule of succession. This rule becomes the basis for H.L.A. Hart's fundamental *rule of recognition*.[60] That is to say, a basic rule accepted in the given society as determining what institutions are able to make binding law, not by virtue of force alone but in the exercise of an accepted 'right'. Its greatest value lies in the abandonment of the misleading personal analogy of sovereignty used by both Bentham and Austin in favour of an analysis which treats sovereignty as a continuing system rather than a structure of individual acts of will.   This analysis satisfactorily accounts both for constitutional laws and for the continuing efficacy of laws in general in ways which were not open to the classical positivist analyses.   Constitutional rules become simply aspects of complex rules of recognition.   The continuity of rules is explained through the analysis of law making as an authoritative process, the products of which are accepted as authoritative until such time as either the rule is changed or abrogated within the system or the system itself loses its authority.   Upon this point Hart commented that,

> When the individual ruler dies his legislative work lives on; for it rests upon the foundation of a general rule which successive generations of the society continue to respect regarding each legislator whenever he lived.[61]

In this respect it is fair to argue that Hart's analysis did indeed improve upon that of Bentham, rather than merely addressing somewhat different issues.

The rule of recognition, which identifies the sources of law, is for Hart the springboard for a wider restructuring of the positivist analysis.   He contended that the rule of recognition is a special example of a general class of rules which he termed 'secondary', which are in their nature power-conferring, in contrast with 'primary', 'duty-imposing', rules.   It is the union of these two types of rule which, in Hart's view, define a 'legal system'. Primary rules are said to be prior in time of development to secondary rules and originally to take the form of static customary practice.   The subsequent need for secondary rules is then argued to emerge from the pressure for change and the effective enunciation of new rules in a dynamic society. These take the particular forms represented by the claimed need for rules of identification, change and adjudication to resolve the fundamental problems of stasis and uncertainty.   It was Hart's contention that once such rules have developed in a society it moves from a 'pre-legal' into a fully 'legal' condition.   This illustrates his argument upon 'developed' legal systems, but his anthropological assumptions must be considered very dubious and could be considered outdated even when *The   Concept   of Law*   was written.[62]

The Question of Hart's Legal Anthropology

Hart made the broad assumption that legal development necessarily proceeds from a pre-legal structure of static primary rules, without effective means of identification and change, to a developed 'legal' order founded upon a union of primary and secondary rules. Such a 'developed' legal system would then be one more or less approximating to western legal practice. Studies of the law of 'primitive', or more accurately non-industrial technological, peoples going back to the study conducted by Llewellyn and Hoebel amongst the Cheyenne Indians[63] and including the work of Gluckman[64] and Roberts[65] tend to suggest that what is observed is not so much a series of steps along a single line of 'development' as the finding of different responses to essentially similar social needs in widely differing conditions. The essence of this idea was expressed by the American Realist thinker Karl N. Llewellyn at about the same time as his work amongst the Cheyenne people in his concept of 'law jobs'.[66] Llewellyn argued that in any society there are certain essentially 'legal' tasks to be performed which amount in the final analysis to the avoidance or safe channelling of disputes which have the potential dangerously to disrupt social order. By what mechanism this might be achieved in a given society is much less important to the society than the fact that it is achieved. To assume, as Hart did, that the formalities of a settled industrial society are distinct in type, as opposed to form, from those of, e.g., a society of nomadic herdspeople, has more than a little of the appearance of unconscious chauvinism. Roberts comments that,

> While the command theory is now seen to be simplistic and in some respects inaccurate, even the most ... sophisticated formulations, such as those of Hart, are for the most part developments of it, and remain difficult to apply outside the context of a western legal system.[67]

He proceeds to make the point that the absence of the institutional framework of western law by no means precludes the performance of the tasks of dispute guidance and resolution. The disparity is dictated by the environment in which a given society lives. It can also be suggested that, notwithstanding Roberts' argument, many so-called 'primitive' societies do develop very sophisticated criteria of identification in the operation of their social norms which may in, this present context, reasonably be termed 'secondary rules'.   Even custom must be distinguished from randomly convergent activity by reference to some set of criteria and it is quite clear that even in so informal a society as that of the Nuer in the Sudan elders are considered to be vested with a conventional wisdom upon what is acceptable as 'right' conduct and that, in general, their view will be supported by social pressure against deviance.[68]   Llewellyn and Hoebel found amongst the Cheyenne people that in response to problems of social dislocation 'warrior societies' had sprung up which played, *inter alia*, a formally recognized 'policing' role within the tribes.   This would seem to indicate clearly the ability of so-called 'primitive' and relatively decentralized societies to develop institutions when the need arises.[69]   There may be suggested to be in such societies functional equivalents of rules of recognition, adjudication and change.

It may further be contended that the three problems of Hart's hypothetical 'pre-legal' society which are said to call forth secondary rules, those of uncertainty, stasis and inefficiency, are to some extent mutually contradictory.   In particular the problems of uncertainty and inflexible stasis seem to be contradictory; it is difficult to imagine that a norm could be at once constrainingly inflexible and uncertain in its authority or substance. This rather unsatisfactory legal anthropology can perhaps be regarded as largely rhetorical in nature and it does not necessarily have an adverse impact upon the union of primary and secondary rules as a mode of analysis in their proper context.   It must, nonetheless, be considered an unfortunate element of Hart's analytical framework.

The Implications of Hart's Theory: The Importance of Officials

The union of primary and secondary rules at the very root of Hart's concept of a legal system is claimed at once to free jurisprudence from the classical positivist 'expositorial' emphasis upon the pragmatic observation of 'facts' of power and obedience and from the embrace of naturalist concepts of legal morality.   However, within Hart's analysis of validation there is seen a subtle distinction in the levels of operation of criteria of identification.   He argued that there are two minimum conditions which must be satisfied for the maintenance of a 'legal system', which are (a) general obedience to those norms which are recognized as 'valid' by reference to the accepted criteria of identification and (b) acceptance of norms as standards of behaviour by officials.[70]   This differentiation between obedience to law on the part of citizens in general and a fuller understanding of the structure of legal norms on the part of officials is set out clearly in Hart's statement that,

> The assertion that a legal system exists is therefore a Janus-faced statement looking both towards obedience by ordinary citizens and to acceptance by officials of secondary rules as critical common standards of official behaviour.[71]

In one sense this is self-evidently the case. 'Officials', or more specifically lawyers, do have a more technical appreciation of law and legal validity than do members of the public at large. But on a more analytical level, granted the claim of distance from the mere fact of obedience, this statement does seem to move far towards a position in which law is defined in terms of the attitude of officials and factually maintained by general acquiescence in their perceptions. Hart tended to dismiss the American realist view that law consists ultimately of 'what courts do', but the distance between this and the idea of law as 'what officials believe' is perhaps not very great. In Hart's model, as in the 'pure theory' of Hans Kelsen to an even greater degree, the logical conclusion would, indeed, seem to be that the validity of law rests upon the belief of officials. Kelsen himself maintained that law becomes 'actual' only at the point of application by officials, remaining up to that point merely potential.[72]   Any such view seems, however, to underrate the importance of the fact that many day-to-day transactions of clear legal import, such as 'normal' contractual activity, take place in a normative framework at an unofficial level. It is true that such transactions are, in the event of dispute, subject to potential adjudication by courts but it is not generally with that thought in mind that they are entered into. Litigation will be an afterthought if things in fact go wrong. Brendan Edgeworth makes the point well in his comment that,

> Why the legal theorist should uncritically accept the discourse of officials at a particular point in history to comprehend hermeneutically the essence of a legal system ... is never convincingly spelt out ... .   One is presented, therefore, with the professional's world view as the yardstick of reality. But all levels of society produce, apply and interpret 'the law', and its social existence cannot be identified in totality without examining the entire range of hermeneutical forms associated with it.[73]

Upon this general level it may reasonably be argued that it is not only the critical awareness of officials which matters for the real functioning of law but that of all participants in the system, even if officials have manifestly a specialist and highly significant role to play.[74]   In this sense it may be suggested that 'obligation', however conceived, must operate at a level broader than that of official critical awareness if it is to have any meaningful general significance.

The Concept of Validity in Hart's Positivism

Validity is a key concept in Hart's theory in the sense that he emphasized the quality of 'authority' associated with the identification of law-constitutive power through the operation of the 'rule of recognition'.   There arises here an important linguistic point which has been usefully set out by H.E. Simmonds in an argument that Hart's concept of validity can only be understood by reference to the linguistic philosophy of Wittgenstein.   Thus,

> The significance of ... propositions [about legal validity] can only be clarified by reference to [a] ... context ... characterised by the existence of a practice involving the ascription of authority to certain sources of norms ... legal discourse is linked to law as fact without itself being reducible to factual descriptive discourse.   This ... is Hart's most valuable insight.[75]

Consequently, Simmonds argues, Hart's concept of validity is separated from moral argument without becoming merely descriptive and that ultimately 'validity is ... a matter of pedigree rather than content'.[76]   In essence this argument returns to the 'internal' nature of Hart's concept of validity. Simmonds adds that just as legal validity is connected with fact, so too it cannot wholly be divorced from issues of moral principle.   The question ultimately is not whether such issues have a bearing upon the concept of 'law' but rather at what level, or perhaps in what context, they do so. This defines the real nature of the relationship between the positivism of H.L.A. Hart and the earlier work of Bentham and Austin.   Hart's theory represents an analysis of law from the 'internal' viewpoint of any given system.   Bentham and Austin's earlier classical positivist analysis is clearly 'external' in conception in both its nature and chosen basic emphases.

Legal systems have, as Hart conceded, both 'internal' and 'external' dimensions. It may, thus, be argued that far from superseding the Classical positivist analyses, Hart's analysis adds another dimension to positivism by addressing different questions, from a critical and reflective standpoint. The clearest 'improvement' which may be found in Hart's system in comparison with that of Bentham and Austin may be the identification of law making as a systemic process rather than as a series of isolated acts of will.

The Sustainability of the Claims made for Hart's Positivism

The claim is made that Hart's model of a union of primary and secondary rules as the basis of a legal system effectively excludes moral argument from *legal* analysis. The central concepts in his analysis are those of *authority* and *obligation*. Returning to the contrast between the bank robber and the Inland Revenue, both of whom - in different ways - are making demands with menaces, the latter acts pursuant to a recognized authority[77] referable ultimately to a rule of recognition. Thus, it is argued, the law has 'authority' and imposes 'obligation', whereas the gunman merely 'obliges', i.e. compels, through the immediate application of coercive force. It is, however, questionable whether the categories of 'being under obligation' and 'being obliged' exhaust the forms of obligation to which the phenomenon of law may be related. The legal 'obligation' to which Hart refers is not characterized directly either by force or moral quality. Instead it is argued that,

> Rules are conceived and spoken of as imposing obligation when the general demand for conformity is insistent and the social pressure brought to bear upon those who deviate or threaten to deviate is great.[78]

This is the pragmatic expression of the 'internal' viewpoint. Once the supposition of minimum practical efficacy is satisfied, rules enunciated in accordance with the accepted criteria of legal identification will be seen as 'right' within the system in question and social pressure for conformity will create some sense of 'obligation' to comply. The deviant with a purely 'external' viewpoint will, however, experience only a coercive compulsion.

The obligation is one created within the social consciousness by pressure to conform in accordance with an 'internal' received perception of authority.[79]

Hart's idea of the obligation to obey law actually rests upon the 'internal' presumptions made by and about the legal system and this necessarily presupposes the 'justice' and good intentions of the law, as in the phrase 'justice according to law'. This has, as Hart emphasizes, no direct or necessary connection with actual or predicted external sanctions. Beyond this, Hartian, model of internal 'authority' and the, Benthamite, model of external 'power' there may be argued to exist what may be termed an overview. It is almost universally admitted, and is certainly conceded by most mainstream positivists, that an evaluatory judgment upon positive law is possible, even if it is denied that such a judgment can bear upon 'law' quality as such. Upon the latter ground the naturalist tradition was rejected by Bentham and Austin, and also by Hart, as an illegitimate attempt to incorporate moral elements into pragmatic or formal criteria of legal identification. It may be argued that this is a misunderstanding of naturalist argument which in fact focuses upon the *purpose* of law making powers rather than upon the identification of their products.[80] This view posits an entirely different type of 'obligation' to obey law, based upon its moral or ethical nature and in particular the extent of and the limitations upon its 'proper' use. Thus, although a law may be formally valid even if it is considered morally bad, the fact of its moral defectiveness impinges upon and damages its standing as 'properly' made law and potentially reflects upon its call upon conscience. In this context Neil MacCormick's view upon the relationship of Hart's model of law with the dynamics of moral analysis is very interesting. He comments that,

> [The fact that] the elements of moral and legal reasoning share a common framework even though they have considerable differences of internal detail ... does not contradict Hart's proposition that criteria of legal validity [do] ... not include [moral] criteria ... . The mistake, if any, lies in his supposition that [standing as practical reasons for action] ... is the only conceptual overlap ... between law and morality.[81]

Properly considered, Hart's argument does not, as it claims, override either the classical positivist or the broad naturalist analyses of law and the obligation to obey law. Hart's argument is in fact an additional element rather than a replacement model. It may rather be suggested that both the positivist and naturalist analyses represent different contexts in which issues of validity and obligation may be raised.   Hart's achievement was not to produce an 'improved' and comprehensive positivism but to enunciate a different argument exposing some of the distortions to which, in an inappropriate search for comprehensiveness, earlier theory had fallen prey. Unfortunately, Hart himself may be argued to have fallen into a different but related pitfall in advancing his idea of a 'minimum content of natural law'.

This is founded upon ideas of basic social viability and involves,

> some very obvious generalisations ... concerning human nature ... which ... show that as long as these hold good, there are certain rules of conduct which any social organisation must contain if it is to be viable.[82]

Thus it is argued that a society must enunciate certain rules or types of rules taking into account basic human characteristics and circumstances, including vulnerability, approximate equality, limited altruism, limited resources, and limited understanding and strength of will,[83] or it will in the long run cease to be politically viable.   It is possible to debate the factors to be taken into account but the basic concept can hardly be found objectionable as an observation of socio-political reality.   In the context of naturalist analysis, however, the model is minimal almost to the point of vacuity.   It is founded upon a false assumption that 'naturalist' thought addresses issues of validity and obligation upon the same level as a positivist analysis.   In fact quite different questions are being addressed.   Hart himself recognized, in his discussion of command theory, that obligation may be analysed at more than one level and his own account is, by the same logic, no more capable of being comprehensive in its analysis than any other.   The 'minimum content of natural law' may, in short, be argued to have little value in a positivist theory and little relevance to the actual concerns of mainstream naturalism.

Positivist Development and Its Implications

The patterns of the evolution and development of the classical and later positivist analyses of legal obligation do not represent a process of refinement leading to a comprehensive legal theory.   That they should be imagined to do so leads to a distorted model.   These approaches are, rather, analyses of distinct phenomena raising different questions andt yielding different answers.   The proposition advanced by Bentham and Austin is broadly that where the state demands a pattern of conduct in a legal form it will seek to secure maximum compliance by the attachment of a consequence to non-compliance (or possibly to compliance).   This, as Hart remarks, is an 'external' view of the motivation to compliance.   Hart's own model of obligation is rooted in the authority flowing from the operation of a rule of recognition.   The first model relates not strictly to an 'obligation' to obey but to a causal motivation without any necessary reference to, in Hart's terms, a critical reflective attitude.   The second model, in contrast, relates to intra-systemic authorization and the definition of formal duties within the assumed authority of a given system.   The rule of recognition, like Kelsen's *grundnorm*, is represented as a *sine qua* non for a 'legal system' and at once as a rule and a descriptive socio-political fact.   Within a formalist analysis the exclusive emphasis upon rules can be criticized, as by Dworkin[84] or by MacCormick and Weinberger.[85]   More generally, such a claim can clearly not address the question of a *moral* claim of laws to be obeyed. MacCormick has argued that this further dimension can be deduced from Hart's analysis, concluding that,

> If unjust laws are made this is not merely morally deplorable in a general sense. It has that special deplorability which inheres in the perversion of a trust. At the back of the obloquy which we cast upon the unjust legislator ... is perhaps the thought that 'an unjust law is ... a corruption of legality'. And that is ... the dictum of no positivist but of the supreme natural lawyer, St. Thomas Aquinas. But how was that judgment reached?   It was reached solely by following through the implications of Hart's hermeneutic analysis of law.[86]

In making this argument MacCormick stresses the point that Hart's use of the terminology of 'obligation' requires the involvement of values, commenting earlier that,

> the most basic laws are those which impose categorical requirements upon persons ... precisely in the sense that infringements of them are stigmatised as wrongs.[87]

However, it is important to notice that the morality in terms of which infringements of positive law are here being stigmatized is a formalistic and systemic morality not involving any objective exterior of comparison. With all due respect to MacCormick's argument the leap cannot be made from the proposition that an act contravenes an intra-systemic morality to the idea that it is more generally 'immoral'. Professional legal discourse, which is replete with quasi-moral terminology, tends to conflate these moralities which may, but do not by any means necessarily, coincide. The issue is, again, one of questions and contexts. There is no reason why Hart's concept of legal obligation should embrace extra-systemic moral judgments, but an attempt to make it do so is, as in the case of the claimed 'minimum content of natural law', problematic The positivist categories of obligation, causal motivation and formal intra-systemic duties, cannot be exhaustive. The moral dimension of obligation, which is the fundamental concern of naturalist theory, is quite different in nature and relates neither to coercion nor to formal duty, but to the claim of a legal norm upon the conscience of its addressees. Even at this stage of argument it may, then, be suggested that there are at least three forms of obligation which may be associated with law. Before a theoretical framework for the relation of these categories can be advanced, the third, moral, analysis requires examination, together with recent re-analyses of the formalist position and the variety of sceptical, deconstructive and critical theories. Only when these differing approaches and usages have been set in context can a useful general analysis of the obligation, or obligations, to obey law be attempted.

Notes

1   H.L.A. Hart, *The Concept of Law*, 2 ed., with postscript ed. by P.A. Bulloch and J. Raz (Clarendon, Oxford, 1994), p.82.
2   J.U. Lewis suggests in 'Blackstone's Definition of Law and Doctrine of Legal Obligation as a Link between Early Modern and Contemporary Theories of Law' (1968) *Irish Jurist*, 336 especially at 347, that conventional positivists misunderstand and misrepresent Blackstone's position which, he argues, actually makes a rather 'modern' distinction between moral obligation and legal validity.
3   J. Bentham, *A Fragment on Government* (Blackwell edn., 1967), Ch.4, p.93.
4   H.L.A. Hart, *Essays on Bentham* (Oxford, 1982), p.82.
5   J. Bentham, in *The Works of Jeremy Bentham* (Edinburgh, 1838-43), Vol. III, p.221. See also H.L.A. Hart, op.cit., Ch. IV, passim.

6   See Chapter 3.
7   D. Hume, *A Treatise of Human Nature* (Oxford edn., 1978, reproducing the 1740 pagination), Book III, Ch. I, para.36.
8   J. Bentham, *A Fragment on Government* (Blackwell edn., 1967), Preface, para.13.
9   J. Harrison, *Hume's Theory of Justice* (Oxford, 1981), p.37.
10 J. Bentham, *Of Laws in General*, ed. H.L.A. Hart (Athlone, London, 1970), Ch.II, para.1.
11 J. Austin, *The Province of Jurisprudence Determined* (1832, Weidenfeld and Nicholson edn., 1954), Lecture 1, pp.16-18.
12 See below.
13 J. Bentham, *Of Laws in General*, p.1.
14 J. Bentham, *An Introduction to the Principles of Morals and Legislation* (Blackwell edn., 1967), Ch.I, para.1.
15 Ibid., para.2.
16 J. Bentham, *Of Laws in General*, p.135.
17 Hart, *Essays on Bentham*, p.135.
18 Ibid., p.134.
19 Ibid., p.136.
20 Ibid., Ch. VI.
21 Ibid., p.136.
22 P.M.S. Hacker, 'Sanction Theories of Duty' in Simpson, ed., *Oxford Essays on Jurisprudence*, 2nd series (Oxford, 1973), p.131.
23 See Chapter 3.
24 See Chapter 5.
25 See O.W. Holmes, 'The Path of the Law' (1897) 10 *Harvard Law Review*, 457.
26 J. Austin, *The Province of Jurisprudence Determined*, Lecture 1, p.1.
27 J. Bentham, *An Introduction to the Principles of Morals and Legislation*, Ch. I, para.2.
28 Expressly in a note added to *An Introduction to the Principles of Morals and Legislation*, Ch. I, para. 13, in July 1822 following a comment made by Alexander Wedderburn, later Lord Loughborough and Earl of Rosslyn.
29 Ibid., Ch. XII.
30 Ibid., para.6 et seq.
31 Ibid., Ch. XIII, para.2.
32 Ibid., Ch. XVI, para.3.
33 Hart, *Essays on Bentham*, p.224.
34 J. Austin, op.cit., Lecture VI, pp.254-5.
35 Ibid., Ch. IV, para.26.
36 Ibid., Ch. IV, paras.32-33.
37 H.L.A. Hart, op.cit., p.328.

38   See J. Bentham, *Of Laws in General*, p.19.
39   Ibid.
40   J. Raz, *The Concept of a Legal System* (Oxford, 1970, 1978 edn.), p.10.
41   See H.L.A. Hart, op.cit., Essay IX, 'Sovereignty and Legally Limited Government', pp.233-4.
42   J. Bentham, *Of Laws in General*, Ch.VI.
43   Ibid., pp.68-69.
44   J. Bentham, *A Fragment on Government*, Ch. IV, para.32. In the USA where there is such judicial power, there is a political process in judicial appointment.
45   Ibid., para.33.
46   J. Austin, op.cit., Lecture 1, p.2.
47   W.L. Morrison, *John Austin*, in the series *Jurists: Profiles in Legal Theory*, ed., W. Twinning (Edward Arnold, 1982).
48   Ibid., at p.146.
49   J. Austin, op.cit., Lecture V, p.185.
50   R.M. Dworkin, *Taking Rights Seriously* (Duckworth, 1977, 1978 edn.).   The Rights Thesis is discussed in Chapter 4 below.
51   Bentham and Austin would probably have seen Dworkin's analysis of adjudication as approaching a judicial usurpation of the legislative function.
52   See Chapter 3.
53   First Published in the Clarendon Law series by Oxford University Press in 1961 and issued in a second edition in 1994 with a postscript edited by P.A. Bulloch and J. Raz.
54   When *The Concept of Law* was written positivist legal theory was known mainly from the work of Austin.   The re-emergence of Bentham's work, in which Hart played a major part, renders some of the points made rather unfair.   For modern comment see R.N. Moles, *Definition and Rule in Legal Theory* (Blackwell, 1987).
55   See *The Concept of Law*, 2 ed., Ch. II, pp.19-20.
56   Ibid., p.21.
57   See ibid., pp.82-83.
58   Ibid., p.53.
59   See ibid., pp.28-91.
60   See ibid., pp.100-110.
61   Ibid., p.63.
62   See H. McCoubrey, review of the Second Edition of *The Concept of Law* in (1995) 15 *Legal Studies*, p.307 at p.308.
63   K.N. Llewellyn and E.A. Hoebel. *The Cheyenne Way* (University of Oklahoma Press, 1941).
64   W. Gluckman, *Politics, Law and Ritual in Tribal Society* (Blackwell, 1977).
65   S. Roberts, *Order and Dispute: An Introduction to Legal Anthropology* (Penguin, 1977).

66 See K.N. Llewellyn, 'The Normative, the Legal and the Law Jobs: The Problem of Juristic Method' (1939-40) 49 *Yale Law Journal*, 1355.
67 S. Roberts, op.cit., p.24.
68 See ibid., pp.49 and 120-1, citing E. Evans-Pritchard, *The Nuer* (Oxford, 1940). Similar points can be found made by E.A. Hoebel, *The Law of Primitive Men* (Cambridge, Mass., 1954) and T. Eckhoff, 'The Mediator the Judge and the Administrator in Conflict-Resolution' (1966) 10 *Acta Juridica*, 148. See also, more generally, W. Goldschmidt, *Sebei Law* (University of California Press, 1967).
69 See *The Cheyenne Way*, Ch.5.
70 H.L.A. Hart, *The Concept of Law*, 2 ed., pp.114-7.
71 Ibid., p.117.
72 See H. Kelsen, *General Theory of Law and State*, trans. A. Wedberg (Harvard University Press, 1948).
73 B. Edgeworth, 'Legal Positivism and the Philosophy of Language: A Critique of H.L.A. Hart's "Descriptive Sociology"' (1986) 6 *Legal Studies*, 115 at 138.
74 This is a point implicit in the Scandinavian Realist analysis. See in particular K. Olivecrona, *Law as Fact*, 2 ed. (Stevens, 1971).
75 H.E. Simmonds, 'Practice and Validity' (1979) *Cambridge Law Journal*, 361 at 364.
76 Ibid., at p.365. The issue of pedigree and content was debated in the context of the law of the Third Reich by H.L.A. Hart and Lon L. Fuller, unfortunately upon the basis of an inaccurate report of a post-war judicial decision. See Chapter 7.
77 The Income and Corporation Taxes Acts.
78 H.L.A. Hart, op.cit., p.86.
79 Ibid., pp.66-68.
80 See Chapter 3.
81 N. MacCormick, *H.L.A. Hart*, in the series *Jurists: Profiles in Legal Theory*, ed. W. Twinning (Edward Arnold, 1981), p.161.
82 H.L.A. Hart, op.cit, pp.192-3.
83 See ibid., pp.194-8.
84 See Chapter 4.
85 See N. MacCormick and O. Weinberger, *An Institutional Theory of Law* (D. Reidal Publishing Co., 1986).
86 N. MacCormick, 'Law, Morality and Positivism' (1981) 1 *Legal Studies*, 131 at 145.
87 Ibid., at p.144.

3 Moral Analyses of Obedience to Law

One of the principal identifying features of a positivist theory of law has come to be an insistence upon the autonomy of law and legal phenomena. This was not implicit in the thought of the founders of the school. Both Bentham and Austin sought to limit the 'province of jurisprudence' for purposes of 'scientific' study but never claimed that questions relevant to law might arise outside that limited 'province'. There is undoubtedly, however, an implication of exclusiveness in the language if not the intention of early positivism. This tendency has been taken much further by later positivists and neo-positivists. The attempt by H.L.A. Hart to generate a 'complete' positivist jurisprudence carries distinct elements of this tendency, which may lead to infelicities which cannot be resolved within the self-imposed limitations of this type of theory.[1] No legal theory has ever succeeded in demonstrating satisfactorily that law is an autonomous phenomenon in the sense of one which can operate free from the impact of external factors. Even the 'pure theory' advanced by Hans Kelsen[2] is ultimately founded upon the extra-legal political 'fact' of the *grundnorm*.

From such a deliberately limited perspective it is, of course, possible to discuss law 'as if' it is indeed an autonomous phenomenon, so long as the limitation is borne in mind. This is what legal practitioners do as a matter of habit and convenience. Error creeps in only when the convenient assumption of autonomy made within the system is elevated into a doctrine. Thus, in a technical discussion of a contract for the purchase of a cabbage it may be reasonable to accept the assumption of autonomy which is made within the system under which the contract was made. It is rather as one may in practice act 'as if' the world was flat for the purpose of walking round the corner, without for a moment believing that the planet actually is flat. In the wider perspective, however, just as the planet Earth is more or less spherical, the question of how and why ownership of cabbages comes to be transferred in just that way in the given legal system raises significant issues which are not capable of being answered by reference to 'legal' phenomena alone.

This is recognized by a number of modern 'post-positivist'[3] theories but it is basic to naturalist legal theory.

The Concept and Claims of Naturalism

The term 'naturalism' encompasses a considerable range of theoretical approaches but the common factor has been suggested elsewhere to be,

> a concern with the moral nature of the power to make laws rather than with the formal identification of state prescription.[4]

Such a concern is of obvious significance in the context of an obligation to obey law and moves beyond the spheres of force and formal obligation into the question of the association of moral and/or ethical obligations with law. The actual claims made by the various strands of mainstream naturalist theory have commonly been misunderstood and misrepresented at least from the time of Bentham onwards. The common perception of naturalist legal theory is that implied by the deceptively simple statement of St. Augustine of Hippo that *lex iniusta non est lex*[5] - a law which is unjust is not 'law'. Taken out of context to mean that an unjust law has no effect, the statement would be evidently fatuous and no less so in the late Roman era in which St. Augustine lived than at present. Clearly governments can, and do, enact iniquitous provisions and enforce them. The question at issue is not, however, that of the *ability* of governments to impose iniquitous laws, but rather that of their *right* to do so. This question leads naturally to that of the degree of obligation which may be associated with 'improper' enactments. Some modern theories, such as Dworkin's 'rights thesis',[6] approach this issue through the 'moral' perceptions of particular societies and the 'constitutional' assumptions which are generated by them. This is not, however, the primary concern of mainstream naturalism. The emphasis of such theory lies much more upon the search general moral and ethical criteria which may objectively be applied in the evaluation of the quality of positive law and the obligation imposed by it. The claim made by St. Augustine related not to legal efficacy in a narrowly intra-systemic sense but to the broader moral claim imposed by a 'whole law' upon its addressees.

The Problems of Method in Naturalist Theory

There are two major methodological problems to be overcome in the naturalist enterprise.   The first and most basic is the determination of satisfactory objective criteria of assessment.   Any taint of subjectivism is clearly to be avoided, essentially for the reasons set out by Bentham in his comment that,

> the natural tendency of such doctrine [i.e. natural law] is to impel a man, by the force of his conscience, to rise up in arms against any law whatever that he happens not to like.[7]

Assuming that the basic problem of subjectivity can be overcome, there yet remains the second difficulty, that of determining the effect of the application of the chosen criteria of evaluation.   Even adopting the cruder interpretation of the Augustinian statement *lex iniusta non est lex*,[8] there are highly complex moral, social and political issues to be resolved in the determination of the appropriate balance between the competing claims of social stability and individual expectation.

There are two broad categories of solution which may be suggested for the first problem.   There may be reference to absolute moral standards, whether found in the will of God or in some more vaguely defined 'cosmic reason', or to principles derived from observation of the dictates of human nature.   These approaches are not necessarily mutually exclusive and many theorists have in fact adopted both.   Thus, St. Thomas Aquinas attributed all morality and justice to the *Lex Aeterna*, the general will of God, which he saw as partly revealed to humankind, in scripture, as the *Lex Divina* and as partly open to rational observation as the *Lex Naturalis*.[9]   In contrast, social contractarian theorists[10] have relied upon observation of the apparent dictates of human social nature without reference to its possible origins.   Whatever method is adopted, however, one fundamental objection must be overcome. This was stated in a more general context by David Hume in his remark that,

> In every system of morality ... I am surprised to find that instead of the usual copulations of propositions, *is* and *is not* I meet with no proposition which is not connected with an *ought* or *ought not* ... a reason should be given for what seems ... inconceivable, how this relation can be a deduction from others which are entirely different from it.[11]

More simply put, a normative *ought* proposition cannot properly be derived from an observational or descriptive *is* proposition.   Can it thus be said that naturalists on an improper basis attempt to define what law 'is' by reference to what it 'ought to be'?   More subtly, perhaps, that they attempt to derive a definition of what law 'ought' to be from an observation of what human nature, for whatever reasons, 'is'?[12]   The first issue may readily be disposed of upon the same basis that the seeming fatuity of St. Augustine's assertion that *lex iniusta non est lex* may be dismissed.   It is not the making of rules or principles but the right to do so which is in question.   The second form of this criticism may also be effectively countered.   J.M. Finnis in his modern reworking of naturalist legal theory approaches the question in the succinct form in which it was posed by Julius Stone - 'Have the natural lawyers shown that they can derive ethical norms from facts?'[13]   Arguing from an essentially Thomist base, Finnis denies that naturalist thinkers did, or had any need to, attempt any such questionable derivation.   He argues that within the Thomist scheme the relationship of morality to human nature, founded upon knowledge by inclination, is in fact non-inferential.   He advances the view that,

> Aquinas considers practical reasoning begins not by understanding [human] nature from the outside, ... but by experiencing one's nature ... from the inside, in the form of one's own inclinations.   But ... there is no process of inference.   ... [B]y a simple act of non-inferential understanding one grasps that the object of the inclination which one experiences is an instance of a general form of good, ...[14]

One is thus invited to consider not that human nature is in itself 'good', but that human inclinations serve as indicators of the rationally conceived goals of human 'good'.   This is implicit in the later statement of Finnis that,

> For Aquinas, the way to discover what is morally right ... and wrong ... is to ask, not what is in accordance with human nature, but what is reasonable. And this quest will eventually bring one back to the *underived* first principle of practical reasonableness, principles which make no reference at all to human nature, but only to human good.[15]

Thus, reason affords an insight by humankind into what may, in Aristotelian terms, be called a teleological 'good'.   A different defence against Hume's attack is advanced by Deryck Beyleveld and Roger Brownsword. They argue that,

> the essential Humean point is that a moral *ought* can be validly inferred only from a supporting moral *is* or ... *ought*. In short, moral *oughts* can only be validly inferred from supporting *moral* premises. Therefore, the key to the Humean principle is the move from the non-moral to the moral, not the move from *is* to *ought* as such.[16]

Thus they conclude that,

> to dispute the Natural-Law theory ... is to deny that to judge legal facts involves moral judgment, and the Humean principle cannot justify this denial. To think that it can is to suppose that statements of legal fact are morally neutral ... but the Humean principle cannot, and does not, in itself show that legal facts, or any other kinds of facts, are morally neutral.[17]

This argument goes further than that advanced by Finnis in a number of respects making the point expressly that the positivist model of morally neutral 'law-fact' is in itself specious rather than merely that 'law-fact' is open to moral evaluation within the 'province of jurisprudence'. A reservation to this proposition must be entered in so far as the treatment of law as an autonomous phenomenon has value for the limited purposes of technical legal discourse, but the basic point is nonetheless strong. Whether the issue is approached through Finnis's or that of Beyleveld and Brownsword, the basic naturalist contention may, when properly analysed, be seen not to fall foul of the fundamental Humean dichotomy between *is* and *ought*.

Upon a somewhat narrower perspective it may be argued that the is/ought dichotomy is anyway not properly in question in consideration of the propriety of the evaluation of positive law by reference to moral criteria derived, in whole or part, from the study of human nature. Positive law is concerned with the prescription and maintenance of structures of communal and individual conduct and it is difficult to discern any good reason why judgment of the performance of that role should not be founded upon the needs of its subjects. Such needs may, in turn, be defined only by some form of reference to 'human nature'.

If the evaluation of positive law by reference to moral or ethical criteria is accepted as tenable, there remains the problem of selecting the criteria to be applied. The only fixed point of reference here must seem, as O'Connor suggests, to be in one form or another, again, the perception of human nature.[18]   It would, however, be curious to suggest that undifferentiated human inclinations may afford adequate criteria of evaluation for the determination of the extent of 'obligation' associated with law.   Such a view would, indeed, lead directly to the gross subjectivism castigated by Bentham. Despite its relative antiquity, a clear exposition of these issues is still to be found in the analysis advanced by St. Thomas Aquinas, who in many ways set out the clearest form of developed classical naturalism.

The Naturalist Model(s) of Good Law

The Thomist conception of law seeks to relate human rationality to the cosmic rationality of God and this involves, through the *lex naturae*, insight into human nature as an aspect of natural order.   As Copleston puts it,

> man cannot read ... God's mind, [but] he can discern the fundamental tendencies and needs of his nature, and by reflecting on them he can come to a knowledge of the natural moral law.[19]

Thus humankind,

> recognizes or can recognize its [i.e. the moral law's] inherent rationality and binding force, and he promulgates it to himself.[20]

This represents the idea of acquisition of 'knowledge through inclination', the through the understanding of human nature.   There are certain evident difficulties in this concept.   In particular there arises the problem of knowing which of the various human inclinations, many in conflict, represent human 'good'.

Kai Nielsen, in a critical discussion of the Thomist position,[21] argues that there is a fundamental inconsistency in claiming a supernatural origin for the moral law whilst yet arguing that human beings can have knowledge of their 'good' by studying the desires of their fellows.[22]   The natural moral law may be rationally self-evident to God, but is not apparently so to human beings. It is thus difficult to know just how those human inclinations which are indicative of 'goodness' can be adequately identified. The basic objection is stated by David N. Weisstub as follows,

> Aquinas invites us to reflect on our nature to seek the good. But, given that he affords us an absolute assertion as to man's nature, devoid of guidelines that indicate... [how] man may achieve the good, he treads an argument of faith rather than reason.[23]

In fact the derivation of insight into human 'good' from the study of human nature, knowledge through inclination, is by no means so uncertain a doctrine as Nielsen and Weisstub, respectively, claim and imply. Thomist theory in this area is in large part teleological in nature and human beings are indeed invited, to an extent, to discern their own developmental 'good' in the inclinations of their nature. It is not, however, the Thomist claim that human nature, however derived, can or should prescribe the ideal form of life for humankind. It is argued, rather, that positive law should serve the purpose of affording provision for the form of social and political community in which aspiration to the best form of life might most effectively be pursued. This goal is advanced bearing in mind the ultimate Thomist concern with the spiritual edification of individual human beings. The key to the mode of derivation of knowledge of human 'good' through inclination can be seen in Nielsen's own statement that 'the standard is supposed to come somehow from the ... inclinations of all men'.[24] It would be unreasonable to suggest that all human desires are 'good', that could hardly be so since many human desires actually conflict. It seems, however, not unreasonable to suggest that the general expectations held by human beings of the societies in which they live can play a proper role in the shaping of the moral structure of those communities.[25] The indication of 'goodness' in an inclination may be argued to lie in its tendency to facilitate the formation of a stable community in which each of its members is afforded due recognition as a co-member within the network of individual and collective claims best fitted to the life of human beings as social and political animals.

In the identification of such inclinations account must be taken of the generality of aspiration. This is not, of course, to say that anything which most or even many people regard as desirable must therefore be considered to be 'good' for human beings. There are in practice very many objects of common desire, such as vast wealth or unaccountable power, which, as relative concepts, derive much of their desirability from the relatively worse position of others. Such desires, far from being indicative of general human 'good', may well fall within St. Augustine's category of 'lusts' to be resisted. Equally, the highly specific desires generated by particular cultures, which may or may not be 'good'in themselves, can, by virtue of their specialization, not be regarded as inherent in the human condition. Such culturally specific inclinations may, however, be particular expressions of more general principles which are so inherent as, in a rather different context, Aquinas himself might be taken to have suggested. The relevant human inclinations in this context are, thus, those which are generally accepted as the basic shared expectations of the members in common of a stable and fair social order. A similar approach underlies the natural rights approach of Finnis and, at a rather greater distance, also Rawls' theory of justice. The comparison of ideas of justice with analyses of the moral nature of law is justified by the masked degree of functional convergence of the concepts, although the two categories are clearly distinct. The nature of the conclusions which may be drawn from such a process of reasoning were stated by A.P. D'Entreves in his comment that,

> Natural law is the basis of political allegiance, the ground upon which social and political relations can be secured and comprehended.[26]

It may thus be argued that 'knowledge through inclination' is an appropriate mode of derivation of minimum legitimate social expectations by reference to which a framework of evaluation of positive law may be set out. Upon such a perspective the variations of substantive opinion within the body of classical naturalist thought becomes comprehensible as variations in reaction to given circumstances, rather than as disagreements destructive of the credibility of the doctrine as a whole.[27]

As to the ultimate origin of human 'good', whether it be a product of the will of God or a biological accident, the matter is a question of fundamental importance in its own right and one which far transcends issues raised by the nature of the obligation to obey positive law. This question is not, however, one which is fundamental to the naturalist argument in jurisprudence as such. For this specific purpose the fact of human nature and human inclination is a sufficient starting point for debate without addressing the question of their source and origin. It may be added that modern debate upon human rights has precisely such a foundation but does not necessarily enter into questions of source or origin.

The Place of Moral Analyses of Positive Law

If it is accepted, as it is contended that it must be, that positive law making is an enterprise undertaken in a moral and ethical context by reference to which its quality and claims may be evaluated, it must also be accepted that the practical operation of law may be affected by its quality. It is here that the naturalist argument impinges directly upon issues of 'obligation' and that the greatest controversy is generated since there necessarily arises the question of the status and claims of a positive provision judged to be 'immoral'.

The moral authority of positive law is one of the most ancient questions of legal theory and one certainly addressed by the ancient civilizations of both the near and far East. In its origin the question seems to relate to the transition from static to dynamic 'law ways'[28] which H.L.A. Hart, arguably misguidedly, considered to mark the point of origin of a recognizable 'legal' system.[29] Customary law has, by definition, the authoritative aura of tradition but the new law emanating from a dynamic system must somehow cloak itself in an equivalent authority if it is to avoid stigmatization as an arbitrary and tyrannical imposition. This is a sub-issue of the general question of the moral nature and authority of government.

The process of legitimation can be seen in the Semitic codes of the ancient near-East, for example in the 'code' of King Hammurabi of Babylon (d. 1750 BC.). This was not the first of the ancient Semitic codes, in 1947 the significantly earlier code of King Lipit-Ishtar of Nippur was discovered, but this does not deprive the Code Hammurabi of its status as a jurisprudential landmark. As C.W. Coram remarks,

> King Hammurabi's great contribution ... was to fuse local laws and precepts into a comprehensive legal code of nearly three hundred paragraphs.[30]

Hammurabi's code was actually less a legislative code than a 'casebook' recording judicial determinations by the King and presumably intended to act as a precedent for future judicial decision making. The nature of the authority claimed for the code is very interesting. The 'Preamble' states,

> Anu and Bel ... [called] me, ... the god-fearing Hammurabi, to establish justice in the earth.[31]

It concludes with the statement,

> Law and Justice I established in the land for the good of the people.[32]

The King, unlike the Egyptian Pharaohs, did not claim divine status, nor is any simple equation made between royal and divine authority. The suggestion made is rather that government is an institution authorized by divine agency 'for the good of the people' and it is not a great leap from this to the idea that government is legitimate only within such a purposive parameter.

A parallel, but much more strongly expressed, view can be found in the Pentateuch,[33] the first five books of the Hebrew Scriptures contained in the Old Testament. The law there stated evidently represents a lengthy period of development from a sanguinary system of clan or kin based obligation typical of nomadic peoples to more 'settled' forms of provision. The primary law, the *Torah*, claims its authority upon an interesting basis. Much of the substantive content is unequivocally attributed to the will of God revealed to Moses on Mount Sinai.[34] It is, however, made clear that the prescription was accepted as part of a 'covenant' and not merely as an act of subjection. Thus it is written that,

> [All] the people answered with one voice and said, All the words which the Lord hath said we will do.[35]

Thus the obligation imposed has a very particular flavour in the Hebrew Scripture viewed as a 'covenant' history.

In the context of Divine law it may be added in parenthesis that in Jewish jurisprudence an ingenious solution was found to the problem of the rigidity of prescription inherent in theocratically conceived laws enunciated in particular historical epochs. The *Torah* is supplemented by a canon of interpretation know as the *Halakah*. This partakes of the same authority as the *Torah* upon the basis that a true interpretation is necessarily inherent in the thing interpreted. This beguiling argument, which largely ignores the question of validation, had an equivalent in Islamic *Shar'iat* jurisprudence in the canonical 'schools'of interpretation. This was, however, frozen as an active source of development with the 'closing of the gates of *ijtahad*'.[36] A more distant, and rather questionable, parallel to this may be seen in the traditional claim of English judges to be able to find the solutions to new problems in the interstices of the common law tradition.[37]

Once accepted the obligation imposed by the *Torah* was seen as absolute. Governmental demands contravening Holy Law were seen as abominations involving not only those making the demand but also those obeying in sin. The effect of this view of government can be seen in the Biblical accounts of the consequences in the reigns of Saul[38] and Ahab.[39]

On the other side of the world the Confucian philosophy of classical China also took a moral view of government, emphasizing its position as a part of a rational cosmic harmony, of which 'bad' government would be a disruption. It may be added that, partly because of the historical experience of *Legalist* political philosophy under the Chin dynasty, the Confucian theorists of the Han and later dynasties relegated positive law to a role of coercive enforcement and certainly not as a 'proper' mode of dispute resolution.[40] The moral authority of government in the Confucian system was symbolized by the *Mandate of Heaven*, a reference to the abstraction of cosmic reason rather than to any concrete divine commission. It was assumed that 'bad', or even simply inadequate, government would tend to lead to social dislocation and eventually dynastic collapse - interpreted as a withdrawal and transfer of the Mandate of Heaven. Mencius (Meng K'e) commented that,

> when those above ignore the rites, those below ignore learning, and lawless people arise, then the end of the state is at hand.[41]

Upon the direct issue of an obligation to obey law, however, Confucian thinkers took a much less straightforward line. It would seem that Confucian theory treated the obligation of subjects to obey as continuing until such time as a transfer of the Mandate of Heaven was taken to have occurred, that is to say until a new dynasty had in practice been established. Here, it may be suggested that there was a considerable, if unacknowledged, survival of earlier Chin *Legalist* thinking in that there was no recognition of any limitation of the citizen's duty to obey the laws made by the state, whilst it endured, however 'bad' they might be.[42] The Confucian analysis was much more one of causality in the sense that it was argued that if the state failed to conduct itself correctly there would result an imbalance in natural order which would manifest itself in civil commotions and even natural disasters with the ultimate potential consequence of dynastic collapse. There was here no call to disobedience.

The Platonic Arguments for Obedience

It is not, perhaps, surprising that detailed consideration of the nature of the obligation to obey positive law as a distinct issue emerged first neither from the ancient Judaic nor from the classical Chinese traditions of jurisprudence. It was first considered in the Hellenistic strand of western juristic thought.[43]

The issue was discussed by Plato in *The Last Days of Socrates*, particularly in the *Apology* and *Crito*. This work purports to be an account of the thought of Socrates during his trial and whilst awaiting execution upon charges of impiety and corrupting youth. In fact, it is an analysis by Socrates' pupil Plato of the duty of the citizen to obey the state and its laws set in a Socratic context. The two central sections of the work, the *Apology* and the *Crito*, represent, respectively, Socrates' speech in defence at his trial and his subsequent refusal of the pleas of his friend Crito that he escape from the condemned cell. It may be added that Socrates' execution was delayed by the requirements of the annual ritual of the 'Mission to Delos' and it may indeed have been the hope of the Athenian establishment that he might escape, thus relieving them of both his unwelcome presence and the odium of killing a famous philosopher.

The burden of Socrates' argument in the *Apology* is that the state has no right to require an individual to do wrong and should it purport to do so a just person would have no honourable option but to refuse. The argument goes, indeed, so far as to suggest that in his day a just person could hardly expect to survive in Athens.[44] Amongst other specific examples, Socrates is represented as citing an order addressed to him and others during the oligarchic rule of the 'Thirty Tyrants' to seize Leon of Salamis and bring him to unjust execution.[45] Socrates alone refused to comply and argued that he himself would undoubtedly then have been slain had not the oligarchy fallen shortly thereafter. The same position is represented in an earlier statement that should the court decide to spare his life upon the condition that he cease teaching his philosophy, he would have to refuse such a condition upon the ground that its implementation would do evil by denying the city the benefit of Socratic teaching.[46] It appears, therefore, that in the *Apology* Plato, speaking through Socrates, strongly denies that there can be any obligation to comply with the requirements of an unjust law. In his account of the arguments advanced by Plato in the *Crito* A.D. Woozley contends that a basic distinction must here be drawn between categories of laws, orders and decisions and that the theoretical condition which is analyzed for us in the *Apology* is not capable of definitive categorization.[47]   This is a matter of some significance in comparisons between the *Apology* and the *Crito*, but it must seem that in the former Socrates is represented as denying the right of the state to command injustice.   He emphatically does not, however, deny that the state may in practice wreak injustice.   Indeed, the burden of the argument is that the just individual should not associate him or herself with state injustice, lest the individual become unjust.   Thus, Socrates is made to remark,

> the difficulty is not so much to escape death;   the real difficulty is to escape from doing wrong, ... [48]

Socrates in fact was condemned to death, perhaps because he sought justice rather than the corrupt 'mercy' for which convention demanded that he plead.

The argument of the *Crito* is concerned directly with the obligation to obey an 'unjust' law, specifically here a judicial decision.   Three responses to an unjust legal decision can be found admitted as permissible in the argument which Socrates is represented as making in denial of his friend Crito's advice to escape.   These are (1) to persuade the state to change its demands, (2) to depart to another state governed by more congenial laws, or (3) to choose to remain and then to submit to the demands of the law.[49] These may be characterized as persuasion, departure or obedience.   What is not permitted is to remain in the state, having failed in argument for legal change, and then to defy the law.

In the argument advanced in the *Crito* the obligation to obey is founded upon three bases set out in a dialogue between Socrates and Crito, although these are presented as discrete elements but rather as parts of a continuous discourse.   The three elements may loosely be termed, respectively, 'filial', 'contractual' and 'destructive'.

The 'filial' argument takes an overtly 'paternalist' view of the state, indeed a direct comparison is made between the relationship of parent and child and that existing between a citizen and the state of his or her residence.[50]   The subject is represented as owing a debt of gratitude to the state for maintaining the society in which he or she must be taken to have acquiesced by virtue of having remained in it.   The subject is also represented as being placed under obligation by the inherent 'authority' of the state, having, again, acquiesced therein through continued voluntary residence in its territory.   Such arguments have, possibly, a much greater viability in the context of the very small political units represented by ancient Greek city states than in the much broader context of modern nation states.

The more general 'contractual' argument may be more readily acceptable in a modern context. In this contention an individual who is free to choose otherwise but elects to remain resident in a state is taken implicitly to have agreed to abide by its laws.[51] In the *Crito*, the personified laws of Athens are made to add that Socrates, by virtue of his long residence and involvement in the life of the city, can be held especially to have entered into such a social contract.[52]

This is a basic version of one of the most common forms of argument for an obligation to obey law. Woozley draws the obvious parallel with the 'loyalist' response to anti-Vietnam war protests in the USA during the 1960s and 1970s, 'America - Love it or Leave it.'[53] The argument is essentially that contained, in a much narrower focus, in the equitable maxim *qui sentit commodum sentire debet et onus* - the person who takes the benefit must also take the burden. Thus, continued residence in a state, having neither obtained change nor accepted an available option of departure, is taken to imply an 'agreement' to abide by the prevailing laws in return for the, again voluntarily accepted, benefits of the social system existing under the aegis of those same laws.

This 'contractual' argument shades into a more strongly phrased argument based upon a view of disobedience as socially destructive. The argument is put concisely through the medium of the personified laws of Athens, which are represented as asking Socrates,

> Can you deny that by [escaping from Athens] ... you intend, so far as you have the power, to destroy us, the laws ... ? Do you imagine that a city can continue to exist ... if legal judgements ... have no force but are nullified ... by private persons ?[54]

This question can be seen as a clear parallel with Bentham's trenchant attack upon the idea of 'natural rights' which was considered in the preceding chapter. The argument is advanced in two broad forms. At *Crito* 50B the suggestion is made that the legal order as a whole may be in danger of collapse if individuals set the laws at nought. That is to say, in Benthamite terms, that a vital habit of obedience may be weakened with effects fatal to the system. The bulk of the argument is not, however, addressed in this 'public' form, but to Socrates personally in terms of his own duty to the laws; why should he wish to act in a manner tending towards the destruction of the authority of the laws? This is not by any means the same thing as a claim that disobedience by Socrates, or any other individual, would in itself have any such extreme effect as destroying the laws. In *Crito* 50D to 51C the point is made that Socrates has obviously been willing to accept the benefits and protection of Athenian law and now that a part of his implied agreement, acceptance of judicial decisions, acts to his detriment he may not withdraw. The point of the contention being, again in some striking parallel with Bentham, that no system can endure if its subjects accept only those parts of it which are beneficial to them.

These three arguments can be seen as variant shadings of one argument upon the implied acceptance of legal authority and the consequent moral unacceptability of a defiance of the court's decision, unjust though it was, by Socrates. There is here an apparent inconsistency between the arguments advanced in the *Apology* and in the *Crito* in so far as one appears to urge that the state has no right to command wrongdoing, whereas the other appears to counsel obedience even to 'bad' or unjust laws, or rather, strictly, judicial decisions. On the basis of these respective positions Socrates, as represented by Plato, has at various times been treated as a pioneer exponent of civil disobedience as a response to injustice and as an 'authoritarian' proponent of an unlimited obligation to comply with positive legal rules.

The apparent inconsistency may be reconciled upon the basis of Socrates' statement in the *Apology* that the state has no right to command wrongdoing[55] and in the *Crito* that to do wrong is always dishonourable.[56] Socrates appears to argue on the one hand that a person should not do evil when so required by the state but should accept wrongful infliction by the state upon him or her, subject to the possibilities of persuasion or prior departure. This refers ultimately to Socrates' clear view that evil is a quality of the wrongdoer and not of the victim.[57] Thus, the subject should not do evil to others, even if so ordered by the law, but should, upon an essentially social-contractarian basis, submit to the adverse action of a legal system which he or she has accepted by a course of conduct. In the one case the individual refuses to do evil, in the latter he or she submits to evil perpetuated by others. The practical implications of this argument may be referred back to the case of Leon of Salamis. Upon this model Leon of Salamis should have submitted to arrest and execution, assuming of course that he had had the prior options of argument or flight. Socrates, on the other hand, was justified in his refusal to participate in the unjust action of the state.

By the same token, had the Thirty Tyrants in consequence condemned Socrates, he should then have submitted to his own fate.

Such a resolution of the conflict leaves open the question of any absolute limits to the duty to obey. What of the 'just' citizen who conspired to frustrate acts of genocide by the Third Reich or acts of political oppression in the Stalinist Soviet Union? Such action would have been entirely proper according to the Socratic argument, but should the 'just' citizen thereafter have submitted to arrest and death at the hands of the *Gestapo* or the NKVD? In such a case the answer must presumably be in the negative because the possibility of 'persuasion' was clearly absent and so, to all intents and purposes, was that of departure. But had one or both of those options been available, would submission, not to an isolated unjust act but to a general scheme of abomination, have been required? F.C. Wade has argued[58] that in addition to the basic requirement of doing no evil to others, the duty to obey laws may also be limited by a requirement that they be just. He contended, therefore, that a distinction can be drawn between the hypothetical command or 'agreement' in the *Apology* that Plato abandon his teaching as a *quid pro quo* for reprieve and the condemnation which is the focus of the *Crito*. For Socrates to have ceased disseminating what he saw as wisdom would have been an evil not only to himself but also to Athens which he should by no means have perpetrated. On the other hand, compliance with a judgment rendered under a system of law which, by continued residence in Athens, Socrates had 'agreed' to accept would be to act 'justly' to the personified laws of the city. Although the condemnation was unjust, the implied agreement of Socrates to abide by judicial decisions was just and not capable of an *ex post facto* differentiation in respect of the substantive content of a particular decision. A broadly similar argument is advanced by R.E. Allen.[59] Woozley, however, argues that such theoretical reconciliations between the views urged in the *Apology* and the *Crito* are untenable. He thus concludes that,

> the conflict between, on the one hand, his [Socrates'] principle that in no circumstances must a man do what is unjust ... and, on the other hand, his three arguments for obedience to the laws cannot be resolved.[60]

It is perhaps true, as Woozley argues, that there is a conflict upon the face of the language used in the *Apology* and the *Crito*. However, there also seems to be a reasonable argument to be made for a certain degree of interpretation in considering the arguments advanced in *The Last days of Socrates* and if undue literality is not insisted upon, the resolutions advanced by, e.g., Wade and Allen may be accepted as reasonable in the context of Plato's concerns.

Later Social Contractarian Theory

The essential 'contractarian' argument upon personal duty to obey as a social obligation set out in *The Last Days of Socrates* is also found, in a variety of forms, in the work of the 17th and 18th century 'social contractarian' thinkers. Of these, Thomas Hobbes, John Locke and Jean-Jacques Rousseau may fairly be taken as a cross section. All three used the hypothetical social contract as a device for the exploration of the fundamental purposes of a legal order.

Hobbes (1588-1679), writing in the context of the English Civil War, urged that the purpose of government was the maintenance of social order in the pursuit of which almost any government, however oppressive, was to be preferred to anarchy. Thus, he argued that individual 'political' powers are surrendered to the state and the individual is then under an obligation to obey so long as social order is in fact maintained. He put this point uncompromisingly in the statement that,

> when a man hath ... granted away his Right, then he is *obliged* or *bound* not to hinder those, to whom such Right is granted ... .[61]

Little or no moral or ethical element is to be found here. Indeed, from an expository point of view Bentham found much to admire in Hobbes. He did not deny that one might reasonably hope for more from a government than mere avoidance of civil war or anarchy, but he nonetheless saw such avoidance as the primary foundation of the legitimacy of the state. Through failure in that alone could obligation to the state be vitiated in his view, it mattering little, otherwise, what form the sovereign power might take.

John Locke (1632-1704), who wrote in the very different political context of the English 'Glorious Revolution' of 1688-89, was by contrast centrally concerned with the forms of sovereignty and the substantive exercise of sovereign powers. In this light he considered that the purpose of government was not merely the provision of order in place of chaos but the protection of 'property'. In his usage the term 'property' included not only land, chattels and other material assets, but also such claims as 'rights' and 'liberties'. The divergence from Hobbe's concerns is evident in the difference between their respective models of the pre-contractual 'state of nature'. Whereas Hobbes imagined a strife-torn existence leading to a 'life of man, solitary, poore, nasty, brutish and short',[62] Locke presented a state of things in which basic rights were already inherent but, in the absence of a state authority, inefficiently maintained. The consequence of failure to protect 'rights' in such a system have been summarized elsewhere in the following terms,

> if a civil government behaves in a manner contrary to the implication of the delegation of powers made to it by the community then its law will to that extent become tyrannical and its authority [will to the same extent be] ... vitiated.[63]

This is a much more substantively purposive model than that of Hobbes. It may also, in its use of images of political and economic 'properties', be viewed as an early capitalist 'enterprise' analysis, although the imposition of such an *ex post facto* coloration onto a late 17th century argument should perhaps be approached with some caution.

Jean-Jacques Rousseau (1712-1778) in *Du Contrat Social* (Of the Social Contract) went further in arguing that the surrender of 'natural' individual powers was not made to any particular form of state authority but rather to the general idea of a social order, the form of which would be determined from time to time by the *volonte generale* (general will) of the community. This 'will' was not conceived by Rousseau as mere popular opinion, but as the opinion which a rational and informed community would hold. Far from leading to the revolutionary populism with which Rousseau is sometimes associated, this concept tends rather towards a form of radical elitism. The formally enshrined 'leading role' of the communist parties of the former Eastern bloc was somewhat similarly conceived,[64] although whether Rousseau would have relished that particular comparison may be doubted. Be that as it may, upon Rousseau's model when a particular form of government, in his case the French *ancien regime*, ceased to be an efficient agent for the rational expression of the development of the political community, the duty to obey would find a new focus in a changed political order, without alteration of the 'social contract' itself.

In their different ways all these theories rely expressly or impliedly upon a purposive model of government. This goes beyond the 'contractarian' element of the argument in *The Last Days of Socrates*, which hints at a purposive model of obligation only in the discussion in the *Crito* of the objection to disobedience as 'destructive' of the law.[65] However, a fuller review of the issue is found in the work of St. Thomas Aquinas. It is not, perhaps, surprising that the most substantial naturalist analysis of the obligation to obey should be found at the mature stage of the fusion of the two principal strands of the western naturalist tradition, a position which led Finnis to describe Aquinas as 'a paradigm "natural law theorist"'.[66]

The Augustinian Background of Thomism

The significance of the work of Aquinas in this field lies in his fusion of the classical rationalist traditions with the Judaeo-Christian ethic, producing a form of Christian Aristotelianism which went further than the earlier Christian Platonism of St. Augustine of Hippo but nonetheless developed from it. For St. Augustine, the perfect society was one wholly submissive to the Divine will, which he termed the *Lex Aeterna* - Eternal Law. Of it he stated that,

> Lex Aeterna est qua justum est ut omnia sint ordinatissima.[67]

That is to say, Eternal Law is that by which all things are justly ordered. This, with the highly significant addition of direct Divine attribution, has clear parallels with both the Platonic 'ideal'and the cosmic reason of the Stoics. Positive law, the *Lex Temporalis*, was for Augustine, a necessary but regrettable expedient raised by the need in a fallen earthly society to restrain the obdurately sinful from acting in ways obstructive to proper modes of life. Positive law in this view is thus seen simply as a coercive restraint which is by no means to be compared with freely chosen submission to the Divine will.

In the analysis advanced by Augustine of Hippo the relationship set out between the *Lex Aeterna* and the *Lex Temporalis* is very much more direct than is that which had been proposed much earlier between the

Platonic ideal and reality. The *Lex Aeterna* is not presented as a critical standard for purposes of comparison and evaluation, but as itself the only truly authoritative 'law'. The *Lex Temporalis* is presented as a partial, pale and coercive reflection which is morally validated only by concordance with the relevant norms of the *Lex Aeterna*, notwithstanding any formalities of enactment. Thus, St. Augustine stated that,

> in temporali lege nihil est justum ac legitimum quod non est lege aeterna homines sibi deriverint.[68]

i.e., no part of positive law is just or 'legitimate which is not founded upon Eternal Law.

The implication of this reasoning in terms of the obligation to obey is set out bluntly in the comment that, *lex esse non videbitur quae justa non fuerit*,[69] meaning that no 'law' was ever seen which was not just. Unfortunately this, along with the simpler and much cited statement that, *lex iniusta non est lex*,[70] an unjust 'law' is non law, has become a significant source of misunderstanding. In positivist analyses this type of remark has been cited with disdain and countered with all too readily available instances of morally dubious positive enactments which have been recognized and applied by the courts. The famous remark of Austin that,

> The most pernicious laws ... have been ... enforced by judicial tribunals. ... [I]f I shall be tried and condemned, and ... I object to the sentence that it is contrary to the law of God ... the Court will demonstrate the inconclusiveness of my reasoning by hanging me up ...[71]

summarizes this form of criticism perfectly. Had St. Augustine, or any other naturalist, actually claimed that a government cannot enact an 'unjust' provision which a court will recognize and apply, the argument would fully merit derision. Such, however, was not the burden of his contention and it would have been incredible, in the context of his time, had it been so. St. Augustine was a Bishop at a time when the Church had, to modern eyes, an almost unhealthy obsession with the macabre details of the agonizing deaths of martyrs. He made the obvious point that all positive rules and decisions cannot be 'good' because if they were so, the Christian martyrs would necessarily have to be concluded to have been justly condemned.[72] This would, of course, be an utterly insupportable conclusion from any conceivable Christian viewpoint and it was certainly not that intended by

St. Augustine.   In fact he was writing of government as an exercise taking place within a moral framework which sets bounds to its 'legitimacy', which is quite distinct from any claim that governments might not in practice exceed their moral 'authority'.

Once this has been accepted it becomes clear that St. Augustine's actual claim was that positive law making is an inherently moral activity constrained by what might be termed a 'proper purposes' doctrine.   In effect, positive provisions are argued to be required not only to satisfy formal criteria of identification but also purposive moral criteria in order to be fully binding upon the consciences of their addressees.   'Laws' made for some other purpose or so perversely devised as to frustrate an originally 'just' intention may be coercively imposed but would yet, to a greater or lesser degree, be defective in their claim upon conscience.

The nature of the Augustinian argument upon this point is illustrated by an example which parallels H.L.A. Hart's consideration of 'power'and 'authority' in his example of the coercive action of a bank robber,[73] although in pursuit of radically different ends.   St. Augustine used the account of a confrontation between a captured pirate and Alexander the Great, adopted from Cicero, to demonstrate the moral nature and limitation of governmental 'authority'.[74]   Alexander asked the pirate, immediately prior to his execution, how he could presume to engage in robbery upon the seas. The pirate replied that there was but one difference between himself and Alexander, he had only one ship and was condemned as a pirate whereas Alexander had a whole navy and was acclaimed a great ruler.   On a purely formal level Alexander could enact and impose such orders as he thought fit, whilst the pirate could only make criminal demands.   However, and here the Augustinian argument differs sharply from that advanced in Hart's 'gunman' example, the coercive demands of a conqueror do not necessarily give rise to any greater degree of *moral* obligation to comply than did those of the pirate.

In short, the spectrum of the types of obligation which may be imposed by law is not limited to the formal recognition of positive 'authority' or any associated potential for coercive enforcement by agencies of the state.   This spectrum embraces also the purposive moral context of positive law making, by reference to which a level of conscientious obligation, which transcends the categories both of formal   duty and possible coercive imposition, is defined.

The Contribution of Thomism

These arguments were more subtly developed by St. Thomas Aquinas (1225-1274) in a manner which diverged from the Augustinian model in its treatment of positive law as such. In this Aquinas was much influenced by the rediscovery of the works of Aristotle, which had been lost at the time of Augustine. Like Aristotle, and unlike Plato and St. Augustine, Aquinas considered law to be a 'natural' aspect of the life of human beings as social animals and to have no inherent or necessary connection with sin. He made explicit reference to the dictum of Aristotle that humankind is a 'political animal' (*politikon zoon*).[75] Aquinas also followed Aristotle in considering law to be an essentially didactic institution calculated, when 'properly' made, to the advancement of the 'good' of its addressees. This 'good' is invested in the Thomist view with an absolute religious quality not found in the Aristotelian analysis, but the teleological nature of the argument is also made clear. The significance of the change as between the Augustinian and Thomist appreciations of positive law is well expressed in the comment by the Dominican editors of Aquinas' great work, *Summa Theologica*, that,

> law is seen as a whole ... freed from Augustinism which stressed the minatory role of law. ... [Aquinas] brings out the *potestas directiva*, relegating the *potestas coactiva* to a secondary office of positive law ... . In brief, law has a dignity greater than that of a remedy *propter peccatum*.[76]

These emphases appear clearly in the basic definition of law advanced by Aquinas,

> nihil est aliud quaedam rationis ordinatio ad bonum commune, ab eo qui curam communitatis habet, promulgata.[77]

That is to say, nothing but a rational provision made for the good of the community by whoever has the charge of it and promulgated. The Thomist concept of law is thus quadripartite, involving (a) rationality, (b) beneficial intent for the community, (c) governing authority and (d) promulgation. This definition was applied not only to human positive law but to all forms of law, up to and including the *Lex Aeterna* - the ordinance of God. It must be admitted that at first sight the basic Thomist definition of law has something of the quality of a moral criterion for the distinction of 'law' from 'non-law' which has classically been scorned by successive positivist commentators.

This can, however, readily be shown to be a false impression. The four elements of the definition can be divided into two quite distinct categories founded, respectively, upon moral/ethical bases and upon formal considerations. The latter two, governing authority and promulgation are straightforward - in effect 'positivist' - criteria of identification. The basis for each is simple. Laws are made by rulers because they must be associated with an identifiable authority which can, although coercion is not in the Thomist scheme a definitive characteristic of law, in the final analysis impose them upon the refractory. Thus, whilst any person of good will may advise or persuade, only a sovereign can 'legislate'.[78] Promulgation is necessary for the obvious reason that a rule or principle for the guidance of conduct can only function effectively if it is communicated.[79] That law making is a sovereign act and one which requires promulgation is an uncontroversial proposition which would seem in no way incongruous in any 'positivist' analysis. The distinctively 'naturalist' element of the Thomist definition lies in the remaining requirements of rationality and intent for the good of the community. These criteria are evaluatory in nature and relate not to the formal identification of law but to its substantive quality.

The case made out by Aquinas for the inclusion of these criteria in the definition of 'law' is simple. He contended that, as an enunciation of principles for the guidance of conduct, law is in some sense an expression of will by the law maker(s).[80] Any will expressed in legislation, or other legal, form must in the Thomist view be 'rational' if it is usefully to be distinguished from mere arbitrary demand.[81] It is assumed in this argument that a rational will is necessarily benevolent, a view also found in the Platonic and Aristotelian analyses but given additional emphasis here by the advancement of the *Lex Aeterna* as the ultimate origin of all rational perception. It is worth noting here in parenthesis that Aquinas related the *Lex Aeterna* to positive law, the *Lex Humana*, through two media. In the Thomist analysis the Divine will is presented firstly as being disclosed through the *Lex Divina*, revelation through scripture, and secondly as being discerned through the *Lex Naturalis*, those aspects of the operation of the Divine will observable through human reason. Aquinas argued that, as the product of a benevolent legislative will, laws which are generally rather than particularly directed - a point also made by H.L.A. Hart in a different context in *The Concept of Law* - must be directed to the common good rather than to the individual benefit of specified persons.[82] The nature of the common good, an obviously central question, is here defined by the teleological framework of the Thomist analysis. F.C. Copleston remarks that,

> moral law is for him [Aquinas] one of the ways in which creatures are directed towards their several ends. ... [I]t is a special case of the general principle that all finite things move towards their ends by the development of their potentialities.[83]

The relationship between positive law and the moral law is not, however, simple and Aquinas did not argue it to be so.

The essential causes of complication are twofold. Firstly, the moral content of positive law varies widely, ranging from the enshrinement of basic moral norms such as 'you shall do no murder'[84] to rules which are morally neutral in their substance, although possibly the subject of moral obligation once made. An example of the latter may be seen in the law relating to traffic regulation - the decision as between driving on the left or on the right is in itself devoid of moral significance, but once the decision has been made there is clearly a moral obligation to observe the same rule as everyone else. Secondly, most positive laws are neither absolutely 'moral' nor absolutely 'immoral', but have mingled moral qualities in relation both to their substance and to their application in particular circumstances.

The moral assessment of law in the Thomist analysis, as in all naturalist analyses, represents in effect a 'proper purposes' doctrine applied in practice. As the Dominican editors of the *Summa Theologica* put it,

> The argument is concerned with the moral force of law, not with its strict morality.[85]

Aquinas presented the proper purpose of positive law as the facilitation of the social life and development of human beings through the appropriate exercise of free will for the fulfilment of the Divine plan for humankind. This concept followed directly from the basic definition of 'law' which he advanced. The idea is well expressed by Dino Bigongiari in his discussion of the political thought of Aquinas,

> A state according to St. Thomas is a part of the universal empire of which God is the maker and ruler. Its laws are, or can be made to be, particular determinations of the empire's eternal code; and the authority which enforces these laws is a power whose origin is also in God.

> Its good and justification is to offer to man satisfactory ... conditions of life as a basis for a moral and intellectual education which ... lend[s] itself to ... spiritual edification.[86]

Aquinas ultimately concurred with the view of St. Isidore of Seville that 'properly' conceived positive law is defined by three basic qualities: (1) consistency with religion (i.e. with the revealed *Lex Divina*), (2) correspondence with natural law (i.e. with the rationally perceived *Lex Naturalis*) and (3) tendency to further the teleological 'good' of humanity.[87] This concept, thus, relates ultimately back to the cosmic, Divine, rationality embodied in the *Lex Aeterna*.

A law which is thus 'just' will, in the Thomist perception, exercise moral suasion over its subjects, for whom obedience will be 'right' and disobedience 'wrong'. This should not, however, be taken to imply any confusion of functions as between the *Lex Aeterna* and the *Lex Humana*, in modern terminology as between ultimate morality and positive law. Although law is argued to have no necessary or inherent linkage with sin, it cannot itself, in the Thomist perception, be the highest form of moral order. In what is broadly a Thomist analysis Georgio Del Vecchio makes the point that Divine Justice, as the highest moral prescription, does not relate to the human condition only through the filter of human positive 'justice'.[88] He quotes the remark of St. Gregory the Great that, '*humana justitia divinae justitiae comparata injustitia est*'.[89] That is to say, that human justice in comparison with the justice of God is not 'just' at all. Thus, positive and Eternal law are not properly to be considered the same thing encountered at different levels, although the former should certainly be founded upon the latter. The highest law, in short, defines the ultimate aspiration of a truly 'just' society, characterized, *inter alia*, by the inherency of mercy. Human law, in contrast, even when informed by the *Lex Divina* and *Lex Naturalis*, can at most do no more than prescribe the base upon which a moral society might be built.[90] Even so, within its appointed sphere a 'just' positive law will bind in conscience by virtue of its moral authority and purposive value.

What, if any, obligation is then imposed by a positive legal provision which is less than perfectly 'just'? Aquinas did not contend that an unjust law would be non-law in the positivist sense of being a formally inapplicable norm. The issue in question is, as for St. Augustine, rather the extent of the claim which a 'bad' law imposes upon the conscience of its addressees. According to the Thomist analysis, legal provisions might be 'unjust' in either of two broad ways. They might contravene the cosmic prescription of the will of God or they might simply be 'unfair' according to human perceptions. A given provision might, of course, fall foul of both criteria, in which case the former would subsume the latter. Any 'law' failing under the first head would be an abomination devoid of claim upon conscience, a view deriving directly from the Judaic and Patristic perceptions. This argument, both in its traditional form and in some secular equivalent forms associated with the concept of human rights, relates to gross outrages. A modern genocidal 'law' would be an example and would now contravene not only moral law but also public international positive law.[91] The second type of 'injustice' is both more commonly encountered and less simple in the questions which it raises. It is more problematic because relative degrees of human injustice require to be balanced against demands of social stability which cannot be set aside in all, or even most, cases.

The central question posed by an 'unjust' law in this context is whether or not all 'true' positive law is founded upon natural law.[92] The Thomist response is founded upon the Augustinian proposition that *non videtur esse lex quae justa non fuerit*, which is to say that no law was ever seen which was not just.[93] Aquinas draws out the implications of this in commenting, *unde inquantum habet de justitia inquantum de virtute.*[94] This is felicitously translated by the Dominican editors of *Summa Theologica* as, 'hence a command has the force of law to the extent that it is just'.[95] This proposition may readily be misunderstood and careful qualification is necessary if modern linguistic usage is not to be allowed to misrepresent Aquinas' intention. T.E. Davitt argues that from the Thomist viewpoint,

> A prime over-all requisite for a law ... is that it be just. If it is not just, if it lacks this essential element, it is not law at all ... rather perversity, corruption, violence and tyranny.[96]

Davitt admits that Aquinas was not strictly speaking of law in the 'positivist' sense in this context, but the distinction requires to be made overt rather than implicit if confusion is to be avoided. In fact Aquinas was speaking of law as a moral phenomenon rather than simply as a structure of formally recognized positive rules and principles. With regard to laws which may be considered humanly 'unjust' he stated, *Et hujusmodi magis sunt violentiae quam legis ... .*[97] That is to say that such 'laws' have more the nature of outrages than that of true law. This remark was made with reference to the Augustinian comment upon the justice of laws quoted above.   Again, with reference to 'tyrannical' laws he stated that,

> lex tyrannica cum non sit secundum rationem non est simpliciter lex sed magis est quaedam perversitas legis[98]

i.e., a tyrannical law made contrary to reason is not truly a 'law' but, rather, a perversion of law.   'Tyranny' in the Thomist usage connotes arbitrariness and irrationality rather than necessarily the abomination implied in modern usage.[99]   These references should be read in the light of what has been argued above to be the essentially 'purposive' nature of the naturalist enterprise.   The claim is not that an immoral legislator will fail to produce and identifiable rule or standard but that an immoral use of legislative power is an abuse of power which is 'properly' exercised only within moral parameters.   A 'law' which is unjust in this sense will then to a greater or lesser degree be defective in its claim upon conscience.

In his *Commentary upon the Sentences of Peter Lombard* Aquinas argued that the (moral) duty to obey law arises from a derivation of authority and is coterminous with that derived authority.[100]   In the case of a humanly 'unjust' law he sought to resolve the issue of obedience or disobedience through a combination of moral and pragmatic considerations.   He argued that even a 'good' law is made for the common good and has authority to the extent of the pursuit of that end but not beyond.   Aquinas gave the example of an order to close the gates of a walled city in time of siege, suggesting that the gates should be opened, notwithstanding the order, when necessary to admit citizens fleeing from the enemy.   Such 'emergency' disobedience was, however, limited by Aquinas to cases in which it would be unreasonable, in consequence of the particular time or circumstance, to refer the issue to the appropriate authorities for resolution.   He made reference to Justinian for authority for the proposition that rules designed for the common benefit should not be applied so harshly as to confound the benefit intended.[101]   Thus a law should not be followed if, in a particular case, its application would not be for the common good.   This proposition amounts, however, in all to little more than the concession of a 'defence of necessity' in certain cases of disobedience to laws which are not 'bad' in themselves.   It cannot be represented as a general denial of claim to obedience in conscience.   Upon this latter and much more significant point in the present context of discussion, Aquinas finally came to the centrally important conclusion that, unde nec in talibus homo obligatur ut obediat legi, si sine scandalo vel majori detrimento resistere possit.[102]

The point being that there is no moral obligation to obey an 'unjust' law unless greater 'scandal' or detriment than that caused by the law itself would result from disobedience. 'Scandal' here means, as the Dominican editors of the *Summa Theologica* point out, 'not shocking behaviour, but the sin of causing moral harm to another.'[103]   Granted the Thomist admission of the 'natural' importance of positive law as a social institution, it is implicit in the argument that some price in 'bad' law must be paid in an imperfect world for the avoidance of the greater perils of chaos and anarchy.   This emerges clearly in Chapter VI of *De Regimine Principum* in which Aquinas argued that a 'tyranny' which does not go to excess should be tolerated because rebellion may bring on the worse perils of a yet greater tyranny or, in the alternative, anarchy.

Nonetheless, Aquinas conceded that when abuse of power by a tyrannical regime becomes a worse evil than   social disruption, it may properly be resisted.   In short, the immoral use of power will ultimately undermine the moral basis of the obligation to obey.   He cited as examples of tyrants thus properly deposed, Tarquinius Superbus, the last ancient King of Rome, and the anti-Christian Emperor Domitian.[104]   If, however, the 'price' in bad government to be paid for social stability is not susceptible to infinite inflation, Aquinas did counsel that in all but the most extreme cases, the alleviation of oppression should be left to Divine rather than human agency.[105]   Thus, upon the Thomist model, a 'bad' positive law may be imposed but does not have a claim in conscience except, in the case of a humanly 'unjust' rather than abominable provision, to the extent that social stability may demand compliance.

The imposition of a 'bad' positive law, or of a 'good' one upon the refractory who are immune to the promptings of conscience, will involve coercion by the state.   Such coercion is, however, in the Thomist analysis bound by the same moral parameters as law-making.   Dino Bigongiari comments,

> God ... has implanted in us the invincible conviction that the power to coerce, which He gives, implies an obligation on the part of the coercer to respect voluntarily that which he compels others to observe. Hence the power which law has to coerce subjects can never be dissociated from the power to make the ruler abide by it.[106]

Aquinas pointed out the limited capacity of coercion as an element of law. He argued that coercion can only be applied to external acts, whereas the moral obligation imposed by law is subject to no such limitation.[107]

The Problem of 'Bad' Government in Thomist Theory

Thomist legal theory was part of a more general analysis of government in a moral context intended to be of direct practical significance. D'Entreves commented upon this that,

> The art of politics ... must not be measured solely by its achievements, ... efficiency and success. ... [T]he reason for this is that politics always imply a moral responsibility ... . They are not a purely pragmatic science. They are a part of morals.[108]

The treatment of 'bad' government, which may, of course, be signified by 'bad' law making, in the Thomist system, is generally similar to that set out in relation to a particular 'unjust' or tyrannical 'legal' provision. Thus, resort to revolt is limited by the imperative of social stability[109] and Aquinas concurred with St. Isidore of Seville in the view that tyrannicide probably involved a greater sin than that committed by the tyrant.[110] In cases of intolerable abuse, however, Aquinas considered, in convergence with, e.g., Mencius, that the overthrow of a 'tyrannical' government would not truly be 'seditious' and indeed the sedition would rather be committed by the tyrant through abuse of power. In this context the basic proposition may be seen set out in the *Commentary upon the Sentences of Peter Lombard* in which Aquinas argued that abomination can have no moral claim but lesser abuses may be sustained by the demands of order.[111]

The practical alleviation of tyranny was considered largely a matter for Divine rather than human action. To the (western) medieval mind this was not, however, a doctrine of political quietism. It was considered, rather, an assignment of the matter to the jurisdiction of the Church in contrast with the secular jurisdiction of, in particular, the Holy Roman Emperor. This related to the Doctrine of the Two Powers, also called the Doctrine of the Two Swords, affirmed by Pope Gelasius I (492-496) in a letter sent to the Emperor Anastasius in 493. The idea was that on earth the undivided sovereignty of Christ is exercised through two powers, the Pontifical and the Imperial, each of which has its proper role and function. Pope Gelasius insisted, however, upon the ultimate superiority of the Pontifical power because it must in the final days render account for the acts of rulers. Translating this doctrine into the area of political activity, Aquinas argued that positive law-making as such fell within the appointed competence of secular rulers, but matters pertaining to the spiritual well-being of the faithful fell, *ex hypothesi* within the jurisdiction of the Church.[112]   Thus, it was implied, the Pope could release the subjects of a temporal ruler from their obligation to obey in extreme circumstances of political abuse or moral corruption.   It must, however, be emphasized that in this model the spiritual and secular powers were seen as parts of an integrated order, not as alien or opposed actors.   As D'Entreves remarked,

> St. Thomas does not conceive of a relation between two different societies, between state and church ... but of a distinction of function.[113]

Thus, in the Thomist model practical law making and moral evaluation of laws are neither confused nor treated as opposed.   They are, rather, considered as complimentary activities within an essentially unitary moral and political framework.

This Thomist view, essentially a neo-Aristotelian development of St. Augustine's Christian Platonism, may be contrasted with that later advanced by John Calvin.   He argued that in rendering obedience to temporal sovereigns, 'obedience is rendered to God, from whom they receive their authority.'[114]   He then added that,

> those who rule in an unjust and tyrannical manner are raised up by Him to punish the iniquity of the people.[115]

That this too was not necessarily taken as an absolute doctrine of quietist submission was amply demonstrated by, e.g., the reaction of John Knox and the Scottish Lords to the unwelcome rule of Mary Queen of Scots.   The analysis of Aquinas must still appear more subtle than that advanced by Calvin, even as it appears more so than that advanced by St. Augustine.

Finnis and a 'Naturalist' Discourse of 'Rights'

The Thomist analysis was, of course, advanced in a very different social context from that now existing. The basic questions raised by the moral-purposive analysis of law are, however, of central modern importance. Within the current conventions of moral and political discourse the essential concerns are most effectively addressed through the language of 'rights'. In this respect the work of J.M. Finnis is of central significance.[116]

Finnis's defence of the legitimacy of the mode of derivation of naturalist criteria of evaluation has been considered above. In *Natural Law and Natural Rights*, Finnis, proceeding from an essentially Thomist analytical base, makes out a case for a rights-based substantive naturalism.[117] He sets out a range of basic 'goods' derived from general value judgments made by the broad range of human societies. These are necessarily categoric rather than specific in nature and thus, arguably, they are able to avoid the peril of culture-specific subjectivity which tends to beset such endeavours. In Finnis's analysis these 'goods' comprise life, knowledge, play, aesthetic experience, sociability, practical reasonableness and religious (meaning spiritual) experience. Preferences amongst these 'goods' are then made subject to canons of 'practical reasonableness'. The canons of practical reasonableness are (1) commitment to a coherent life plan, i.e. 'harmonious purposes and orientations, not ... specific projects',[118] (2) no arbitrary preferences amongst values, (3) no arbitrary preferences amongst persons, (4) detachment from specific objectives to the extent consonant with (5) commitment to general objectives forming part of a coherent life plan, (6) adoption of 'efficient' means in the pursuit of objectives, (7) respect for all basic 'goods' in each decision, (8) respect for the common 'good' of the community, and (9) adherence to the dictates of personal conscience. The combination of basic 'goods' and 'practical reasonableness' is argued by Finnis to produce a practical morality[119] which gives rise to certain absolute rights.

These absolute rights attached to the human condition are founded upon the basic proposition of 'practical reasonableness' that,

> it is always unreasonable to choose directly against any basic value, whether in oneself or in one's fellow human beings. And the basic values are not mere abstractions; they are aspects of the real well-being of flesh and blood individuals. Correlative to the exceptionless duties entailed by this

requirement are ... exceptionless human claim-rights ... .[120]

These 'exceptionless claim-rights', which relate directly back to the 'basic goods', are not to be deprived life as a direct means to an end, not to be deceived in situations involving factual communication, not to be condemned upon charges known to be false, not to be deprived or required to deprive oneself of procreative capacity and, lastly, to be given 'respectful consideration'[121] in any assessment of the common 'good' of the community.

This is a 'rights thesis' which is different in kind from that advanced by R.M. Dworkin[122] and one with a clear claim to inclusion in the corpus of general naturalist legal theory. Finnis's particular conclusions are open to some question. Lists of 'rights' are inevitably specific derivations from more general principles and can be argued not to be autonomous phenomena capable of exhaustive specification, but derivative expressions with some dependency upon their context. This appears to be what Dworkin had in mind in his argument that 'rights' are essentially generated as a response to positive demands made in contravention of legitimate moral expectation, even if the argument does, arguably, sit somewhat oddly in the intra-systemic context of his own analysis.[123] One may, of course, accept that exceptionless claim-rights arise from such a moral background, amongst which those advanced by Finnis have a very strong claim to consideration. However, the nature of the moral context would seem to have priority as an issue of theory over the specific listed rights which may emerge from its focus in a given condition of society. In this respect a more abstract Kantian argument perhaps offers the most satisfactory foundation for discussion in this area.

It may here usefully be remarked in parenthesis that the work of Immanuel Kant (1724-1804) does not afford a direct model of the obligation to obey law as such, but can be argued to afford a rational abstract model of a minimum substantive purposive naturalism in the combination of his *Categorical Imperative* and *Principle of Right*.[124] The deontological cast of Kant's ethical analysis would, however, raise considerable difficulties in a 'rights' analysis in the determination of the maxim is to govern a given situation.

In his theory of 'natural rights' Finnis identifies four basic senses of the term 'obligation' in this context of usage. The four models which he identifies for this purpose are (i) 'empirical liability to ... sanction', (ii) 'legal obligation in the intra-systemic sense', (iii) 'legal obligation in the moral sense' and 'collateral' moral obligation.[125]   He dismisses, rightly, as 'unsound'[126] those jurisprudential methods which seek to remove one or more of these senses of obligation from the province of jurisprudence or, indeed, to dismiss them altogether.   The value of the distinction drawn by Finnis between 'legal obligation in the moral sense' and   'collateral' moral obligation might, however, be debated.   The internal morality of law is largely bound up with its formal structure whereas a 'moral' obligation of fidelity to law is, if it is to avoid circularity, necessarily founded upon a moral structure which is external, or 'collateral', to the law itself.   If this is accepted, one is then left with the tripartite categorization of 'obligations' in the context of law suggested above.   That is to say, coercive imposition, formal duties and moral obligations.

In his analysis of the interface between the formal and moral 'obligations' to obey law Finnis makes the point that,

> There are, legally speaking, no degrees of legal obligation, just as there are no degrees of legal validity.[127]

He adds that the apparent variability of legal expectations do not derogate from the uniformity of legal obligation per se.   Upon the basis of this uniformity of formal obligation Finnis denies the 'penal' or 'sanctions' based approach to obligation, commenting in particular upon the widely variable predictive effects of the threat of the application of sanctions.   The actual relationship of moral and formal obligations is then set out, in terms of the 'practical reasonableness' of the 'good citizen', as a three stage process of reasoning. This is,

> A. We need for the sake of the common good to be law-abiding;
> B. But where (x) is stipulated by law as obligatory, the only way to be law-abiding is to do (x);
> C. Therefore we need [it is obligatory for us] to do (x) where (x) has been legally stipulated to be obligatory.[128]

Finnis argues that in formal legal reasoning step A is assumed so that only B and C remain relevant and that this, by and large, will hold good most of the time also for the 'good citizen' - in implied contrast with the 'bad man' postulated by Oliver Wendel Holmes.[129]   It is, however, possible for the 'good citizen' to reclaim step A of the reasoning process and thus to make informed   choices amongst the variously 'moral' but uniformally 'valid' propositions of positive law. Finnis, like Aquinas, stresses the moral 'weighting' in favour of obedience in most situations.[130] The argument advanced is essentially neo-Thomist, but it is shaped valuably in the forms of modern discourse with, in particular, an emphasis upon the relationship between morality and 'internal' legal reasoning which was of little or no interest to scholastic theorists.

The Work of Beyleveld and Brownsword

A somewhat different modern naturalist view is set out in *Law as a Moral Judgment* by Deryck Beyleveld and Roger Brownsword.[131] They commence from the basic naturalist proposition that law is inescapably a moral phenomenon. They also contend that such a proposition in no way conflicts with the Humean is/ought dichotomy[132] in an argument considered above. Upon the specific issue of legal obligation(s) Beyleveld and Brownsword contend that is common ground between the naturalist and positivist approaches that 'obligation' and 'validity' are closely linked concepts, but deny the positivist concept of 'validity'. Thus they state that,

> Unlike the legal positivists, who tie their notion of legal obligation to a morally neutral concept of legal validity, we tie our idea of legal obligation to a moral view of validity. Laws, for us, are morally legitimate prescriptions ... and they straightforwardly generate legal-moral obligations.[133]

As such this appears to be a statement of the basic 'naturalist' position. It may, perhaps, be regretted that it refers to the traditional naturalist/positivist divide which has been argued above to be founded largely upon terminological misunderstandings. In the light of this argument it is, of course, entirely proper for Beyleveld and Brownsword to state the divergence between their, naturalist, view of obligation and that which the positivists set out. It does not, however, follow from this, evident, difference, that the positivists are therefore 'wrong', if it is accepted that 'obligation' is a term which may carry distinctively different meanings, *inter alia*, in 'naturalist' and 'positivist' usages. The analysis which is advanced by Beyleveld and Brownsword clearly relates to issues of moral obligation associated with law, but this need not exclude the relevance of distinct arguments upon formal obligation or the *potestas coactiva*.

In general the view of law advanced may be related to the Thomist analysis in which a 'complete' law must meet both formal and moral criteria of identification.   Such a law will impose a moral obligation to obey upon those to whom it is addressed.   Where a purported 'law' is 'incomplete', in the sense of failing to satisfy one or more of these criteria, it is argued that there may, even so, be some 'obligation' to obey.[134]   Beyleveld and Brownsword suggest four such situations: (1) 'an internal collateral obligation to comply with a 'provisionally valid' legal rule', (2) a similar obligation to comply with a 'subjectively valid' legal rule (i.e. one believed by an official to be valid) until the question of its status has been resolved, (3) 'a standing internal obligation' not to disrupt the accepted polity by disobedience, even though there is no collateral obligation to comply where a rule is applied *ultra vires*, and (4) an 'external synthetic collateral obligation' to obey even a rule lacking 'official authority', if, 'as the lesser of two evils', compliance would better promote the accepted legal/moral order than would disobedience.[135]   As a result of the attempt to analyse 'obligation' as a unitary concept under a 'naturalist' umbrella, these four situations straddle the areas of 'formal' and 'moral' obligation suggested above.   Thus, (1) and (2) are essentially concerned with the formally internalized morality of a positive legal system and may reasonably be considered to fall within the sphere of 'positivist' rather than 'naturalist' analysis.   Situations (3) and (4), however, raise the basic 'naturalist' concern with the 'price' in 'bad' law which may reasonably be expected to be paid for social stability in a system which is in general morally acceptable.   Beyleveld and Brownsword cite with approval the comment of Finnis that,

> the good citizen may (not always) be morally required to conform to that [morally questionable] stipulation to the extent necessary to avoid weakening 'the law',[136]

The framework within which such decisions are to be made, and also a defence to Bentham's fundamental charge of subjectivism, is set by Beyleveld and Brownsword by reference to the linked theories of 'Accountability' and 'Restraint'.[137]   These linked theories may reasonably be considered to function as a split-purposive model of the parameters of obedience to positive law.   The theory of 'Accountability' refers to what might best be termed the essential 'trusteeship' of government in the exercise of power and answerability therefore. The theory of 'Restraint' refers precisely to the claims of social stability over expectations of the moral quality of substantive provision.

This analysis may be seen to stand in the mainstream of purposive naturalist argument and, again, usefully advances the naturalist case in a modern form of discourse. The focus upon the moral nature of obligation in this context is, also, entirely appropriate, even if it may be regretted that adherence to a unitary model seems to perpetuate the questionable naturalist/positivist 'debate', when, as it is here suggested, the case is more one of differing 'answers' being given to different questions.

Conclusions: The Place of Moral Obligation in Legal Theory

Across the broad spectrum of naturalist thought it may be contended that, properly understood, the true concern of this type of theory in relation to the obligation to obey is with the moral sense of the term and not with its intra-systemic or, possible, coercive senses. Confusion between the first two seems to stem, as Finnis implies,[138] from the undifferentiated use of 'obligation' based terminology in general legal discourse. The moral claim of positive law to obedience is argued to be extra-systemic in nature and entirely distinct from the formal obligations arising from intra-systemic concepts of validity. It is founded upon the purposive bases of the legal enterprise, in both its legislative and judicial aspects, and not upon its own internalized assumptions. Positive legal provisions made beyond the purposive parameters set by legitimate human expectations, however expressed, are argued by the broad spectrum of naturalist thinkers to be to a greater or lesser extent defective in their moral claim. irrespective of their formal status.

Upon this view, naturalism can be seen to be a legitimate part of a holistic jurisprudence which ranges wider that the narrowly defined Austinian 'province of jurisprudence' and addresses the moral context in which law making takes place. The focus of this argument is distinct from that of positivism and, once this is accepted, the apparent conflict between the two approaches is not so much resolved as shown to be founded upon false premises. This said, there is nonetheless an interface between moral and formal obligations in a functioning legal system. In many instances extra-systemic moral obligation and intra-systemic duty will of course coincide. Many naturalists have conceded that the moral 'weighting' of social stability may attach some degree of moral obligation even to 'bad' laws, although not to the extent of an acceptance of outright iniquity. Such judgments involve delicate shadings of emphasis in an interface between different species of 'obligation'.

Judgments derived in the interface between formal and moral obligations, often involving an examination of the soundness of the presuppositions underlying formal discourse upon intra-systemic obligation, have become a major focus of modern jurisprudential enquiry, even if not necessarily expressed in quite those terms. The evidence for this can be seen in a range of theories which attempt to explain the relationship between the moral and formal elements within legal systems. For the most part such analyses have focused upon intra-systemic concerns and cannot be catgorized as 'naturalist', they may, however, usefully be considered 'post-positivist'. These arguments raise issues which are distinct from naturalism *stricto sensu* but, equally, form part of a broader examination of the nature and quality of obligation(s) to obey law. As such, these theories demand separate discussion as a distinctive series of contributions to the corpus of theory in this area, reflecting in many ways the very particular concerns raised by 20th century experience.

Notes

1 See Chapter 2.
2 See H. Kelsen, *General Theory of Law and State*, trans. A. Wedberg (Harvard, 1948).
3 See Chapter 4.
4 H. McCoubrey, *The Development of Naturalist Legal Theory* (Croom Helm, 1987), Introduction, p.xii.
5 St. Augustine of Hippo, *De Libero Arbitrio*, Book I, V:33.
6 See Chapter 4.
7 J. Bentham, *A Fragment on Government* (Blackwell edn., 1967), Ch.IV, para.19, p.93.
8 See note 5.
9 See St. Thomas Aquinas, *Summa Theologica*, 1a2ae. 93,6.
10 E.g. Thomas Hobbes, John Locke and Jean-Jacques Rousseau. In a modern context the 'liberal' theory of justice advanced by John Rawls is founded upon a social contractarian methodology.

11 D. Hume, *A Treatise of Human Nature*, Book III, Part 1, Section (a) (Oxford edn., 1983, reproducing the pagination of the 1740 text), at p.469.

12 For an interesting discussion of the relation of Hume's work to 18th century naturalism see Philip Milton, 'David Hume and 18th Century Conceptions of Natural Law' [1982] 2 *Legal Studies*, 14.

13 J. Stone, *Human Law and Human Justice* (Stevens, 1965), p.212. Cited by J.M. Finnis in *Natural Law and Natural Rights* (Clarendon, Oxford, 1980), at p.33. Finnis also cites the claim made by D.J. O'Connor in *Aquinas and Natural Law* (London, 1967) at p.68 that '[A]ny natural law theory entails the belief that propositions about man's duties and obligations can be inferred from presuppositions about his nature'.

14 J.M. Finnis, op.cit., p.34.

15 Ibid.

16 D. Beyleveld and R. Brownsword, *Law as a Moral Judgment* (Sweet and Maxwell, 1986), p.21.

17 Ibid., at p.23.

18 See note 13.

19 F.C. Copleston, *Aquinas* (Penguin, 1955, 1982 edn.), p.221, making reference to St. Thomas Aquinas, *Summa Theologica*. 1a2ae. 91,2.

20 F.C. Copleston, op.cit., at p.222.

21 K. Nielsen, 'An Examination of the Thomistic Theory of Natural Law' (1959) 4 *Natural Law Forum*, 44.

22 Ibid., at p.50.

23 D.N. Weisstub, 'Law and Telos - Some Historical Reflections on the Nature of Authority' 12 *U.B.C. Law Review*, 225 at 246.

24 K. Nielsen, op.cit., p.56.

25 This is one of the bases of human rights analyses.

26 A.P. D'Entreves, *Natural Law*, 2 ed. (Hutchinson, 1970), p.xiv.

27 Aquinas stood at a focal point in the synthesis of Judaeo-Christian and Graeco-Roman traditions. The process of fusion commenced as Christian doctrine spread amongst the Gentile population of the Roman Empire but gained a rapid impetus with the 313 AD 'Peace of the Church' following the adoption of Christianity by Constantine the Great as an official religion of the Empire. This forced the Church to engage in detail with Imperial policies and laws, rather than regarding them as the dubious products of a hostile state. St. Augustine of Hippo represented a median stage in the process of fusion, embodying a form of Christian Platonism, whereas Aquinas, in the 13th century, worked with the, by then, rediscovered works of Aristotle.

28 This phrase is borrowed from the American Realist thinker Karl N. Llewellyn. See in particular K.N. Llewellyn and E.A. Hoebel, *The Cheyenne Way* (University of Oklahoma Press, 1941).

29 See Chapter 2.

30   C.W. Coram, *Gods, Graves and Scholars*, trans. E.B. Garside and S. Wilkins, 2 ed. (London, 1971), p.305.
31   *Code Hammurabi*, Front, Column I, trans. Chilperic Edwards, *The World's Earliest Laws* (London, 1934).
32   Ibid., Front, Column V.
33   Detailed codes will be found especially in Exodus 20:1 to 23:19 and in Deuteronomy 12:1 to 26:15.   For discussion see J. Blenkinsop, *Wisdom and Law in the Old Testament* (Oxford, 1983).
34   See Exodus 20:1 and Deuteronomy 5:6.
35   Exodus 24:3.   The text is taken from the Authorized 'King James' version (Oxford University Press).
36   For discussion see N.J. Coulson, *Conflicts and Tensions in Islamic Jurisprudence* (University of Chicago Press, 1969), pp.25-57.
37   The function of choice in common law adjudication has been considered, *inter alia*, by R.M. Dworkin (see Chapter 4) and the American Realists (see Chapter 5).
38   1 Samuel 15:10-34.
39   1 Kings 21:20-22:37.
40   See Confucius, *Analects*, 12:xiii.   For discussion see H. McCoubrey and N.D. White, *Textbook on Jurisprudence* (Blackstone, 1993), pp.119-123.
41   *Mencius*, trans. D.C. Lau (Penguin edn., 1970), Book IB, 8.   See also IVA,1; VB,9 and VIIA,31.
42   Evidence of Legalist influence may clearly be seen, e.g., in the work of Hsun Tzu.   See *Basic Writings*, trans. Burton Watson (Columbia University Press, 1963).
43   See also note 28.
44   *The Last Days of Socrates: Apology*, trans. H. Tredennick (Penguin Classics edn., 1969), pp.31-2.
45   Ibid., 32C-D.
46   Ibid., 28D-30A.
47   See A.D. Woozley, *Law and Obedience: The Arguments of Plato's Crito* (Duckworth, 1979), pp.55-8.
48   *The Last Days of Socrates: Apology*, p.73.
49   *Crito*, 51D-52A.
50   Ibid., 50E-51.
51   Ibid., 51C-E.
52   Ibid., 52B-C.
53   A.D. Woozley, op.cit., p.81.
54   *The Last Days of Socrates: Crito* 50A, pp.89-90.
55   *Apology* 31D-33B.
56   *Crito* 48D.
57   See, e.g., *Crito*, 54B-C.

58 F.C. Wade, 'In Defence of Socrates' (1971) 25 *Review of Metaphysics*, pp.311-325.

59 R.E. Allen, 'Law and Justice in Plato's *Crito*' (1972) 69 *Journal of Philosophy*, pp.562-6.

60 A.D. Woozley, op.cit., p.59.

61 T. Hobbes, *Leviathan*, Ch. XIV (Penguin Classics edn., 1977, referring to the pagination of the 1651 edition), p.64.

62 Ibid., Ch.XIII, p.62.

63 H. McCoubrey, op.cit., p.71. Locke's theory can be found set out primarily in his *Two Treatises of Government* (1690).

64 See Chapter 5.

65 See note 54.

66 J.M. Finnis, *Natural Law and Natural Rights* (Clarendon, Oxford, 1980), p.28.

67 St. Augustine of Hippo, *De Libero Arbitrio*, I.VI:15.

68 Ibid.

69 Ibid., I.VI:50.

70 Ibid., I.V:33.

71 J. Austin, *The Province of Jurisprudence Determined* (1832, Weidenfeld and Nicholson edn., 1954), Lecture V, p.185. See also Chapter 2.

72 St. Augustine, op.cit., I.III:18-19.

73 H.L.A. Hart, *The Concept of Law*, 2 ed., with postscript ed. by P.A. Bulloch and J. Raz (Clarendon, Oxford, 1994), Chapter II, pp.19-22.

74 See St. Augustine of Hippo, *De Civitate Dei*, Book IV, Ch.4.

75 St. Thomas Aquinas, *Summa Theologica*. 1a2ae.95,4. The reference is to Aristotle, *Politics*, 1253a, 2-7.

76 St. Thomas Aquinas, op.cit., Dominican Edition (Blackfriars with Eyre and Spottiswoode, 1964), Introduction to Vol. 28, pp.xxi-xxii.

77 St. Thomas Aquinas, op.cit., 1a2ae. 90,4.

78 Ibid., 1a2ae. 90,3.

79 Ibid., 1a2ae. 80,4.

80 A proposition denied by the Scandinavian Realists, see Chapter 5.

81 St. Thomas Aquinas, op.cit., 1a2ae. 90,1.

82 Ibid., 1a2ae. 90,3. A similar point is made in *De Regimine Principum*, 1,15. This latter work comprises advice upon the conduct of government addressed probably to Hugh III de Lusignan, King of Cyprus, but possibly to his father Hugh II.

83 F.C.Coplston, op.cit., pp.219-20.

84 The Sixth Commandment, Exodus 20:13.

85 Aquinas, *Summa Theologica*, Dominican edn., Vol. 28, p.104, note (b).

86 D. Bigongiari, ed., *The Political Ideas of St. Thomas Aquinas* (Hafner Press, 1953), Introduction, p.viii.

87   St. Thomas Aquinas, *Summa Theologica*, 1a2ae. 95,3, citing St. Isidore of Seville, *Physics*, II.9.200A 10.

88   G. Del Vecchio, 'Divine Justice and Human Justice', a lecture delivered to the XIIIth Course on Christian Studies at Assisi on 1 September 1955, trans. H. McN. Henderson (1956) *Juridical Review*, p.147.

89   St. Gregory the Great, *Moralium*, LVC, xxxvii, para.67, cited by G. del Vecchio, op.cit., at p.162.

90   A similar point is made in a different context by R.M. Dworkin in his distinction between moralities of 'aspiration' and 'duty'. See Chapter 4.

91   See the 1948 Genocide Convention, which is widely ratified and generally held to have the status of customary international law.

92   The term is used here in its general sense of a higher moral law rather than in the technical Thomist sense of the *Lex Naturalis*.

93   See St. Thomas Aquinas, *Summa Theologica*. 1a2ae. 95,2, citing St. Augustine of Hippo, *De Libero Arbitrio*, 1,5.

94   Ibid., 1a2ae. 95,2.

95   Ibid., Dominican den., Vol.28, p.105.

96   T.E. Davitt, S.J., 'Law as a Means to an End - Thomas Aquinas', 14 VLR, 65 at 69.

97   St. Thomas Aquinas, op.cit., 1a2ae. 95,2.

98   Ibid., 1a2ae. 92,1.

99   The Dominican editors of *Summa Theologica*, sub nomen *Summa Theologiae*, remark that such a law is not 'necessarily an atrocious ordinance but one aimed at the private benefit of the ruler' (op.cit., Vol.28, p.44, note (h)).

100 In particular in Book II, Dist. 44, Qu.2, Art.2.

101 St. Thomas Aquinas, *Summa Theologica*, 1a2ae. 96,6, citing *Digest* I,III.25.

102 Ibid., 1a2ae. 96,4.   A similar point is made in ibid., 2a2ae. 104,6.

103 Op.cit., Vol.28, p.131, note (d).

104 St. Thomas Aquinas, *De Regimine Principum*, VI.44.

105 Ibid., VI.51. In the context of medieval political thought this formula did not carry quite the tone of fatalistic resignation implied to the modern reader. The Divine agency was assumed by Aquinas to function on earth through the Church and, in particular, the Papacy.

106 D. Bigongiari, op.cit., Introduction, p.xx.

107 St. Thomas Aquinas, *Summa Theologica*, 1a2ae. 60,6.

108 A.P. D'Entreves, ed., *Aquinas - Selected Political Writings*, 8 ed. (Blackwell, 1981), Introduction, p.xii.

109 St. Thomas Aquinas, *Summa Theologica*, 2a2ae. 42,2.

110 Ibid., 2a2ae. 42,1.

111 Book II, Dist.44,3.

112 St. Thomas Aquinas, *Summa Theologica*, 2a2ae. 60,6.

113 A.P. D'Entreves, op.cit.,p.xxi. See St. Thomas Aquinas, *Summa Theologica* 2a2ae. 60,6; 67,1 and 147,3: see also *Commentary Upon the Sentences of Peter Lombard*, Book II, Dist. 44,3.

114 J. Calvin, *Institutes of the Christian Religion*, 'On Civil Government', xxiii, ed. J.T. McNeill in *Calvin on God and Political Duty*, 2 ed. (Bobbs-Merrill Educational Publishing, 1956), at p.72.

115 Ibid., 'On Civil Government', xxv at p.74.

116 Some modern analyses, such as Dworkin's 'Rights Thesis', seek to introduce moral ideas into discussion of the formal processes of law, but this type of argument rests upon a rather restricted type of morality. See Chapter 4.

117 Op.cit., the citations following are from the edition of 1984.

118 Ibid., pp.103-4.

119 Ibid., p.126.

120 Ibid., p.225.

121 Ibid.

122 See Chapter 4.

123 Ibid.

124 For discussion of this use of the Kantian argument see H. McCoubrey, *The Development of Naturalist Legal Theory* (Croom Helm, 1987), pp.76-81 and 188-206.

125 J. Finis, op.cit., Ch. XI.

126 Ibid., p.354.

127 Ibid., p.309.

128 Ibid., p.316.

129 Ibid., pp.322 ff. Holmes' model of law is considered in Chapter 5.

130 Ibid., p.319.

131 Op.cit.

132 See above.

133 Op.cit., p.325.

134 Ibid., p.335.

135 Ibid.

136 Ibid., at p.338, citing J. Finnis, op.cit., p.362.

137 Ibid., pp.370 ff.

138 J. Finnis, op.cit., p.320.

4 Obligation in Post-Positivist Theories

For much of the second half of the 19th and the first half of the 20th centuries Anglo-American, and most particularly English, jurisprudential thought was dominated by what may reasonably be termed a 'positivist' consensus.[1] There was more than one reason for the general acceptance of a conventional, and often rather unreflective, 'positivist' approach. Amongst these, the strengths of the analyses set out by Bentham and Austin and, later, H.L.A. Hart, must obviously be numbered. Perhaps more importantly, however, a 'positivist' approach represents in many ways a 'common sense' theory of law which accords well with the practising lawyer's experience. For the most part law in practical application does indeed appear to consist of 'rules' which are produced in an exercise of political power through whatever constitutional processes exist in the state concerned. Thus a supposedly uniform positivism had, and continues to have, a great attraction for the practising legal profession as the base of jurisprudential assumption. That positivism should play this role is by no means in itself undesirable, except in so far as the assumption is made that no place remains within jurisprudence 'properly so-called' for questions to be posed outside a 'positivist' context. Unfortunately this latter assumption has to a considerable extent been made in much conventional legal discourse.

In the second half of the 20th century the conventional positivist consensus has increasingly come to be questioned from a number of points of view. This questioning has sometimes been given the character of a 'naturalist revival',[2] but such a general categorization would over-simplify the pattern of development, even if the moral and ethical nature of law making has indeed been a central focus of concern. The origins of this modern unease go back at least to the early 1930s and the rise of modern political totalitarianism in Europe. The pre-1914 world order had largely been shattered by the impact of the First World War together with the various more or less violent political upheavals which occurred during its course or as a result of the major changes made by the Versailles settlement aftermath. The process of mutation leading from Marxism through Marxism-Leninism to Stalinism in the former USSR[3] and the rise of Fascism in Italy and Nazism in Germany raised uncomfortable questions about the nature of positive law and its uses which found no ready answers in conventional positivist analyses. During the years immediately before and during the Second World war Stalinism tended to be dismissed, in the west, as a peculiarly 'Russian' aberration and even, by some western intellectuals who were well distanced from its real effects, admired as an inevitable accompaniment of 'progress'. Mussolini in Italy and Hitler in Germany also attracted a variety of reactions, including admiration for the supposed 'efficiency' of these systems. It is, in retrospect, startling that Julius Stone in a highly critical review of Fascist legal theory published in 1937 felt it necessary to preface his remarks with the statement that,

> the prevailing approach to Fascism in democratic literature is ... [that] Fascist theories may be more advanced than those of the most progressive democracies, but Fascist practice falls far behind the practice of even the most backward democracies.[4]

The end of the Second World War in 1945 raised the issue of abuse of positive law in an unavoidable form with the detailed exposure, following military collapse, of the extent of legal iniquity and malpractice in the Third Reich. The issue, seemingly buried by Austin if not by Bentham, of the role of moral and ethical criteria in legal analysis was raised again in mainstream jurisprudence in a variety of forms.

The impact of this concern can clearly be seen in the principal post-war development in positivist legal theory as such. In advancing a 'minimum content of natural law', however questionable the innovation might be in its original context,[5] H.L.A. Hart in *The Concept of Law* implicitly acknowledged the problem of the 'moral' dimension of law.[6]

It may reasonably be argued that in much even of the modern development of legal theory the expression of this concern has, unfortunately, come to be significantly misdirected. Two principal sources of misdirection appear to have been central in this context. The first is a continuing problem in the identification of the context in which given questions about law and obligation are actually being asked. The second lies in a continuing adherence to the, highly questionable, notion that positive law can be said to possess phenomenological autonomy to a genuinely significant degree.

Lon L. Fuller and Procedural Natural Law

One fruit of the renewed concern with the moral dimension of law may be seen in the idea of 'procedural natural law' advanced in *The Morality of Law* by Lon L. Fuller.[7]   Perhaps curiously, in the light of his central concern with the internal morality of law, Fuller agreed with H.L.A. Hart in treating law as a structure of rules about which the most fundamental questions to be asked lie in the definition of the rule making process.   However, Fuller took issue with Hart upon the value of the 'rule of recognition'[8] as an ultimate criterion of identification.   He made the point that despite Hart's denial that 'government' is no more than a 'gunman' situation written large, the rule of recognition serves only as a formal identificatory criterion of 'official' coercive power.   Fuller emphasized that Hart's rule of recognition contains no element of reciprocity, commenting that,

> Every step in the analysis seems almost as if it were designed to exclude the notion that there could be any rightful expectation on the part of the citizen that could be violated by the lawgiver.[9]

To remedy this lack Fuller advanced an internal legal morality which demands certain procedural qualities as intrinsically necessary for the recognizable exercise of 'legislative' powers.   In a parallel with Hart's use of the hypothetical 'Rex' dynasty in *The Concept of Law* to demonstrate the development of a 'rule of recognition'[10] Fuller advanced a lengthy analysis of failed 'legislative' endeavours by a hypothetical King Rex.[11]   This leads to an analysis of eight defects in purported legislative action which are in effect negative procedural criteria of legislative identification.

These defects include such matters as the making of self-contradictory or incomprehensible rules with which compliance is impossible, as well as a simple failure to enact rules at all.   If a purported legislative effort were to fail upon all eight tests then, Fuller argued, it would not be recognizable as 'law'.   Indeed it may well be doubted whether Bentham or Austin themselves would have been willing to recognize so sorry an object as a viable 'law'.   In practice, however, most legislative endeavours will score neither 'full marks' nor zero or 'fail' standard upon the scale implied by Fuller's theory.   They will tend rather to fall somewhere in a middle range.   An interesting question arises here as to whether it is possible to define a 'pass mark', some minimum necessary level of legislative attainment,   in   relation   to Fuller's scheme. It may be remarked in passing that very delicate judgments would be required in making any such decision, especially since some of the general, and undoubted, 'vices' listed amongst Fuller's negative criteria may in some circumstances actually become positive virtues. For example, retroactivity of effect can in general be considered an evil and is so considered by Fuller, but it may become highly desirable in correcting a specific unjust infliction. Be that as it may the question of minimum attainment is not really germane to the immediate issue.

It is clear that Fuller's procedural naturalism must be limited in nature precisely because it addresses a procedural morality rather than one of substance. It is true that procedural morality may prevent certain forms of substantive iniquity from finding 'legal' expression. An example may be seen in the Nuremberg Race Laws of Nazi Germany. These in effect rendered it unlawful to be of Jewish race, which was a demand with which compliance was impossible since no-one can change their race in order to meet a requirement of the state and thus fell foul of one of Fuller's specific negative criteria. In many other situations, however, such would not be the case, as, for example, with a decree proscribing religious practice. The essence of Fuller's views upon the problem of substantive iniquity appears in his comment that,

> It is a great mistake to treat questions of the design and administration of ... institutions as if the problem was merely one of weighing substantive ends against one another. For institutions have an integrity of their own which must be respected if they are to be effective at all.[12]

It remains, however, the case that such a procedural 'screen' may still leave a considerable latitude for substantive iniquity. Robert S. Summers remarks that,

> Fuller devoted more sustained thought to legal processes that to any other facet of law. But surprisingly enough he did not stress the necessarily moral value of certain legal processes. Yet he arrived at the idea even earlier (1949) than he did his views on the moral value of his principles of legality, which were not published until the 1960s.[13]

Fuller's refusal to address the substantive morality of law, other than obliquely, had major implications for the impact of his ideas upon theories of legal obligation. His concentration upon procedural issues means that for the purposes of his analysis once an adequate and acceptable means for the 'legal' expression of a norm has been found, it will impose 'obligation' irrespective of its substantive content. This is significant even granted the fact some forms of iniquity might be incapable of finding procedurally adequate 'legal' expression.

Two points may be made about this. Firstly, Fuller objected to the formalistic nature of Hart's theory and yet ultimately his own analysis seems to do little more than engraft a sort of 'moral' formalism onto a scheme still fundamentally concerned with the definition of rules. This leads to the second point, that despite a basic concern with the 'internal' morality of law, or rather a legal system, Fuller adheres to a 'rules' model of law and may be argued thereby to have perpetuated some of the defects of the positivistic formalism which he opposed. The resulting considerable limitation of the potentially significant impact upon ideas of obligation of Fuller's emphasis upon reciprocity as between law-maker and subject is perhaps the more surprising in the light of his consideration of the abuses of law under the Third Reich referred to by Summers.[14]

Fuller debated with H.L.A. Hart upon the subject of post-war reaction to the 'grudge informer' cases which arose in Nazi Germany. As such this debate will be considered at a later stage of argument,[15] but it does here afford some guidance to Fuller's general view of the nature of the obligation to obey law. In brief, it is well known that there were in the Third Reich a large number of highly repressive laws and regulations which were widely regarded within the Reich itself as 'terror laws'. In a number of cases people maliciously reported minor infractions to the state or party authorities knowing very serious penalties to be likely and hoping for their infliction in the satisfaction of personal grudges. It may readily be accepted that such conduct was morally reprehensible but its jurisprudential implications are problematic. The action of a grudge informer was, *ex hypothesi*, formally lawful and possibly even mandatory at the time of its commission and it may be regarded both at the time and subsequently as a gross abuse of 'legal' process. In *ex post facto* consideration major difficulties arise. Should the action of the grudge informer be retrospectively penalized by reason of its moral turpitude, even though it was formally lawful at all material times, or would the apparent injustice of the retrospective penalty raise an equal and opposite wrong and thus counsel inaction?[16] In the context of disentangling the affairs of a tyrannical regime such as the Third Reich this question must self-evidently be considered a very serious one. It is clear in this context since former injustice requires redress without, by the very processes of redress, occasioning further harm.

In an appendix to *The Morality of Law* Fuller listed various possible responses to this problem in relation to the conduct of a hypothetical 'purple shirt' regime which is a thinly disguised model of the Third Reich.[17] Five responses are advanced. These are, (1) an idea of a rule of law requires acceptance of the validity of known law at any given time, therefore grudge informers may not retrospectively be penalized. (2) A regime like that of the 'purple shirts' has so little actual respect for law that juristic standards cannot reasonably be applied to occurrences under it and therefore, again, no action should be taken. (3) No blanket decision can be made upon the legality of the 'purple shirt' regime, some matters will have retained a recognizably 'legal' basis and some will not. It may, therefore, be appropriate to penalize actions standing outside the recognizable 'legal' framework. (4) A selective approach such as that advocated under (3) is not permissible because it leads back to the very subjectivity which was so objectionable under the 'purple shirts'. The only solution would then be express legislation dealing with all liabilities arising from the time of the 'purple shirts'. Finally, (5) there is in fact no jurisprudentially adequate solution so the 'post-purple shirt' authorities should simply turn a blind eye to any private acts of retribution meted out to grudge informers. Of these possible responses only (1) and (3) can be said to address directly the issue of the obligation to obey and in *The Morality of Law* the choice amongst them is thrown back to the reader. Only scattered clues to Fuller's opinion upon this issue are found elsewhere.

So far as the issue of obligation is concerned, Fuller's 'debate' with H.L.A. Hart upon the 'grudge informer cases' must be considered rather unfortunate. Unfortunately the original report of the particular case which was the focus of discussion[18] was highly misleading and gave the false impression that the post-war [West] German court had found the Nazi laws in question to be straightforwardly invalid upon the basis of the application of moral criteria of evaluation. The subsequent 'debate' was consequently focused upon questions of formal validity and was set against the implicit background of the much misunderstood statement of St. Augustine of Hippo that *lex iniusta non est lex* - an unjust law is no law.[19] Unfortunately in this context the issues of obligation which are in fact central to an analysis of the 'grudge informer' cases were largely excluded from consideration. It may be noted, however, that in writing elsewhere Lon L. Fuller did make the comment that,

> [It is a] grotesque ... notion that the moral obligation of the decent German citizen to obey these [morally iniquitous] laws was in no way affected by the fact that they were in part kept from his knowledge, that some of them retroactively 'cured' wholesale murder, that they contained wide delegations of administrative discretion to redefine crimes they proscribed, and that, in any event, their actual terms were largely disregarded when it suited the convenience of the military courts appointed to apply them.[20]

This returns to Fuller's central concern with the 'internal' procedural morality of a legal system. The conventional argument upon the moral obligation to obey appears to be turned upon its head with the view that gross breaches of procedural morality may lead to an actual failure to produce 'law' at all and that, consequently, no obligation of any description will be imposed. Support for this interpretation is found in a comment made by Fuller in the context of his hypothetical incompetent legislator King Rex,

> A mere respect for constitutional authority must not be confused with fidelity to law. Rex's subjects ... remained faithful to him as King throughout his long and inept reign. They were not faithful to his law, for he never made any.[21]

There appears to be here a failure to distinguish between the categories of formal and moral obligation. One returns again to the fact that if Rex could find a procedurally adequate way of enacting an iniquitous provision, there is nothing in Fuller's analysis to deny that an obligation to obey would be imposed. The idea that a formally 'valid' provision might still be defective in the total obligation which it imposes is, if not expressly excluded, certainly not directly admitted.

Perhaps such a result was inevitable in the light of the basic 'rules' model adopted by Fuller. There is, however, some reason to suggest that Fuller came close to questioning this basic assumption at least once in the course of the development of his theory. Evidence for this proposition can be found in his statement that,

> It is truly astounding to what an extent there runs through modern thinking in legal philosophy the assumption that law is like a piece of inert matter - it is there or not there.[22]

It is perhaps unfortunate that Fuller did not pursue the logic of this perception to the conclusion that the 'province of jurisprudence' may extend into realms beyond the validation of rules. Be that as it may, there is little evident room in Fuller's argument for the idea that the obligation to obey law may be addressed according to different criteria in different contexts. The assumption is seemingly made that obligation is essentially unitary and does indeed exist or not exist according to whether or not a recognizably 'legal' rule is produced in a given instance. In this sense Fuller's work must ultimately be seen as a 'moral' annex to an essentially formalist analysis of law, albeit one which points out the inadequacies of an exclusively 'positivist' description of the identification and operation of legal rules.

The Duty to Obey in Dworkin's 'Rights Thesis'

A more wide-ranging and more currently influential post-positivist analysis is found in the work of R.M. Dworkin. Dworkin shares with Fuller the view that moral and ethical considerations play an internal role in law which far transcends the merely external role which is, at most, allowed to them by classical positivism. However, the logic of this perception is pursued much further by Dworkin than it was by Fuller. In brief, Dworkin argues in *Taking Rights Seriously* that no absolute division can be drawn between the categories of law and morality and that in deciding 'hard cases', those in which established legal rules provide no clear answer, judges are able to look beyond the content of rules without resorting to the arbitrary judicial 'legislation' which Bentham condemned as a usurpation of the legislative function.[23] Instead, Dworkin argues, adjudication takes place in a political and moral context which generates non-rule 'standards' by reference to which a 'right answer' may be found in 'hard cases' and arbitrary judicial preferences may effectively be excluded. Such standards are not formally generated or abrogated by reference to some 'rule of recognition' in the manner advanced in H.L.A. Hart's theory, but arise instead from a judicial and public 'sense of appropriateness' in relation to adjudication.[24] In adjudication upon particular cases the test for their application, once deemed relevant, is not, as it is for rules, one of 'validation'. It is, rather, one of relative 'weighting' in comparison with other standards which may be thought relevant to the decision which is to be made in the case.

As a theory of adjudication this can be seen as a useful insight and, possibly, one which is far less controversial than some of its supporters and opponents seem to suggest. Dworkin himself categorizes his work as generally 'anti-positivist' in the sense of being opposed to the basic rules model of law. However, in an interesting discussion W.I. Waluchow has questions whether positivism is necessarily committed to the simple Austinian proposition of an absolute division between the existence of law and argument upon its merits.[25] He suggests that within the positivist canon there may be found both 'strong' positivism in the Austinian mould and 'weak' positivism which admits values in a legal analysis without falling into a 'naturalist' posture, with the implication that Dworkin is in fact a 'weak' positivist in this sense. In detail Waluchow's argument may be questioned. No avowed positivist can be identified as a member of the 'weak' branch of the school and the distinction drawn between positivism and naturalism is founded upon the conventional misconstruction of St. Augustine's remark that *lex iniusta non est lex*[26] as implying the formal invalidity of an immoral law rather than a defect in its absolute claim upon those to whom it is addressed.[27] In the context of Dworkin's work, however, the argument is by no means without merit. No positivist denies that there are influences upon law other than the content of rules, Hart certainly did not, the question is rather one of the place, if any, of such factors in jurisprudential analysis as such. Indeed the existence of non-rule factors in adjudication is a legal commonplace. To take an example, judicial interpretation in England and Wales, as well as Scotland, may involve reference to certain 'presumptions' about Parliamentary intentions, an especially entrenched example being the presumption against exclusion of resort to the courts for the determination of legal issues.[28] These are not rules of law in the positivist sense but adjudicatory expectations of a sort which may be thought to fit well into Dworkin's analysis and are indeed very difficult to displace. Thus, there is in the United Kingdom no 'constitutional' guarantee against expropriation of property[29] but there is a strong judicial presumption in favour of compensation for compulsory acquisition which may in turn be seen as reflective of a value judgment upon the moral claim of private ownership. In so far as Dworkin's theory allows account to be taken of such matters in a far more satisfactory way than does the approach of classical rules-based positivism, there may be some case for treating it as a development of positivism in the 'weak' sense advanced by Waluchow. The case is strengthened when it is further considered that Dworkin's adjudicatory 'standards' ultimately reflect 'constitutional' value judgments rather than the wholly external morality which is argued to be the hallmark of naturalist analyses.

Dworkin's argument extends beyond techniques of adjudication, which in themselves have an impact only upon the determination in a given case of the existence or otherwise of a formal obligation, and enters a moral dimension of much wider significance. Dworkin divides his adjudicatory 'standards' into policies and principles. The former are goal-oriented and 'quasi-legislative' in nature whilst the latter are derived from general expectations of 'justice or fairness or some other dimension of morality'.[30] In this context the argument focuses upon principles rather than upon the less 'weighted' policies. This proposition of 'moral' principles raises the basic methodological problems of any theory which is naturalist or tends in a quasi-naturalist direction - how can it be determined what is in some sense objectively 'right' in distinction from a mere product of cultural preference?[31] Dworkin's response to this problem and his core argument upon the moral nature of law and legal obligation is found in his central 'rights thesis'. The essence of this is that 'principles' are founded upon communal expectations which are enshrined in the 'constitutional' commitments of a state and these give rise to 'rights' within the society concerned. Dworkin seeks to distance such 'rights' from merely 'popular' entitlements founded upon a 'decibel morality' and argues that they reflect basic abstract commitments which in concrete application to disliked minorities might be decidedly 'unpopular'. It cannot, however, be sufficient to avoid the charge of populism merely to argue that 'rights' represent abstract commitments, it is also necessary to explain the substance of such 'rights'. Here Dworkin's argument seems somewhat questionable. He seeks to confine the argument within the analysis of a functioning legal system and expressly disavows any 'metaphysical' concerns. In anticipation of possible 'philosophical objection' he states that,

> I [may] ... be charged with the view that there is always a 'right answer' to a legal problem to be found in natural law or ... [some] other transcendental strong box. ... [Any such view] is of course nonsense ... I intend no such metaphysics. I mean only to summarize ... the practices that are part of our [i.e. the United States] legal process.[32]

The tenability of this disclaimer must to some extent be questioned in the light of a closer examination of the content of the argument which Dworkin actually advances upon the substance of 'rights'.

Dworkin argues that certain rights transcend what he elsewhere terms an 'associative' social contractarian duty to obey.[33] These are rights in the 'strong' sense of the term and a citizen is entitled to exercise them without restraint by the state except in the face of some countervailing and yet stronger claim. Such 'strong' rights are contrasted with 'weak' rights which are merely individual judgments of what it is 'right' to do without any necessary connotation of entitlement.[34] Dworkin argues that certain 'constitutional' expectations are 'rights' in the strong sense and a government does not merely act 'wrongly' in legislating in defiance of them but commits a further 'wrong' in enforcing such a provision.[35] This, however, merely restates the problem and Dworkin himself comments that,

> if a man has a ... moral right against the Government, that right survives contrary legislation or adjudication. But this does not tell us what rights he has ... .[36]

In response to this issue he propounds principles of *Human Dignity* and *Political Equality*.[37] The first of these is, as Dworkin says, essentially Kantian and is put in the form that,

> there are ways of treating a man that are inconsistent with recognizing him as a full member of the human community, and ... such treatment is profoundly unjust.[38]

This is in effect a derivation from Kant's *Principle of Right* which proposes that an action which is to be considered 'good' in respect of a person will always tend to enhance his or her humanity rather than to diminish it. The second principle provides that,

> the weaker members of a political community are entitled to the same concern and respect of their government as the more powerful members have secured for themselves.[39]

The principle thus advanced may be seen to have obvious affinities with the basic social contractarianism which also informs John Rawls' liberal distributive theory of justice.[40] This striking parallel or convergence might reasonably be anticiapted from the nature of the two theories. Dworkin himself states the combined consequence of the two principles as follows,

It makes sense to say that a man has a fundamental right against the government, in the strong sense, ... if that right is necessary to protect his dignity, or his standing as equally entitled to concern and respect, or some other personal value of like consequence.[41]

This conclusion has many of the characteristics of a doctrine of substantive naturalism and, in its partially Kantian derivation, might even seem somewhat to tend towards the 'transcendental'. Such a categorization would, however, rather misrepresent Dworkin's purpose. He is in fact seeking a conceptual framework for the analysis of the 'rights' generated, in particular, within the constitutional system of the United States and is highly significant that in his combination of principles he prefers the principles of 'political equality' over the Kantian *categorical imperative* that all actions should be founded upon a principle which might be made a maxim for general action.[42]

For Dworkin's purposes it is necessary to distinguish simple liberties from the preferred and 'weighted' liberties which constitute 'rights' and the particular combination of principles which he selects provides a means of doing this. The principle of human dignity, which is borrowed from the 'transcendental strongbox', sets an agenda for the content of entitlement and the liberal principle of political equality supplies an identificatory criterion which seeks to avoid what Dworkin sees as the danger in 'crude' utilitarianism. This danger lies in the distribution of 'goods', including liberties, to others in accordance with the external preference[43] of a majority, bearing in mind that upon a utilitarian analysis the greatest good of the greatest number might involve the greatest misery of the few.[44] This is avoided by reference to the principle of political equality which excludes a distribution of liberties by reference to external preferences because such a criterion would be a denial of the claim of those who would then be disadvantaged to 'equal concern and respect'. Thus, in the resulting system of modified liberalism 'rights' symbolize internal preferences conducive to 'human dignity' which might be denied by reference to majority external preferences in an unrefined utilitarian system, an example of such a 'right' being freedom of speech - including a right to say things that are unpopular.

The 'anti-utilitarian' aspect of the model of rights which is advanced by Dworkin has been criticized from a number of quite different points of view. The criticisms advanced have been various in their nature, but the principal objection which has been taken relates to the essential 'negativism' of an account which seems to define 'rights' by reference to the extent to which the operation of external preferences in an unrefined utilitarian system would tend to exclude or restrict liberties. H.L.A. Hart pointed out that this seems to lead to the conclusion that the incidence of 'rights' is in direct proportion to the degree of repression existing in any given society.[45] Hart also made the point that,

> rights ... are needed as shield not only against a predominance of external preferences but against personal preferences also. ... We cannot escape ... the assertion of the value of ... liberties as compared with advances in general welfare, however fairly assessed.[46]

This emphasizes a most important factor for consideration. If basic rights are to be propounded, in comparison with less 'weighted' liberties, then - as Hart argued - they must be accepted as having an intrinsic value which is independent of any utilitarian or quasi-utilitarian assessment. In the Introduction to *Taking Rights Seriously*, which was written later than the main part of the work, Dworkin himself seems to have moved some way towards this point and to have distanced himself from the modified-utilitarian position. He remarks that,

> particular rights [are derived] from the abstract right to concern and respect taken to be fundamental and axiomatic. ... [It] is a right so fundamental that it is not captured by the general characterization of rights as trumps over collective goals ... because it is the source both of the general authority of collective goals and of the special limitations on their authority that justify more particular rights.[47]

This however seems, as Rolf Sartorius suggests,[48] to be an afterthought upon the status of the principle of political equality which is not reflected in the actual form of argument upon rights advanced in *Taking Rights Seriously*. The Rights Thesis itself seems, therefore, to remain substantially linked to a modified-utilitarian model.

This view of Dworkin's Rights Thesis is reinforced by consideration of its impact upon the idea of an obligation to obey law. The issue arises with the question of the consequence of an attempt by a state to legislate against a liberty which is defined as a 'right' within the terms of the Rights Thesis. In the course of his argument Dworkin considers a number of examples, of which two are especially illuminating in this context. These are the important questions of the existence of a 'right' to pornography and of the position of conscientious objectors in the United States to the military draft for service in the Vietnam War.

Dworkin's discussion of an alleged 'right' to pornography was clearly related to the issues involved in the Williams Report.[49]   The Williams Committee, like the Wolfenden Committee on Homosexuality and Prostitution before it,[50] reported in terms essentially founded upon the liberal principle advanced by John Stewart Mill[51] that the only legitimate cause for interference with the liberty of a person is the potential for actual harm to others and the moral quality of an action can never in itself be a sufficient ground for restriction of liberty.   In making this argument Mill emphasized the value of diversity of preference, both as an end in itself and as a means of social experimentation and development.   His contemporary critic, Sir James Fitzjames Stephen, quoted his brother Leslie Stephen making the obvious counter point that a nation which is half drunk and half sober is more diverse but by no means necessarily better than one which is wholly sober.[52]   This may be disclaimed, at any rate by a moderate liberal, upon the grounds that evils of drunkenness are well known and would, in extreme cases, fall within the remit of the qualifying 'harm' principle.   Dworkin agreed with the conclusion of the Williams Committee but not with the processes of reasoning by which it was reached.   He commences from his basic argument that,

> Rights are best understood as trumps over some background justification for political decisions that state a goal for the community as a whole.[53]

He then sets out the classic liberal dilemma, can there ever be a 'right' to do 'wrong' ?   What, in short, happens in a liberal society when a right of moral independence is exercised in pursuit of an 'objectionable' preference? Dworkin urges a basic right of moral independence which 'trumps' utilitarian arguments in contrast with the weaker claim made by Mill in relation to the value of diversity as such.   He therefore claims that the suppression of pornography would not merely be an illiberal restriction of a preference but a breach of right in the 'strong' sense and therefore 'wrong'.   However, Dworkin concedes that restriction upon the *public display* of pornographic material may, in deference to public distaste, be justified because this would not be a denial of a preference merely a restriction of permitted sources. This   cannot   be   considerecd   an   entirely   satisfactory   argument. Notwithstanding Dworkin's carefully stated concession,   acceptance of a restriction upon public display does admit an external preference since majority dislike is the only conceivable motive for such a constraint once a liberal 'right' to pornography has been advanced. Dworkin's position seems to be that his liberal modified-utilitarianism does in fact allow a compromise to be made with majority external preferences so long as the basic right to equal respect and concern is not breached. There is, nonetheless, a compromise of the basic liberal principle of neutrality amongst preferences and, as T.R.S. Allen has pointed out,[54] in practice restriction upon public display, and therefore upon the availability, of pornographic materials might be little if at all different from actual suppression. If a hierarchy is admissible in a liberal lexicon of values, freedom of expression - the principal victim of the Williams 'compromise'- may indeed reasonably be thought superior to the dubious joys of the perusal of titillating 'literature'.

No liberal theory is in fact entirely value neutral. Even Mill's argument in *On Liberty* proceeds from an assumption of the inherent 'goodness' of diversity subject to the qualifying 'harm' principle and is then 'neutral' only as between the various derivative 'rights' arising from the central proposition. In Dworkin's liberal modified-utilitarian approach this is even more clearly the case. The principle of political equality may to a marked extent be seen as a theory of 'good' which comes as close to an abandonment of scepticism about the 'good life' as is possible in a 'liberal' form of theory. This is, as H.L.A. Hart implied in a slightly different context,[55] symptomatic of an argument in transition between a 'utilitarian' past and a 'human rights' focused future and this results in a certain awkwardness in dealing with issues such as a claimed 'right' to pornography. This point is emphasized when it is considered that the whole debate upon the existence of such a 'right' might be avoided not only in the context of Dworkin's argument but also in relation to that of Mill. A 'right' to pornography could clearly only be derivative and is therefore open to a qualifying 'harm' principle. If it could be shown that pornographic material actually encourages abnormal sexual appetites and may, therefore, increase the incidence of rape and other sexual assaults, the case for suppression is made out even upon a simple 'liberal' theory. If, however, an opposite view is taken, that pornography affords a vicarious satisfaction for inclinations which might otherwise be more dangerously gratified, then a 'liberal' theorist might be driven back to an argument founded upon the claimed 'good' of diversity for its own sake. In the theory which is advanced by Dworkin, however, the 'good' of diversity, represented in the principle of political equality, is not the only 'good' but stands with the principle of 'human dignity'. This, as it has been remarked above, is to a large extent a restatement of Kant's Principle of Right. Upon this base a very clear case against pornography may be constructed. Briefly to restate the Principle of Right, any action in respect of a human being should tend to enhance rather than to diminish the humanity of the subject. The application of this to the question of pornography has been stated elsewhere as follows,

> The subject ...., usually a woman, is by definition being treated as an object ... as an impersonal ... means to the end of the sexual stimulation of the recipient ... . The humanity of the subject is thus degraded and the fundamental 'immorality' of pornography is thereby exposed. ... No-one, whether recipient or subject, can be 'right' to participate in the degradation of ... [a] person ... .[56]

Pornography can indeed be seen as an attack not only upon the human dignity of the subject but also upon that of people generally. Since the agenda for Dworkin's Rights Thesis is largely set by the principle of Human Dignity with the principle of Political Equality as a distributive criterion, there seems to be no good reason why, in the context of Dworkin's theory, it should not be contended that there can be no 'right' to pornography whatever. If this view is taken, a far more sound basis for the actual conclusion of the Williams Committee than those found either by Dworkin or the Committee itself might be suggested. If there is no derivative 'right' to pornography then there can be no theoretical objections to total suppression. The necessary compromises, dictated by the exigencies of political reality rather than 'liberal' theory, might then none the less demand the concession of a carefully limited exception which would in no way be reflective of any 'right'.

Dworkin's discussion of a potential 'right' to pornography is an important example in the context of the obligation to obey law because it illustrates the extent of the parameters of legitimate action by the state in the context of his liberal modified-utilitarian theory. For evidence of the effects upon the obligation to obey where these parameters are considered to have been exceeded it is necessary to turn to Dworkin's consideration of the position of conscientious objectors to the military draft for service in the United States armed forces during the Vietnam War. The involvement of the United States in the Vietnam War was a deeply divisive political issue through the 1960s and 1970s which ultimately severely damaged the capacity of the Johnson administration to govern and contributed very largely to the bitter conflicts of the ensuing Nixon administration. Considerable numbers of young men called up for service in Vietnam refused the draft and thereby came into conflict with the law. Those who so acted on grounds of conscience raise directly the question of the circumstances in which a citizen may properly disobey a law upon the basis that the state is seeking through it to deny him or her a 'right'. Dworkin commences his discussion of this issue with a statement of the 'conventional' response.

> In a democracy [which] ... in principle respects individual rights, each citizen has a general moral duty to obey the law, even though he would like some of them changed ... . But this general duty cannot be an absolute duty, because even a society which is in principle just may produce unjust laws ... . A man must honour his duties to his God and to his conscience, and if these conflict with his duty to the state, then he is entitled ... to do what he judges to be right. If he [does] ... break the law ... then he must submit to ... punishment ... in recognition of the fact his duty to his fellow citizens was overwhelmed but not extinguished by his religious or moral obligation.[57]

This is in effect a version of the social contractarian argument for submission to injustice advanced by Plato in *The Last Days of Socrates*.[58] An uncompromising version of this view expressed in the particular context of the Vietnam 'draft dodgers' is quoted by Dworkin[59] from Erwin Griswold, sometime United States Solicitor-General and Dean of the Harvard Law School,

> [It] is of the essence of law that it is equally applied to ... all irrespective of personal motive. ... One who contemplates civil disobedience out of moral conviction should not be surprised [by] ... criminal conviction [and] ... must accept the fact that organized society cannot endure on any other basis.

This statement is open to some considerable question and is, as Dworkin contends, false in at least two material particulars. Laws are not applied equally ignoring personal motive. For example, a motorist who violates a speed limit on a deserted street in the small hours of the morning whilst rushing a desperately sick member of the family to hospital commits precisely the same offence as a hoodlum who does the same in the middle of the day out of self-centred unconcern or, indeed, to terrorize other road users. As between these two 'equal' offenders it is probable, and entirely proper, that the former would be treated very differently from the latter and would in all likelihood not be prosecuted at all. As Dworkin argues, discretion is brought into play at every stage of the criminal process from decision whether or not to prosecute to sentencing in event of conviction and even beyond, for example in relation to parole decisions where a custodial sentence is imposed. It is also not the case that organized society must rigorously punish all perpetrators of crime in order to survive. Dworkin, by implication, relates this argument to the Benthamite concern with the potential for anarchy if subjects are admitted to be entitled to ignore positive legal provisions upon moral grounds. It has already been suggested that upon a moral purposive view of the naturalist argument this is a somewhat illusory fear.[60] Dworkin, however, responds in a different fashion which focuses upon the implications of civil disobedience upon moral grounds in a theory of principled adjudication in a constitutional, specifically the United States constitutional, system.

Dworkin's starting point is the clarity of the constitutional validity of the law to which moral exception is taken. So far as the draft for the Vietnam War was concerned the most basic question was clearly the lawfulness of American military involvement. Constitutionally the decision to enter armed conflict is, in terms of municipal law, a power vested in Congress and this was not exercised in relation to Vietnam, unless the 1964 Tonkin Gulf Resolution by which Congress authorized President Johnson to escalate military involvement in the Indo-Chinese sector is so considered. With this doubt in principle about the strict municipal lawfulness of the military involvement in mind, Dworkin questions whether the draft might not, therefore, be considered frivolous or perverse and thus to have placed an unfair burden upon a defined class of citizens - men of draft age not covered by religious or higher educational exemptions. If that view were to be taken, the draft might be argued to have contravened the fifth (due process) and fourteenth (equal protection) amendments to the United States Constitution.[61] In fact the US Supreme Court did not address these issues since they felt the issues to fall within an area of 'political' controversy into which the Court usually, but not invariably, declines to venture. Dworkin also refers to another highly controversial issue which was raised in connection with the Vietnam War. That is the question of the lawfulness of some of the methods and means of warfare, i.e. tactics and weapons, which were used during the conflict. So far as this is concerned he contends that the legal argument which was being advanced was essentially tantamount to a claim that,

> The constitution makes treaties part of the law of the land, and the United States is a party to international conventions and covenants that make illegal the acts of war the dissenters charged the nation with committing.[62]

This reference is to the body of the *jus in bello* treaty law, including the 1899 and 1907 Hague Conventions and the 1949 Geneva Conventions, together with a considerable body of other international agreements and custom.[63] Unlawful acts were undoubtedly committed during the Vietnam War, the My Lai massacre being a notorious example.   This was, however, dealt with in the case of *United States* v *First Lieutenant William L. Calley* under US military law,[64] buts such particular unlawful acts by no means necessarily render involvement in an armed conflict as such unlawful.

Whilst, however, the law thus remained variously open to some degree of doubt, it could be argued that assertions of an unqualified associative duty to obey or to accept the adverse consequences of refusing to do so must be doubted because the law itself was not clear.   Dworkin argues further that even after the court has made a decision upon such an issue the law may remain to some extent unclear.[65]   He points out that the US Supreme Court may alter its opinion, taking as an example a requirement of West Virginia state law for students to salute the American flag which was upheld in 1940 and then declared unconstitutional in 1943 and raising the question of whether objectors to this law were 'wrong' between 1940 and 1943 and 'right' thereafter.[66]   He finally suggests that since the US Constitution admittedly incorporates a large measure of political morality, moral dissent remains a possibility within the system even in the face of an adverse Supreme Court decision, granted the possibility of a change in the Court's moral-constitutional view.   He proposes three hypothetical positions which might be taken by a conscientious objector in the face of a law which is in some degree 'doubtful' in status.[67]   These are (1) to assume that moral judgment is barred and that the law should be obeyed whilst campaigning for change through the political process, (2) to follow moral judgment until a competent authority clarifies the situation, at which point the law must be obeyed whilst, if necessary, campaigning for change through the political process, (3) to follow moral judgment even if a competent authority has found against the relevant conclusion, although taking that decision into account in forming the judgment.   Dworkin urges that the third of these options is the correct one.   He argues that, in the light of relevant principles and policies and the appropriate exercise of discretions, courts should give weight to the stance of moral dissidents in their decision making and possibly thus be led to change their initially adverse position. Where, despite continuing adverse decisions, widespread dissent continues Dworkin argues that a good case is made out for political action to change the law.[68]

This is an interesting analysis but not one which can be regarded as wholly satisfactory. Apart from the matters of derivation and the general viability of a liberal modified-utilitarian theory which have been considered above, there are major difficulties arising from Dworkin's thesis in the context of the obligation to obey law. An obvious, of rather superficial, criticism is that the theory is set in terms of a highly specific, United States, constitutional context and modifications of expression are clearly necessary for more general application. Such modifications are, however, quite possible. Thus, in the instance of the United Kingdom, which has no written constitution and is by no means necessarily 'liberal' in its approach to 'constitutional' issues, the decisions of the High Court, the Court of Appeal and the House of Lords in *Attorney-General* v *Guardian Newspapers* (No.2),[69] the 'Spycatcher' case, is plainly open to Dworkinian analysis. It was held that in determining whether or not an interim injunction restraining discussion by the media in the United Kingdom of a book which had already been published abroad, a balance had to be drawn between the public interest in freedom of speech and the principle of confidentiality applied to members and ex-members of the security services. The conclusion reached was in essence that there is some 'right' to freedom of expression which can be overturned only by very substantial contrary requirements. In other words, a 'right' to freedom of expression, which forms no part of the 'black letter' law of England and Wales, Scotland or Northern Ireland, will 'trump' a rule of confidentiality in any other than the most compelling circumstances. An added interest in this context lies in the fact that civil action upon the basis of breach of confidence seems to have been chosen in preference to criminal proceedings under the very widely drawn s.2 of the Official Secrets Act 1911 in the 'Spycatcher' affair because of the increasing difficulty in persuading juries to convict even in the clearest apparent cases arising under that section. 'Perverse' jury verdicts have in fact a long and honourable history as a response to legal provisions or their application which have been seen as oppressive or perhaps merely unpopular, going back in England at least to the reign of King James II. An historically important example of this type of response to perceived abuse of law may be seen in the acquittal of the seven Bishops upon charges of seditious libel in 1688.[70] Despite their major constitutional differences, the legal systems of the United Kingdom and of the United States are very much of the same, common law, 'family', but similar, if more extensive modifications may be made for any other democratic and even many non-democratic systems.

A more serious difficulty arises in the relationship between internal and external moralities in Dworkin's analysis. Dworkin explicitly denies that he resorts to any 'transcendental strong box' or 'metaphysics' in his Rights Thesis,[71] but, as has been suggested above, this is rather questionable in the light of the nature and derivation of the principles of human dignity and political equality. This is emphasized by the clear assertion, which bears repetition, that '[a] moral right against the government ... survives contrary legislation or adjudication'.[72] In common with many 'liberal' theorists Dworkin pays little attention to the substantive 'associative' claims to which 'rights' set, or, more precisely, define, limits and yet this has been a vitally significant part of the argument upon the nature of the obligation to obey law since at least the time of Plato.[73] Similarly, Dworkin does not really address the problem of a legal system founded upon principles and assumptions which are, upon an external moral analysis, thoroughly 'bad'. He does examine and rule out the preferences underlying the practice of the Third Reich in his analysis of 'liberal' rights theory, mainly on the basis of the principle of political equality,[74] curiously, however, ignoring the principle of human dignity which, having been introduced, seems rather to fade from the development of Dworkin's argument. It is implicit in the argument that in any legal system rights survive adverse action by government or courts, but where the action results not from 'error' in a 'liberal' system but from the correct application of 'bad' principle there would seem to remain only recourse to a campaign for political change. This is not a particularly useful conclusion since the more repressive a regime is, the less scope there is likely to be for the mounting of such a campaign. The issue of the proper scope of civil disobedience outside a 'liberal' constitutional context is not much explored in Dworkin's theory, nor should it be expected to be granted the stated principal endeavour 'to summarize ... the practices that are part of our [the United States] legal process',[75] but this does limit the scope and application of the theory.

In a somewhat more general argument in *Law's Empire* Dworkin suggests that 'integrity' in the application of law is an independent virtue capable in itself of founding an obligation to obey. 'Integrity' in this sense is advanced essentially as a virtue of consistency and as a means by which judges may deal with any divergence between 'background morality' and substantive law. Dworkin gives this account of 'integrity',

> we know that people disagree to some extent about right principles of behaviour, so we ... [require] that they act in important matters with integrity, that is, according to convictions that inform and shape their lives as a whole, rather than capriciously or whimsical ... . This becomes a political ideal when we make the same demand of the state ... [in terms of its acting] on a single coherent set of principles even when its citizens are divided about what the right principles of justice and fairness really are.[76]

In some respects this may be seen as a very 'weak' form of the Kantian categorical imperative in its demand that particular decisions should be referable to general principles and is, as such, an elementary part of any concept of 'justice as fairness'.[77] As Dworkin specifies,

> It requires government to speak with one voice, to act in a principled and coherent manner toward all its citizens, to extend to everyone the substantive standards of justice or fairness it uses for some.[78]

It would be difficult to take exception to this principle as such. The claims made for integrity as an independent virtue are, however, somewhat more problematic. If 'integrity' is to be treated as an independent virtue the question must arise as to the claim of legal demands which concord only with a structure which is, on external moral evaluation, inherently 'unjust'. Dworkin concedes the existence of the difficulty and remarks that,

> [If] no competent account of ... an institution can fail to show it as thoroughly ... unjust, and [one which] should ... be abandoned ... the obligations it purports to impose are wholly cancelled by competing moral principle.[79]

An obligation founded upon internal integrity may thus be overborne by ..considerations of substantive morality, this being in effect a 'naturalist' statement. This important concession casts some doubt upon the actual degree of independence of the virtue of integrity. In a critical account of Dworkin's theory of integrity Denise Reaume remarks that,

> Despite Dworkin's assurance that consistency is valued for own sake, ... [f]airness, justice and procedural due process are all general standards and

> each internally requires consistency.   ... This shows that consistency is parasitic upon other ideals.[80]

Clearly in the assessment of the total obligation imposed by a legal provision 'integrity' cannot stand as an isolated factor and Dworkin implicitly concedes this in the statement quoted above.   To describe 'integrity' as wholly 'parasitic' seems, however, to overstate the case.   The 'social contractarian' arguments advanced, for example, in the *Crito* dialogue in *The Last Days of Socrates* by Plato[81] rest in part upon a principle of consistency in which acceptance of a system generates an obligation to accept its particular, and especially its adverse, applications so long as that application is part of the system accepted.   In this sense 'integrity' may indeed be seen as a virtue in its own right, even if one which may be discounted in the light of stronger claims of substance.   Reaume's criticism also fails to take account of the inherent limitations dictated by the context of Dworkin's argument.   His argument is centrally concerned with adjudication and in that context 'integrity' becomes of self-evident importance, if only as the basic requirement that like cases should be decided alike which is the foundation of the doctrine of precedent - both in the strict common law doctrine of *stare decisis* and in the more general *practice* of almost any judicial system.   As an intra-systemic virtue 'integrity' has a reasonable claim to be an independent virtue and is clearly a legitimate expectation of those who are subject to a system of adjudication.   Within this context integrity is significant and may itself be 'weighted' as against other values.   Thus, Dworkin concludes that,

> any successful constructive interpretation of our political practices as a whole recognizes integrity as a distinct political ideal that sometimes calls for compromise with other ideals.[82]

Such an 'internal' principle necessarily rests upon certain assumptions about the system itself, including that it is broadly 'just'.   Where these assumptions prove to be false, the claim of integrity as a source of obligation is necessarily reduced and may ultimately even be vitiated.   There is a clear analogy to be drawn here between Dworkin's 'integrity' and the procedural values advanced by Lon L. Fuller.[83]   It also relates primarily to formal intra-systemic obligations, even though it may play a subsidiary role in the evaluation of the moral claim exerted by a given system.   Dworkin's Rights Thesis   as   such   can   thus   be   argued,   like   Fuller's   procedural natural law, to be symptomatic of a 'post-positivist' recognition of a clear, if limited, role for moral factors in the intra-systemic working of positive law. However, notwithstanding the generality of Dworkin's principles of human dignity and political equality, his focus upon the approach of courts to issues of formal obligation tends rather to relegate the distinct issues of 'associative' obligation to obey law and the general limitations set to the propriety of law making to the periphery of legal theory. Ultimately, therefore, Dworkin's theory, like that of Fuller - if much more subtly - has a greater impact upon the formal analysis of obligation than upon its moral analysis. The analysis is in its proper context very significant, but the use of largely unqualified moral discourse in what is essentially a formal context does carry some danger of the type of pre-Benthamite argument found in the work of Blackstone.[84]

The Institutional Theory of MacCormick and Weinberger

A related but distinct objection to the implications of classical positivist legal theory can be found in the 'institutional' theory of law advanced by Neil MacCormick and Ota Weinberger.[85] The aim of this theory is succinctly stated by its authors to be,

> to explain and account for the existence of norms and legal institutions and other similar thought-objects ... [avoiding] the traps of idealism to which realists and materialists [object] ... [but also] the pitfalls of reductionism to which realist theories have always tended.[86]

The theory advanced is eclectic in its content but highly original in its combination and conclusions. The essential argument is that law and legal phenomena must be analysed as facts, but as thought-facts rather than physical or 'brute' facts. There are said to be two forms of such 'thought-facts' in a legal system. These are 'philosophical facts' which are validated by a combination of 'institutive', 'consequential' and 'terminative' rules. This analysis of rules as philosophical thought-facts bears a passing resemblance to Scandinavian Realist thought, especially to that of Olivecrona,[87] but the argument is different in kind and much less deconstructive in intention. There is also some affinity with H.L.A.

Hart's presentation of primary rules[88] but the mode of 'validation' is utterly different.   It is argued that 'institutive', 'consequential' and 'terminative' rules guide the recognition, effect and limits of given legal philosophical 'thought-facts', such as a 'contract', but that this is not in itself sufficient to describe the operation of law.   Legal thought-facts operate in a social context and are required to adjust to it through a capacity for flexibility. This necessary capacity is argued to be found in the second relevant category of thought-facts, which are the 'sociological facts' underlying the institutions which make, sustain and interpret law and which account for the determination of 'hard cases' such as *Riggs* v *Palmer*,[89] in which it was held that a murderer cannot benefit from the victim's will.   Such sociological thought-facts have an obvious relationship with Dworkin;s 'standards'.[90]   It is the combination of institutional and sociological thought-facts which are argued to form the basis of a legal system.   Thus MacCormick argues that.

> many important elements of law can be profitably contemplated as institutional facts in the philosophical sense, but we cannot squeeze the whole of law into that category;   in other aspects it can only be comprehended as an institutional phenomenon in the sociological sense. Jurisprudence is and must remain a joint adventure of lawyers, philosophers and sociologists.[91]

This, however, leaves open the question of the 'reality' of thought-facts in law and this is obviously of fundamental significance in determining the implications of the institutional theory for arguments upon the duty to obey law.   In addressing this issue MacCormick argues that it determines the whole question of the possibility of legal knowledge, agreeing with Richard Tur that 'the primary role of jurisprudence is to provide a legal epistemology, a theory of legal knowledge'.[92]   MacCormick concludes that legal knowledge in a meaningful sense is possible, essentially by turning a materialist conception of 'fact' upon its head.   He points out that even the perception of brute (physical) facts rests upon assumptions and ontologies, as for example demonstrated by the relationship between the apparent 'reality' of a physical object and the theories of atomic structure which interpret it as a concentration of energy, and concludes, therefore, that thought-facts have no less a claim to be considered 'real' than apparent brute facts.   Legal knowledge then becomes possible and the role of jurisprudence is presented as that of the investigation and elucidation of the 'implicit ontologies' of unreflective professional and lay legal discourse.[93]

If it is accepted that legal thought-facts in general are 'real' then it follows that the associated sense of obligation(s) is also 'real'. In this the Institutional Theory differs from Scandinavian Realism which treats 'obligation' as a fiction, albeit one having effects in the real world.[94]

Within the theory the nature of obligation in an intra-systemic sense may thus readily be deduced as an aspect of the generality of legal thought-facts such as 'contracts'. In a wider context the implications of the Institutional Theory appear more ambiguous. In his essay upon the relation between institutional morality and constitutions MacCormick comments that,

> Institutional morality has two dimensions: on the one hand, it has to fit as well as possible with the actual legal and political institutions of the civil society contemplated. On the other hand, so far as is consistent with this requirement of 'fit', it should approximate as closely as may be with our ideal 'background' political morality. It comprises a set of principles so devised as to make the maximum moral sense of the political institutions we have. Institutional morality is thus ideal morality relativized - relativized to a particular set of political institutions.[95]

This formulation has a clear relationship with Dworkin's conception of 'standards' and 'rights', although pitched at a much greater level of generality and without the specific linkage with the particular political structures and assumptions of the United States. It is also, like Dworkin's model, an analysis of the internalization of political moralities within any given legal system and, again, the political moralities concerned might, upon external evaluation, prove to be highly objectionable. This is not as such a criticism of the Institutional Theory but, as for Dworkin's analysis, there does arise an important question of context.

Like most, if not all, of what has here been termed the post-positivist group of legal theories, the Institutional Theory tends towards a 'convergence' of positivism and naturalism. Indeed the point is made expressly by MacCormick and Weinberger.[96] This appears, however, to be founded upon a conventional misapprehension of the naturalist enterprise. The point is made that there appears to be a clear linkage, not to say confusion, between legal and moral discourse. Thus, it is remarked that,

> Laws conceived in terms of the ought purport to be and are dogmatically represented as being *obligatory*. But they can be so only on the footing of

some ... moral reason for their obligatoriness. On this view the task of the ... black letter lawyer is inescapably a morally loaded one. For what he or she represents as legally obligatory has to be in some way ... morally obligatory; and if it could not be so it could not be legally obligatory either (though of course it might be mistakenly, misguidedly or even wilfully and wickedly enforced as such by officials).[97]

Clearly there is here an interface between social and legal 'obligations' made manifest by the common recourse to quasi-moral terminology found in technical legal discourse. The direct interface is, however, with an internalized morality which is recognized, indeed assumed, intra-systemically but which is essentially subjective seen from an extra-systemic viewpoint. It is in this that the dangers of modern arguments upon a 'convergence' of naturalism and positivism lie. Weinberger argues for 'convergence' between positivism and a 'weak' naturalism,[98] by which he means one which does,

> not assume that valid law is deducible from natural law principles, nor that legal maxims originating in positive law should simply be regarded as invalid because of their incompatibility with ... natural law.[99]

In so far as Weinberger is arguing the essential speciousness of the so-called naturalist/positivist debate he can readily be accepted to be on strong ground and much the same point has been made above.[100] Doubt must, however, be expressed about the juxtaposition of a model of 'weak' naturalism which does not advance moral criteria of validity per se and, presumably, a contrasting model of a 'strong' naturalism which does make such claims. It has also been suggested above[101] that what Weinberger advances as a model of 'weak' naturalism has always been the essence of the mainstream naturalist approach. The mistaken assumption of a false 'strong' naturalism can be argued to derive from basic misapprehensions of both the cultural contexts of classical naturalist thought and the associated linguistic usages. St. Thomas Aquinas, termed by Finnis a 'paradigm natural law theorist',[102] was arguing in the context of a moral universe as the very title of his principal work, *Summa Theologica*, implies. In that context the fact that secular sovereigns might in practice make and enforce enactments upon whatever moral or immoral basis they thought fit seemed both self-evident and not relevant to the questions at issue. The suggestion that a 13th century writer could seriously have considered all legislative action 'good' would seem most odd. In short, the argument related not to the formal dimension of obligation or even, directly, to intra-systemic moralities, but to the broader extra-systemic moral context in which the legislative and judicial enterprises are set. The recognition of legal phenomena as 'thought-facts' implicitly recognizes the interface with a much broader morality. Unfortunately, the evident existence of this interface, which can hardly be denied unless it is to be claimed that legal norms are generated in a moral and ethical vacuum, is taken by MacCormick and Weinbeger as by others, to imply a 'convergence' of naturalist and positivist concerns. Thus MacCormick comments,

> We can set up caricatures or ideal types of so-called legal positivism and natural law theory. But we delude ourselves in supposing that there remains nowadays any sharp division between these approaches so named. The best forms of positivism lead to conclusions similar in important ways to those derivable from the more credible modes of natural law thought, when we pursue rigorously the matters in hand.[103]

This can be argued to be a dangerous misconception in the same manner as the general doctrine of convergence found in a number of post-positivist theories. The observation of the internalized intra-systemic morality of legal systems should not be seen as identical with the basic naturalist concern with the external moral or ethical evaluation of a legal system from an extra-systemic viewpoint. Indeed, the quality of the internal moral assumptions of a legal system are in significant measure the focal point of naturalist criteria of evaluation. MacCormick and Weinberger's joint work is subtitled *New Approaches to Legal Positivism* and this may reasonably be accepted as a precisely accurate description of their endeavour. The Institutional Theory is, like Dworkin's Rights Thesis if in a different fashion, a valuable addition to analyses of the intra-systemic phenomena of law, and the obligation to obey, which is appropriately distanced from the variously inadequate 'rules' models. It is not, however, at all to be considered an all-embracing theory which is able to transcend the distinctions between categorically different intra-systemic and extra-systemic concerns in the analysis of positive law and legal systems. Any 'universal' theory of law would, to be viable, have to include responses to so many quite different questions that it would in reality be a portmanteau which would not have any genuine claim to be 'a theory' at all.

Legal Rules and Systems in the Theory of J.W. Harris

Similar basic issues to those treated by MacCormick and Weinberger are found in the work of J.W. Harris. In *Law and Legal Science*,[104] published in 1979, he examines the nature of the concepts of rule and system in the descriptive and predictive aspects of legal analysis. He proceeds to draw a distinction between momentary (i.e. present descriptive) and non-momentary (i.e. historic systematic) analyses of legal systems. With reference to the issue of legal 'validity', Harris makes the basic point that,

> There is nothing at all odd in legal science attributing 'validity' or legal bindingness to positive legal rules without thereby committing itself to value judgments about the contents of the rules described. Legal science is primarily ... informative ... and takes as its immediate subject matter the field of normative meaning which, consistently with legality and constitutionality, dictates or authorises behaviour on the part of officials and citizens. ... Thus, morality is not of the essence of a momentary legal system. ... It is also ... a proper ... function of legal science to offer moral or political criticisms of individual valid ... rules.[105]

This statement is made in the context of an argument advancing no less than five possible concepts of 'validity' and reflects the vital contextual and linguistic distinctions which have been urged in the present discussion.

There is in the distinction between momentary and non-momentary systems a superficial resemblance to the 'time frame' analysis advanced by R.W.M. Dias.[106] Dias argues that the operation and selection of criteria of legal validity is temporally determined. Thus, in a present 'time frame' only formal criteria of validity can operate, whereas in a continuum moral criteria can come into play and may ultimately lead to the vitiation of 'immoral' laws which may currently be valid. However, as is implicit in Harris's argument, Dias's model falls into the trap of conflicting intra-systemic and extra-systemic moralities, which his own analysis does not. Thus Harris remarks that,

> There is no reason to suppose that all historic legal systems correspond with any principles of critical morality claiming to have universal application. ... One who disapproves of the political institutions of a particular society may always deny that its [formally] valid ... laws are [morally] invalid ... .[107]

Once this fundamental distinction of context is accepted the most obvious defect in Dias's model, that the action of moral criteria appears to be postponed to some infinitely recessive future time, is readily resolved in the realization that different questions are being asked and may therefore be posed simultaneously.

To some extent like MacCormick and Weinberger, Harris deals with legal rules as 'intellectual constructs'[108] but he comments that,

> Mental constructs do not have a meta-reality which parallels the reality of concrete things; but [they] ... may help us to understand the social life of man and as integral constituents of certain human institutions they are part of the social life of man ... .[109]

Harris's general analysis of 'rule' and 'system' in legal science is not, obviously, directly concerned with the question of the obligation to obey law, but it equally clearly does carry implications for that area. The most important relates to acceptance of the fact that law may be analysed upon a number of distinct but interlocked levels. Thus, Harris remarks in his conclusion that,

> law ... is a series of fields of normative meaning and of historic collections of written doctrine, and [the requirement is] to move out into society to discover its practical effects.[110]

In accepting the existence of enmeshing but distinct concepts of law it is implicitly accepted that there may also be distinct but enmeshing ideas of the obligation to obey law. There may thus, as is here urged, be no necessary inconsistency between seemingly divergent analyses of causal motivation, formal obligation and moral obligation. On the contrary, all these various analyses may usefully play a role in the development of a full framework for the understanding of the obligation(s) to obey law, whilst none of them can be accepted as comprehensively explanatory in isolation.

Conclusions

For the purposes of this discussion a number of theoretical approaches have been grouped together as 'post-positivist' in nature. It is not claimed that these theories constitute an exhaustive grouping of approaches capable of being so designated.[111] However, such theories are characterized by concern with the inadequacies of the simple rules model of law advanced by the 'positivist' analyses and a concomitant search for a framework of theory within which non-rule elements of the legal enterprise may satisfactorily be taken into account. For the most part these theories nonetheless retain, in common with strict positivism, an essential intra-systemic focus which suggests categorization as extensions of the scope of formalist theory rather than excursions into wholly different analytical contexts. Within this spectrum of theory four broad propositions may usefully, if somewhat over-simply, be separated out. These are: (1) the content of legal rules is subject to inherent limitations resulting from the parameters of what may formally be identified as a 'legal' system. (2) Although a rule of law of any content might be capable of formal recognition, a legal system contains inherent inhibitions in principle which in fact serve to shape and limit the content of and application of rules. (3) Legal rules exist in an institutional and sociological (or political) context from which they cannot be divorced and which moulds what may be expressed through them. (4) Law exists in a historical perspective which moulds the content of rules both in their generation and possible ultimate abrogation or desuetude (including in the latter case both *de facto* and *de jure* disuse).

Of these, (1) is represented in Lon L. Fuller's 'procedural natural law', (2) and (3) in Dworkin's 'Rights Thesis', (3) in MacCormick and Weinberger's 'institutional' theory, (3) and (4) in Harris's model of 'legal science' and (4) in Dias's 'temporal approach'. With the possible exception of (1), all of these are in various ways concerned with the internalization of moral, ethical or other limitations upon the content and/or application of rules within a legal system. They do not go on to examine the possibility of limitations being set to the propriety of the principles or other non-rule factors which are being internalized by a legal system. Thus, for example, Dworkin does not really answer the question raised by the possibility of a legal system founded upon internalized 'constitutional' standards which may be judged objectively 'bad' according to some external criteria.[112] There is no particular reason why he, or any other 'post-positivist' should address such issues, so long as it is accepted that their theories are extensions of intra-systemic analysis and not newly comprehensive models of legal phenomena. J.W. Harris recognizes this expressly but whether this recognition is common to all theories which may be termed 'post-positivist' may seriously be questioned.

The implications of 'post-positivist' theory for the obligation to obey law are likewise important but circumscribed. Such theories seek essentially to derive an interpretive canon beyond the rules model(s) of law, freed from its crudities whilst retaining an intra-systemic analysis rooted in the pragmatic workings of a legal system. In the context of an obligation to obey, therefore, these theories are primarily concerned to put a gloss upon the analysis of the formal duties created at law which extends into a dimension beyond the mere intra-systemic validation of rules. The analysis remains, however, essentially intra-systemic in focus and concerned primarily with internalized values. Concern with extra-systemic concepts of moral or ethical obligation is largely as foreign to 'post-positivist' theories as it is to positivism itself. The variety of insights afforded by 'post-positivist' theory go some way to meeting a point made by the Rt. Reverend David Sheppard, then Bishop of Liverpool,

> Kafka's man on trial cannot get at authority ... . The law is rigid, impersonal, totally external to his life. ... Authority is remote, emerging with its rigid set of rules from the world of 'them'.[113]

The 'post-positivist' analyses seek to explain the internalization of values in the process of enunciation of formal legal norms and in so doing facilitates avoidance of the infelicities in analysis of obligation which arise in a crude rules model of law. In particular they are able to avoid any confusion of causal motivation and formal obligation. In so far, however, as such theories claim a 'convergence' of formal and moral categories of the obligation to obey law, they threaten to revive another and no less infelicitous confusion of categories. Ultimately there remains the question of the quality of the constitutional and or ethical assumptions underpinning a legal system. This question arises in a moral context which transcends formalism and it is greatly misleading to suppose otherwise.

All the theories considered in this and the preceding chapters have in common, despite their wide divergences of emphasis and with the possible exception of the 'command' theories, an acceptance of 'obligation' as a useful concept which has 'real' effects, whether or not it is itself viewed as a meta-reality. This is not a universal view amongst legal theories and any adequate theoretical model of the obligation to obey law must take account of theories which treat such a concept as at best a *chimera*, if not actually a calculated deceit contrived as a means for the concealment of an unhelpful or disreputable political agenda.   These theories, also highly diverse in form and content, express a far more radically sceptical view than the 'post-positivist' questioning or 'rules' models and form the subject matter of the next chapter.

Notes

  1   This is not to suggest that there was any exclusively 'positivist' dynamic in legal theory, merely to say that this approach dominated conventional, and especially professional, thinking.

  2   In this context the title of C.G. Waines' book, *The Revival of Natural Law Concepts*, originally published in 1930 but republished thirty-five years later (Russell and Russell, NY., 1965) may be seen as significant.

  3   See Chapter 5.

  4   J. Stone, Book Review (1937-38), *Modern Law Review*, 177 at 178.

  5   See Chapter 2.

  6   First published in 1961, 2 ed., with postscript ed. by P.A. Bulloch and J. Raz (Oxford, Clarendon, 1994), for the 'minimum content' see Chapter IX.

  7   2 ed., with revisions (Yale University Press, 1969).

  8   For consideration of this aspect of H.L.A. Hart's theory see Chapter 2.

  9   Lon L. Fuller, op.cit., p.140.

10   H.L.A. Hart, op.cit., Ch. II.

11   Lon L. Fuller, op.cit., Ch.II.

12   Ibid., p.180.

13   R.S. Summers, *Lon L. Fuller*, in the series *Jurists: Profiles in Legal Theory*, ed. W. Twinning (Edward Arnold, 1984), p.40.

14   Ibid.

15   See Chapter 7.

16   In fact the choices may not be quite so stark, as the Courts of the former Federal Republic of West Germany demonstrated in their consideration of some of the 'grudge informer' cases, see Chapter 7.

17   Lon L. Fuller, op.cit., pp.245-53.

18   The case was decided in 1950 upon facts arising in 1944.   The initial erroneous report appeared in (1950-51) 64 *Harvard Law Review*, 260.   The debate between Hart and Fuller can be found in (1958) 71 *Harvard Law Review* at 593-673.

19   St. Augustine of Hippo, *De Libero Arbitrio*, Bk.I,V:33. See also Chapter 3.

20 Lon L. Fuller, *The Morality of Law*, 2 ed. (Yale University Press, 1969), p.123.
21 Ibid., p.41.
22 Ibid., p.123.
23 Duckworth, (1976).
24 R. Dworkin, ibid., p.40.
25 W.I. Waluchow, 'Herculean Positivism' (1985) 5 *Oxford Journal of Legal Studies*, 187. A comparison may be made with the argument advanced by Richard Tur in 'Positivism, Principles and Rules' in Elspeth Atwooll, ed., *Perspectives in Jurisprudence* (University of Glasgow Press, 1977). See also, N. MacCormick, 'Dworkin as Pre-Benthamite' in Marshall Cohen, ed., *Ronald Dworkin and Contemporary Jurisprudence* (Duckworth, 1984).
26 See *De Libero Arbitrio*, Book I, V:33. 27 For discussion of this point see Chapter 3.
27 See Chapter 3.
28 For an example see *Anisminic Ltd.* v *Foreign Compensation Commission* [1969] 2 AC 147.
29 See *Belfast Corporation* v *O.D. Cars* [1960] AC 490.
30 R. Dworkin, p.22.
31 For discussion of this in the context of naturalism *stricto sensu*, see Chapter 3.
32 R. Dworkin, op.cit., p.218.
33 R. Dworkin, *Law's Empire* (Fontana, 1986), pp.202-6.
34 See R. Dworkin, pp.188 ff.
35 Ibid., pp.190 ff.
36 Ibid., p.197.
37 Ibid., pp.198-9.
38 Ibid., p.199.
39 Ibid.
40 See J. Rawls, *A Theory of Justice* (Oxford, 1972). Dworkin discusses Rawls' theory favourably in *Taking Rights Seriously*, Ch.6.
41 R. Dworkin, op.cit., p.199.
42 The value of the Kantian Categorical Imperative and Principle of Right in the development of substantive naturalism have been considered elsewhere, see H. McCoubrey, *The Development of Naturalist Legal Theory* (Croom Helm, 1987), Ch.10.
43 An 'external' preference is that of an individual in the distribution of 'goods' to others, an 'internal' preference is that of an individual in the distribution of 'goods' to him or herself.
44 Bentham's 'ideal' prison, the Panopticon, might be cited in support of this. See also M.D.A. Freeman, *Lloyd's Introduction to Jurisprudence*, 6 ed. (Sweet and Maxwell, 1994), at p.208, citing G. Himmelfarb, 'The Haunted

House of Jeremy Bentham' in *Victorian Minds* (1968). The Panopticon has not been without modern supporters, see J. Semple, 'No Slops for Bentham' *The Independent* (London), 7 May 1990.

45 H.L.A. Hart, 'Between Utility and Rights' (1979) 79 *Columbia Law Review*, reprinted in Marshall Cohen, ed., op.cit., p.214.

46 Ibid., at pp.223-4.

47 R. Dworkin, op.cit., Introduction, p.xv.

48 R. Sartorius, 'Dworkin on Rights and Utilitarianism' (1981) *Utah Law Review*, reprinted in Marshall Cohen, ed., op.cit., p.205.

49 (1979) Cmnd. 772.

50 (1957) Cmnd. 247. This report revived a debate originally conducted between J.S. Mill and Sir James Fitzjames Stephen. See H.L.A. Hart, *Law Liberty and Morality* (Oxford, 1963), and Lord Devlin, *The Enforcement of Morality* (Oxford, 1965).

51 J.S. Mill, *On Liberty*, 1859, reprinted with an Introduction by G. Himmelfarb (Pelican Classics, 1974).

52 Sir James Fitzjames Stephen, *Liberty, Equality, Fraternity*, 1872, reprinted, ed. R.J. White (Cambridge, 1967), p.80.

53 R. Dworkin, 'Is there a Right to Pornography?' (1981) 1 *Oxford Journal of Legal Studies*, 177.

54 T.R.S. Allen, 'A Right to Pornography?' (1983) 3 *Oxford Journal of Legal Studies*, 376.

55 See H.L.A. Hart, 'Between Utility and Rights' in Marshall Cohen, ed., op.cit., at p.214.

56 H. McCoubrey, op.cit., p.80.

57 R. Dworkin, *Taking Rights Seriously*, pp.186-7.

58 See Chapter 3.

59 See R. Dworkin, op.cit., p.206.

60 See Chapter 3.

61 For detailed discussion of this see R. Dworkin, op.cit., at pp.208-210.

62 Ibid., p.208.

63 For discussion of this law see H. McCoubrey and N.D. White, *International Law and Armed Conflict* (Dartmouth, 1992).

64 For discussion see L. Friedman, *The Laws of War: A Documentary History* (Random House, NY., 1972), Vol.II, p.1703.

65 See R. Dworkin, op.cit., pp.211-212.

66 Ibid., p.213.

67 Ibid., pp.210-211.

68 See ibid., pp.215-222.

69 [1990] 1 AC 109.

70 30 June 1688.

71 R. Dworkin, op.cit., p.218.

72 Ibid., p.197.
73 See Chapter 3.
74 R. Dworkin, *Law's Empire*, pp.102-8.
75 R. Dworkin, *Taking Rights Seriously*, p.218.
76 R. Dworkin, *Law's Empire*, p.166.
77 A phrase used by John Rawls in his initial model of justice, see 'Justice as Fairness' (1958) LXVII *Philosophical Review*, 164-174.
78 R. Dworkin, *Law's Empire*, p.165.
79 Ibid., p.203.
80 D. Reaume (1989) XXXIX *University of Toronto Law Journal*, 380 at 390.
81 See Chapter 3.
82 R. Dworkin, op.cit., p.215.
83 See above.
84 For an extended discussion of Dworkin as a pre-Benthamite see, again, N. MacCormick, Dworkin as Pre-Benthamite' in Marshall Cohen, ed., op.cit.
85 N. MacCormick and O. Weinberger, *An Institutional Theory of Law* (D. Reidel Publishing Co., 1986). This book is a collection of essays by the authors which represents a coincident development of theoretical perceptions which were originally set out separately.
86 Ibid., p.6.
87 See Chapter 5.
88 See Chapter 2.
89 115 NY. 506; 22 NE. 188 (1889). This example is used by Dworkin in his analysis of 'hard cases', see *Taking Rights Seriously* (Duckworth, 1978).
90 There are again, of course, vitally significant differences of context.
91 N. MacCormick and O. Weinberger. op.cit., p.74.
92 Ibid., p.96, citing R. Tur, 'What is Jurisprudence?' (1978) *Philosophical Quarterly*, at 149.
93 N. MacCormick and O. Weinberger, op.cit., p.102.
94 See Chapter 5.
95 N. McCormick and O. Weinberger, Ch. VIII at p.174.
96 Ibid., Introduction at p.7.
97 Ibid., p.2.
98 See ibid., pp.111-2.
99 Ibid., p.112.
100 See Chapter 3.
101 See ibid.
102 J. Finnis, *Natural Law and Natural Rights* (Clarendon, Oxford, 1980), p.28.
103 N. MacCormick and O. Weinberger, op.cit., p.141. Also published as 'Law Morality and Positivism' (1981) 1 *Legal Studies*, 131 at 145.
104 Oxford, 1979.
105 Ibid., pp.124-7.

106 See R.W.M. Dias, *Jurisprudence*, 5 ed. (Butterworths, 1985), Ch.22, also 'Temporal Approach towards a New Natural Law' (1970) 28 *Cambridge Law Journal*, 75.

107 J.W. Harris, op.cit., p.126.

108 Ibid., p.130.

109 Ibid.

110 Ibid., p.171.

111 The model of legal systems advanced by Joseph Raz in *The Concept of a Legal System* (Oxford, 1970), to which brief reference is made in Chapter 2, would be one of the other potential members of this grouping.

112 There is an argument that such a system existed in the Third Reich, see Chapter 7. In *Law's Empire* at p.263 Dworkin does state, in relation to the concept of 'integrity' in adjudication, that 'it makes no sense except among people who want fairness and justice as well'.

113 Rt. Revd. D. Sheppard, *Built as a City* (Hodder and Stoughton, 1974, edn. of 1985) p.430, referring to Kafka, *The Trial*.

5 Sceptical Analyses

The central importance of the normativity of positive law and, thus, of the resulting appearance of the reality of an obligation to comply with its demands is by no means an inevitable assumption. A number of approaches to legal theory deny this proposition and may, for present purposes, therefore be categorized as 'sceptical'. The basis for such scepticism varies widely. An important consideration of the sceptical case was advanced in 1973 by M.B.E. Smith[1] who summarized his approach in an initial statement that,

> although those subject to a government have a *prima facie* obligation to obey particular laws (e.g. when disobedience has seriously untoward consequences or involves *mala in se*), they have no *prima facie* obligation to obey all its laws'.[2]

In an extended discussion Smith dismisses most of the conventional bases for a *prima facie* obligation to obey positive law and finally concludes that there can in fact be none such. As a practical demonstration he advances the case of one 'Jones' who is said to have 'broken a law', without any indication of the seriousness or triviality of the transgression, and asks,

> Would you ... be willing to say that what he did was morally wrong? ... I would wager that the great majority would answer 'I can't yet say - you must tell me more about what Jones did'.[3]

This, very plausible, conclusion is expressed more formally as follows,

> If ... we have specific information about an illegal act which tends to show it to be right, then the rule is irrelevant to our determination of the act's moral character. .... [O]ur conclusions about its moral character must be based on this specific information, and not on the supposed reasonableness of holding illegal conduct wrong ... .[4]

This argument appears to address what may be termed an 'external' moral obligation to comply with positive law and, in that context, the conclusion reached is hardly controversial.   There may indeed be *prima facie* moral arguments for compliance, founded upon 'consent' or otherwise, to some of which Smith makes reference, or upon more basic arguments resting upon the claims of order over disorder which are found in the work of Aquinas. The moral evaluation of a duty to obey is external to any *a priori* assumptions of obligation made within the legal system itself.   In short, Smith can be argued to have distinguished between formal analyses which, at least, assume a *prima facie* duty to obey the law and moral analyses which focus upon the quality of the demand rather than its 'legality' as such. This is, indeed, hinted at by Smith in the distinction which he draws between the 'general' questions of obligation, which he seeks to answer, and the 'lawyer's question' which he does not.   Both the general and the 'lawyer's' questions are phrased in   'moral' terms and this may be contended to reflect the form of a legal discourse which tends to confuse formal and moral categories of obligation.   Seen in this light, Smith's argument may be suggested to be 'sceptical' not so much as regards the duty, if any, to obey law, but rather in relation to the implicit assumptions which underlie conventional legal discourse in the context of that issue.

In one sense Bentham and Austin might be considered to have been 'obligation sceptics'.   However, although in their search for an objective 'science' of jurisprudence ideas of 'obligation', and certainly of moral obligation, were excluded from consideration, this was only for the narrow purposes of the descriptive identification of positive law.   Classical positivism did not deny that such issues might usefully be discussed in other, non-jurisprudential, contexts.[5]   Fundamentally 'sceptical' theories, in contrast, do not merely deny the place of 'obligation' in the discipline of jurisprudence, but consider the concept to have no place in any legal analysis, dismissing it either as a misconception or as a deceptive construct serving to conceal some other agenda.

The Spectrum of Obligation Scepticism

A diverse range of legal theories can be considered 'sceptical' in the present sense.   They do not constitute a natural group for any other purpose and are far from being in agreement *inter se* even upon the question of 'obligation'. In the more general context of 'normative' theory Roger Cotterell has summed up the linking thesis of sceptical theories as follows,

> They suggest that doctrine is less important than those who create it; ... the values are relevant to legal analysis only insofar as they represent the particular preferences of influential decision makers; that legal outcomes reflect configurations of political power, not overarching social or political values. ... that law is a human creation to be [studied as] ... it is and not as it might or should have been.[6]

The concept of obligation may, upon such a model, be treated as an artificial construct of legal discourse without 'real' foundation. The actual 'reality' advanced by such theories varies widely, from the economic determinism of classical Marxism to the psychological bases of Scandinavian Realism. Interestingly, both the Marxist-Leninist E.B. Pashukanis and the Scandinavian Realist Karl Olivecrona considered analytical positivism, with its formalist emphasis, to be no more than a variant upon the basic 'voluntarist' heresy which they saw in naturalism and to share, from a sceptical viewpoint, most of its major faults.[7] The particular theories which most clearly fit the 'sceptical' mould here suggested are Marxism and its derivatives, Scandinavian Realism, American Realism and the Critical Legal Studies movement.

Marxist and neo-Marxist Theories

The collapse of communist rule in Eastern Europe and the former Soviet Union has been seen as representing an end to an 'age of ideology' and, by implication, the redundancy of Marxist thought. In fact the 70 year experience of Soviet jurisprudence and the general tradition of Marxist thought, from which Soviet practice was in some respects an aberration, cannot so easily be dismissed from account.

Classical Marxism rests upon an economic determinism which informs an adaptation of the Hegelian dialectic amounting to a form of socio-economic 'catastrophe theory'. The doctrine is well known but, in brief summary, the 'real' basis of social and political relations is argued by Marxists to be economic and that base is considered to develop more rapidly than the social 'superstructure' which rests upon it. The latter consequently adjusts its form periodically, more or less violently, through successive revolutions to concord with new economic realities. This process is seen as being fuelled by class conflict in which successive classes establish their dominance through revolutionary displacement of the preceding ruling class until the revolutionary progression ends, for want of further subordinate classes, with the proletarian revolution. For Karl Marx and his associate Frederick Engels, the proletarian revolution was to be the immediate prelude to the establishment of a stateless and classless communist 'ordering of things' in which the repressive apparatus of the institutional state, including its law, would 'wither away' for want of utility. In this context law was seen simply as a coercive instrument through which an economically dominant class maintains and enforces its advantage, although an instrument particularly associated with the 'bourgeois' phase of social development for a variety of reasons. This class-instrumentalist view was plainly expressed by Engels in the statement that,

> law is sacred to the bourgeois, for it is ... enacted ... for his benefit ... . Because the English bourgeois finds himself reproduced in his law ... the policeman's truncheon which, in a certain measure is his own club, has for him a ... soothing power. But ... [t]he working man knows ... the law is a rod which the bourgeois has prepared for him; and when he is not compelled to do so he never appeals to the law.[8]

There is no place for a Marxist 'legal theory' as such, since law is seen merely as a superstructural incident, and indeed such theorizing is seen as tending towards 'legal fetishism', meaning the elevation of legal forms beyond a subservient status in relation to economic forces. It follows from this that upon a classical Marxist view any idea of an 'obligation' to obey law amounts to a misrepresentation, conscious or otherwise, of the consequences of advantage or coercion. Despite its strongly anti-legalist stance, however, Marxist thought necessarily deals with legal phenomena. As Hugh Collins remarks,

> Marxists reject [legal fetishism] ... and it follows that they are not inclined to develop a general theory of law as an end in itself. Nevertheless much remains for Marxists to say about law.[9]

This is of course most particularly the case where states are controlled by governments committed to a Marxist-related ideology. The obvious examples are found in the former USSR and the People's Republic of China.

The October 1917 Bolshevik Revolution in Russia was not strictly in accordance with Marxist expectations. The Russian Empire in the latter half of the 19th century had, in Marxist terms, been moving from a 'feudal' into a 'bourgeois' condition, commencing most significantly with the abolition of serfdom under Alexander II in 1861. The orthodox Marxist position in such a situation would have been that the next step in development should have been a 'bourgeois' revolution, suggesting support for the February 1917 Menshevik Revolution.

Be that as it may, the last half century of Tsarism had been a significant period of legal development, impelled not least by the sudden gaining of legal *locus standi* by huge numbers of ex-serfs in the 1861 liberation. A major reform of 1864 radically modernized the Russian legal system[10] and, contrary to both revolutionary and reactionary expectations, some elements of the new system, notably jury trial and the small civil claims and minor criminal jurisdictions of the 'Peace Courts' were very well received. There is, indeed, good reason for thinking that jury trial gained strong popular support as a constraint upon what was perceived as official or semi-official abuses. This could be seen in a number of cases, such as, e.g., the *Zasulich case* (1878) and the *Beilis case* (1904).[11] It is of incidental interest that throughout the last half-century of Tsarism the Bar retained a freedom of speech in court proceedings which was in many ways without Russian parallel. Both Kerensky, the Menshevik leader, and Lenin were, significantly, members of the pre-revolutionary Bar. The reactionary regime of Alexander III (1881-94) and the early years of Nicholas II, up to 1905, largely eliminated the Peace jurisdiction as politically undesirable, although its principal elements were restored in 1912. The image of an inherently anti-legal Russian culture upon which alien western forms were artificially imposed is belied by the historical record. Exclusion from legal remedies, through servile status, is by no means the same thing as a rejection of such remedies when available.

After the Bolshevik seizure of power the practical exigencies of power forced the party to make certain ideological accommodations, the product of which came to be known as Marxism-Leninism. The first important step in this decidedly dramatic process of ideological development was the concept of the 'dictatorship of the proletariat', more accurately a dictatorship of the Communist Party, as a period of transition from revolution to full communism, during which residual class antagonisms and 'bourgeois ideology' would be extirpated.   During this period certain 'bourgeois' institutions, including positive law, were to be retained and used as a 'club' in the hands of the 'proletariat' in a final exercise of class domination for the consolidation of the proletarian revolution.   In 1927 P.I. Stuchka, then President of the Supreme Court of the USSR, wrote that,

> Communism means not the victory of socialist law, but the victory of socialism over any law, since with the abolition of classes with their antagonistic interests, law will die out altogether.[12]

This was also, of course, the view of the principal Soviet jurist of the period of 'War Communism', the New Economic Policy and the Five Year Plans, Evgenny Bronislavovich Pashukanis.   He followed an orthodox line in seeing legal rules and principles as contrived means whereby 'real' economic relations are expressed in a formalistic mode.   In particular, in the present context, he saw constitutional law not as the formal expression of some arm's-length 'bargain' between state and people, but as an ideological distortion of the power relations imposed by a dominant bourgeois class.   He wrote that,

> The Constitutional state (*Rechtsstaat*) is a mirage, but one which suits the bourgeoisie very well, for it replaces withered religious ideology and conceals the fact of the bourgeois hegemony from the eyes of the masses.   ... Power as the 'collective will', as the 'rule of law', is realised in bourgeois society to the extent that this society represents a market.[13]

Obligation was also dismissed as an aspect of a 'mystifying' analysis which seeks to conceal the 'reality' of power relationships.   Pashukanis was especially contemptuous of positivist claims to differentiate between 'legal' and other 'obligations'.   He stated that,

> strict differentiation of the moral and juridical sphere is the source of insoluble contradiction for the bourgeois philosophy of law.   If legal obligation has nothing in common with 'inner' moral duty, then there is no way of differentiating between subjection to law and subjection to authority as such.   Yet if ... duty is an important feature of law, even if with only the

faintest subjective tint imaginable, then the significance of law as a socially necessary minimum is immediately lost. Bourgeois legal philosophy exhausts itself in this fundamental contradiction, the endless struggle with its own premises.[14]

This passage is in effect a denunciation of the whole idea of obligation in law as hopelessly chimerical.

This analysis can be argued to have been to a large extent perceptive. The contradiction to which Pashukanis referred may indeed be thought to exist in what he labelled as 'bourgeois legal philosophy'. The long-standing, but it is argued,[15] misconceived naturalist/positivist 'debate' and also the weakness of H.L.A. Hart's idea of a 'minimum content of natural law'[16] seem to derive from precisely such a basic contradiction. However, the 'insolubility' claimed by Pashukanis rests upon a very narrowly defined coercive class-instrumentalist model of law. It is true that the rather scattered nature of the references made by Marx and Engels to law may allow some latitude for different interpretation,[17] but the narrow view set out by Pashukanis does appear to represent an originally accepted Soviet orthodoxy.

However, both in the former Soviet Union and in Marxist opinion beyond it, narrow class-instrumentalism came increasingly to be questioned. In the USSR the triumph of Stalin and the idea of 'socialism in one state' produced a transition of view marked by extreme violence. Pashukanis was denounced as a 'wrecker' and liquidated in 1937 upon the orders of his successor as Party jurist, A. Ia. Vyshinski, who became the choreographer of Stalin's 'show trials'. In place of the temporary and crudely class-instrumentalist view of law there was set up the idea of 'socialist legality' advanced by Vyshinski in his principal published work[18] which is now notable more for the vituperativeness of its invective than for the lucidity of its exposition. The basic idea was, however, simple enough. As part of the stabilization of Soviet institutions there was also to be a 'stability of laws', a phrase used by Stalin himself, in which the norms of a socialist society were to be accepted as being as much capable of 'legal' expression as those of a 'bourgeois' society. The form of this change, in the context of the highly repressive Stalin dictatorship, masks to a large extent the real significance of a shift in emphasis which might have occurred, more benignly, in any event. In some ways the 'rehabilitation' of law in a Marxist-Leninist context was a less dramatic shift than it might at first seem. To some extent the idea of 'socialist legality' may be argued to have initiated the definition of a post-revolutionary 'ordering of things'which Marx and Engels had not defined, but freed from what Hugh Collins terms,

> the dubious definitional fiat that rules which serve any other purpose than class oppression cannot be law.[19]

The general significance of the shift in Soviet jurisprudential thinking is expressed by Harold J. Berman in his statement that,

> It was rediscovered that law is not a luxury but a necessity, that at the very least it satisfies a basic need for some outlet for feelings of justice, of rightness, of reward and punishment, of reciprocity, which exist in all peoples. Stalin did not want the Russian people merely to obey; he wanted them also to believe in the rightness of the order which had been established.[20]

The idea of 'socialist legality' remained, with many fluctuations in emphasis, the essential basis of Soviet legal thought from Stalin to the policies of *glasnost* and *perestroika* in the closing Gorbachev era. It was being suggested, indeed, that the idea of law not merely as an instrument of state but as a potential constraint upon it was gaining ground. W.E. Butler remarked in 1988 that,

> there is some indication that human rights discussions of the 1970s have made Soviet legal theorists aware that citizens' rights cannot always be reliably protected by the State but must be protected against the State. Perhaps the trend ... in Soviet law to place greater reliance upon the courts to resolve disputes [is] reflective of this concern.[21]

It is, however, important to emphasize that the sense of 'rightness' embodied in 'socialist' legality' was not considered to extend to those who were ideologically deviant, those who, in the terms found in H.L.A. Hart's modern positivism, did not share in the 'internal' view of Soviet society. For such people the *potestas coactiva* remained in full force and was used by Vyshinski[22] as the justification for the startling dichotomy between the claimed 'stability of laws' and the blood bath of the Stalinist purges and 'show trials'. The tension between the claims of the state and those of citizens is perhaps inevitable in any community of individuals but arose in an especially intractable form in the former Soviet Union. This was a dichotomy which, along with fundamental economic problems, the USSR failed to resolve. In this sense the compromised 'scepticism' of Marxist-Leninist theory did not meet the developing needs of the society in which it originated.

In China the Communist government established by Mao Xse Dong (Mao Tse Tung) from 1 October 1949 swept away the remnants of the pre-1911 Imperial Legal Code[23] and the, mainly German and Japanese derived, legal innovations of the post-1911 Nationalist government and put in their place a Marxist-Leninist structure of post-Pashukanis type. In one sense the compromised obligation-scepticism which this implied was by no means incompatible with the established Chinese legal tradition. Over a very long period Imperial China had displayed a markedly ambivalent attitude towards law. Confucian orthodoxy emphasized *Li* (rites) which incorporated quasi-moral social obligations as a guide to proper living, relegating *Fa* (positive law) to the role of a coercive power with an almost exclusive emphasis upon criminal process. In the *Analects* Confucius (K'ung Ch'iu) is reported to have said,

> I could try a civil suit as well as anyone, but better still to bring it about that there were no civil suits.[24]

The point being that good citizens should resolve their disputes in accordance with social morality rather than through litigious wrangling. Indeed, all law in Imperial China was criminal in form and was so much perceived as a *potestas coactiva* directed against deviants that private lawyers were considered trouble-makers and condemned as 'tricksters'.[25] Law was thus seen as a coercive and 'external' instrument with 'obligation' in any 'internal' sense the province of the moral norms encompassed in *Li*. The coercive function of law was emphasised by the deliberately intimidator nature of the judicial process that derived, without admission, from the practice of the first Imperial Dynasty, the Chin (221-206 BC), which was committed to a harsh 'legalist' philosophy abandoned in favour of Confucianism by the succeeding Han dynasty. In this concealed 'legalist' heritage there may even be seen some element of 'legal fetishism', along with a marked emphasis upon 'stability' of norms.

In the post-1949 People's Republic of China the pattern of 'socialist legality' was violently disrupted by the application of Mao's theory of development through continuous revolution during the period of the 'Cultural Revolution' in which all ideas of 'legality' were swamped by the Red Guard terror. Following the death of Mao Xse Dong there was a marked swing back to ideas of 'socialist legality' not vastly different from pre-*perestroika* Soviet practice. This was shown clearly in the trial of the disgraced leftist faction led by Jiang Qing (Chiang Ching), Mao's widow, and known as the 'Gang of Four'. Although in one sense a 'show trial', these proceedings were carefully prepared in a 'legal' context with recognition of norms of due process. The official record of the trial made the point that,

> The years of lawlessness ended with the arrest of the Gang of Four in 1976 ... It was recognized that socialist legality must prevail.[26]

This trend of thought was emphasized by the restructuring of the courts in the 1978 Constitution, again stressing the nature of socialist law as a formal expression of ideological rectitude. Thus, the President of the Supreme People's Court, Chiang Hua, reported to the Fifth National Congress in 1980 that,

> We must ensure that peoples' courts are independent ... subject only to the law [as] ... an important principle of a socialist legal system [but] ... [s]upervision of judicial work by people's congresses [is] ... important.[27]

The dramatic political events in Eastern Europe which led to the collapse of the former USSR did not leave China untouched. A Democracy Movement led to protests in Beijing (Peking) in the Spring of 1989 which culminated in the occupation of Tienanmen Square by protesters and the killing of many of them. This clearly marked the blockage of any Chinese movement along the lines of Soviet-style *glasnost* or *perestroika*. The violent suppression of protest is not a uniquely communist or Chinese phenomenon, but the Tienanmen Square deaths did emphasize in an extreme degree the limitation of 'socialist legality' to those who have 'internalized' the system.

Generally, the state of Chinese law in 1996 may be compared in many respects with pre-*perestroika* former-Soviet practice. Some western Marxist commentators have, however, denounced even this as revisionist in tendency. In a strongly anti-legal statement James P. Brady stated that,

Pashukanis demonstrated that ... reliance on law ... was a feature of developing capitalism; ... recent trends in China indicate that [social isolation and fragmented consciousness] ... can not only continue, but even deepen if expedience sets the course of socialist transition and if 'New Class' elites form to undermine egalitarian reforms and democratic decision-making.[28]

Brady admits the perpetration of injustices by the Red Guards during the Cultural Revolution, but the characterization of this era as either 'egalitarian' or 'democratic' seems to demand a very particular ideological perspective.

The implications of the idea of 'socialist legality' for concepts of obligation in relation to law are profound. The crudely coercive aspect of the law is, of course, a significant part of the initial Marxist and Marxist-Leninist models. The acceptance of socialist legality and, therefore, of a normative legal influence within a socialist society beyond the mere repression of 'class enemies' raises immediately the question of the quality of the formal obligations raised in a legal context. In practice it would seem that the structure of formal obligations generated under the law of the former USSR was not vastly different from that generated under other systems. Thus, the obligation generated under former Soviet law by a contract entered into with *Aeroflot* would have had much in common with that arising from a contract with an airline under any other system. There remains the controversial issue of the moral and ethical obligations raised by legal provision. There is here a cautious and limited parallel to be drawn with the early development of the Christian forms of naturalist thought.[29] St. Augustine of Hippo, writing in the late Roman era, considered law to act usefully in repressing sin pending the governance of the City of God, but to have no role in a fully Christian polity. If, for the purpose of a limited discussion, 'bourgeois ideology' is substituted for sin and the post-revolutionary 'ordering of things' for the fully Christian polity, a rough functional equivalence with the model advanced by Pashukanis becomes clear. Both the Bishop of Hippo and the Vice-Commissar saw law as a *potestas coactiva* of strictly limited and temporary utility in the course of progression towards a much better and non-legal order. In both cases the view rested upon a very narrow definition of 'law' founded upon coercion to be applied in cases of obdurate 'error'. The widening of definitional horizons, in the one case through the advanced synthesis symbolized by Thomism and in the other through the development of the idea of a 'socialist legality', opened the doors to an extension of the role of law beyond the repression of residual 'error' to the formal expression of norms perceived as representing a 'right' ordering of society. With this very sense of 'rightness' there comes an implicit 'obligation' to comply with legal norms which derives from their quality and not merely from the potential or actual application of coercive force.

Pashukanis was, not surprisingly, dismissive of 'bourgeois morality' and of naturalism. He identified individualist morality with 'bourgeois' commodity-exchange social mores and claimed that naturalism, in its social contractarian form, was the 'revolutionary ideology' of the bourgeoisie. As a political analysis of the 1688-89 Whig Revolution in England, which displaced James II and brought in William III and Mary II on a basis which was the foundation of modern English constitutional arrangements, there is something to be said for this view. Interestingly, Pashukanis suggested that the reason for the later anti-naturalism of the positivists lay precisely in these revolutionary antecedents, which is to some extent borne out by Bentham's horrified reaction to the French Revolution and its partially 'social-contractarian' underpinning. Pashukanis wrote that,

> natural law ... reduces the function of state power to keeping the peace, and sees the state's sole determining feature as being the instrument of law. ... [I]t deduces the state from the contrast between isolated individuals. This is the entire theory in skeleton form, which admits of the most diverse concrete variations ... . [I]t was the revolutionary banner [of] ... the bourgeoisie [in its] ... struggles against fuedal society. ... [S]ince the bourgeoisie became the ruling class, ... the prevailing theories cannot wait to consign it [naturalism] to oblivion.[30]

The equation of naturalism in general with its particular social contractarian forms is highly questionable and its identification with 'bourgeois class domination' may be considered a crude over-simplification. Once this is abandoned, however, the way might seem open in a neo-Marxist context not for the adoption of naturalist argument as such, but for the adoption of a purposive view of law which would admit functionally similar arguments upon the particular matter of the obligation to obey. In a Marxist context this would indeed be a radical admission. No hint of it appears in the early western Marxist writing of Karl Renner[31] which, despite its emphasis upon the stability of forms, in contrast with the mutability of functions, sets out a basically instrumentalist view of law not far removed from that expressed by Pashukanis. In recent writing, however, this step is to be found approached by Hugh Collins. He remarks that,

> There seem to be only two possible ways in which Marxists might ascribe
> moral worth to the pursuit of particular principles such as legality and liberty.
> The first is to assess institutions and practices according to a functional test
> which considers to what extent they hasten progress towards a revolution.
> The second uses the theory of alienation and evaluates institutional
> arrangements and political principles in the light of Man's true nature to
> discover whether freedom for self-affirmation through labour is permitted or
> encouraged by them.[32]

In effect variants upon a purposive test for the quality of principles and
action are beings suggested and, once narrow class-instrumentalism has
been abandoned, this seems a logical direction for the development of legal
theory in Marxist thought.

In the light of this type of argument the claim of Marxism to be
included without qualification in a 'sceptical' category for present purposes
may be questioned. It is possible that the implications of Marxist thought
for the idea of obligation(s) to obey law are both less dramatic and more
interesting than its original instrumentalist stance might seem to suggest.
The non-autonomy of legal phenomena insisted upon by Marxism may
readily be accepted. Indeed the idea of legal autonomy must appear to be
insupportable in any theoretical context beyond the most uncompromising
forms of classical positivism.[33]   Whether the Marxist claim to find the
'real' base of social and political development in economic relations is
accepted or treated in itself as a form of 'economic fetishism' is another
matter.[34]   Otherwise, the obligation-scepticism of Marxism seems to
become largely definitional. If 'law' is defined as an instrument of class
repression then, *ex hypothesi*, questions of an obligation to obey cannot
arise in Marxist theory. If, however, a less restrictive definition is adopted,
allowing 'socialist' as well as 'bourgeois' norms to be expressed in 'legal'
forms, it would seem that a functional equivalent of the tripartite
categorization of obligations in a legal context which has been suggested
above could equally be applied about certain forms of Marxist theory.

Forms of 'Realist' Theory

More seemingly absolute 'sceptical' views are expressed within the two 'Realist' schools of legal theory. 'Realism' in this context has the same implication as the 'materialism' claimed by Marxists. That is to say that there is a claimed focus upon the 'real' basis of legal phenomena in contrast with 'idealistic', but obfuscatory, models of law. The two schools of thought which take the name 'realist' differ markedly in their choice of 'real' base. The Scandinavian Realist School took law to rest fundamentally upon a psychological base whereas the American Realist School took the behaviour of courts to be the 'reality' of law. In this sense they have in common only their claim to 'realism' and are best considered as distinct each from the other.

The Implications of Scandinavian Realism

Scandinavian Realism originated at the turn of the 19th and 20th centuries in the work of Axel Hagerstrom and denied the 'reality' of legal concepts such as 'validity', 'justice' and 'obligation', treating them instead as psychologically conditioned responses to certain forms and uses of language. Thus, when it is said that a person is placed under (formal) 'obligation' by entering into a contract it is argued that no real phenomenon termed 'obligation' is created, there is merely a psychological response to the stimulus of the formalities of the contractual process. These, in short, associate a feeling of 'oughtness' with the transaction which urges compliance. Again, the idea of ownership is argued to create no 'real' relationship between a person and the property 'owned', instead a psychological and emotional climate is generated by certain recognized rituals as a result of which the person 'owning' the property and the bulk of his or her fellows are brought to 'feel' that interference with his or her control of it would be 'wrong'. On a broader scale the same analysis may then be applied to the general 'obligation' to obey which is seen as a psychological response to the forms of law making and legal expression rather than a 'real' relationship founded upon force or upon 'authority'. The basis for this psychological analysis of law was set out at the beginning of the 20th century by Axel Hagerstrom who argued, largely by reference to a historical study of Roman law, that the generation of a sense of normativity in relation to law is ultimately related to primitive word magic.[35] Interestingly, a similar psychological analysis was advanced at the same time by Leon Petrazycki, Professor of Legal Encyclopaedia at the University of St. Petersburg until the Russian Revolution and thereafter Professor of Law at the University of Warsaw. Despite the convergence of their thinking it seems that Hagerstrom and Petrazycki were each unaware of the work of the other.[36] Petrazycki, who is now an undeservedly neglected theorist, made a significant contribution to psychology through his development of the theory of impulsions.[37] An 'impulsion' is an experience in which a passive response, cognitive or emotional, to a stimulus is combined with an active, volitional, response. The particular impulse of normativity was defined by Petrazycki as an 'ethical impulsion' and, when elevated beyond a mere sense of 'rightness' into one of actual 'obligation', as a 'legal impulsion'. For Petrazycki 'legal impulsions' were not limited to positive legal provisions but embraced all 'obligatory' norms including positive law as a particular category. He divided legal impulsions into two broad categories, *intuitive law*, meaning varieties of 'moral' imperative, and *positive law*.. The category of positive law was then further sub-divided into *official positive law* and *unofficial positive law*. The former was presented as positive law in its normal sense, the latter included such 'normative' influences as public opinion and fashion. This categorization offers an obvious superficial parallel with Austin's laws 'properly' and 'improperly' so-called.[38] The parallel is, however, more apparent than real. Whereas Austin's categories were intended to separate positive law from, in his opinion, misleadingly similar phenomena, Petrazycki's served, *inter alia*, to emphasize the essential unity of the operation of 'obligatory' norms on the psychological level. Thus the nature of the impulsion behind compliance with a moral or social norm will not, on this model, differ materially from that associated with a norm of positive law, although the external stimuli will, of course, differ markedly. For this purpose the question of coercive force may be left aside since forced compliance falls outside the immediate concern of Petrazycki's analysis.

In the sphere of positive law Petrazycki concluded that the concept of (formal) obligation found in such a proposition as a borrower under a formal contract of loan is under obligation to pay the stipulated interest to the lender does not, as a strict positivist would suggest, disguise some material link such as the threatened application of a sanction, nor, as a Marxist or other iconoclastic thinker might suggest, serve to conceal class or some other group instrumentalism. Such concepts are, rather, suggested not to correspond with any material reality but to express experiences in the mind of the person subject to them which have real effects upon his or her conduct. Thus, for Petrazycki, 'ownership' must be seen as an artificial concept which, through the belief of the 'owner' and other people, will produce real and effective patterns of behaviour.

Petrazycki has attracted much odium in Marxist writing, including the work of Pashukanis.[39] The main reason for this seems to have been the fact that his theory of impulsions necessarily emphasizes individual reactions in a way incompatible with the class-collective perceptions of Marxism and neo-Marxism.

A fundamental link in this type of psychological analysis which was not really explored by Petrazycki, but which was implicit in the work of Hagerstrom, is the means by which a sense of 'oughtness' is attached to provisions of positive law. This issue was considered in detail by Karl Olivecrona. He dismissed both positivism and naturalism as variations upon the same misapprehension, terming them both 'will' theories, and argued that in asserting a higher 'will', whether that of a political sovereign or of a higher or Divine reason, as the mainspring of law such theories invert the true nature of a legal order. Thus he commented that,

> The fundamental error of naturalistic positivism is its misinterpretation of the relationship between legislative power and the existing legal order. The legal order is represented as being given and maintained by the actual holders of independent power while in reality their power depends upon the existing legal order as a functioning system. The legal order remains for generations, though subject to continuous change, partly through the lawgiving activities of the temporary holders of power, partly because of other factors.[40]

In rejecting the varieties of 'will' theory Olivecrona also denied that there is any single 'binding force' associated with law. Instead he advanced a model of legal effectiveness founded upon the association of psychological responses with certain modes of enunciation of norms. He treated the attachment of apparent imperation to a norm as essentially the same in all cases, whether issued as a personal command or in the form of general legislation. Olivecrona analysed 'obligatory' norms as composed of two broad elements, an *ideatum* and an *imperantum*.[41] The *ideatum* defines both the relevant situation (the *requisitum*) and the action or abstention required in it (the *agendum*). The *imperantum* then attaches to the *ideatum* the idea that compliance with the *agendum* is non-optional. The *imperantum* may differ widely in form, from the tone of voice of a Sergeant-Major on the parade ground to the legislative formalities of the United Kingdom Crown in Parliament, but in all cases it is the psychological effectiveness of apparent imperation rather than the language of 'rights' and 'authority' in which it is conventionally presented which is important. Thus, Olivecrona stated that,

> there can only be a question of the psychological requirement for the efficacy of a command. From the psychological point of view ... only the idea in the mind of the addressee, concerning the right to command, can be of importance. The right itself ... can exert no influence upon the behaviour of the addressee except through the mediation of his idea of its existence; and if the addressee has got the idea, it is irrelevant whether the right really exists.[42]

The *imperantum* in the case of law consists of the whole formal setting of legislative action which is accepted as effective, thus rendering its products 'valid'. This amounts to the constitutional provision of the country concerned but, as for any *imperantum*, it is not the constitution itself which generates 'valid' norms but the attitude of the population towards it. As Olivecrona expressed the point,

> the ability to make laws with practical effect results from the general attitude among the population with regard to the constitution, this attitude being the immediate source of the law-making power of the legislators. They are in a position to invest a text with the quality of law, in the eye of the public; when it becomes a law, it belongs to the great body of rules commanding universal respect. ... It is an effect upon the psychological level.[43]

Olivecrona's analysis emphasizes the 'constitutional psychology' of the population as a whole. A variant is found in the work of Alf Ross, who emphasized the psychology of the judiciary.

Ross started from the basic proposition that,

> the science of law is a branch of the doctrine of human behaviour, therefore the legal phenomenon must be found within the field of psycho-physical phenomena constituting the domain of psychology and sociology.[44]

He stressed the social psychology of judicial implementation of law and, in doing so, moved closer to the American Realist analysis than any other Scandinavian Realist thinker. He concluded that,

> a 'valid' law means the abstract set of normative ideas which serve as a scheme of interpretation for the phenomenon of law in action ...[45]

adding at a later point that,

> the norms are actually operative in the mind of the judge because they are felt by him to be socially binding and therefore obeyed.[46]

This model of the 'valid' legal rule as a hypothesis about future judicial conduct and its motivation was criticized by H.L.A. Hart as bringing Ross perilously close to the crude judicial determinism of some American Realist writers.[47] It would certainly seem a fair comment that in an analysis of the psychological efficacy of law concentration upon the judiciary seems unduly restrictive since litigation is only one aspect of the total operation of law. In that sense the broader perspective adopted by Olivecrona may be preferred.

Whatever the relative strengths of their analyses, neither Hagerstrom, Olivecrona or Ross offer much, or any, guidance upon the question of how in the first place psychological efficacy should come to be vested in any particular law-constitutive process. Nor is it indicated to what, if any, limits such psychological efficacy may be subject. The model advanced by Olivecrona affords a reasonable description of the practical efficacy of positive law in an established legal order but does not explain the effective establishment of a constitution or the implied limitation of action under its terms. The closest approach to such an account in Scandinavian Realist thought is found in the work of Vilhelm Lundstedt. Lundstedt, a Member of the Swedish Riksdag and Professor of Civil and Roman Law in the University of Uppsala, found the reality of law in the psychology of social welfare. In a posthumously published work he defined 'law' as,

> nothing but ... the conditions which make possible the peaceful co-existence of masses of individuals in social groups and their co-operation for other ends than mere existence and propagation .... . [Law works through] psychological impulses arising in various ways from the nature of [humankind] ... .[48]

Dismissing 'legal ideology', what a Marxist would term 'legal fetishism', as misleading, Lundstedt argued that laws are made and applied according to evaluations of their effect upon social welfare, meaning assessments of the aspirations of people within the society concerned. Thus he commented that,

> The social valuations which become directly decisive for legislation (and interpretation of law) do not ... come immediately from the 'people' but from the legislator (or interpreter) himself, ... The law-giver makes the valuation because he understands the meaning [of] ... his activity to be to benefit society.[49]

Ross objected strongly to this analysis upon the basis that it set up an absolute criterion for 'good' law and affronted the Scandinavian Realist aversion to 'metaphysics'. Lundstedt defended himself vigorously with the argument that,

> this is pure romance from Ross's side. I have as emphatically as possible proclaimed that I proceed from the establishable factual aspirations and efforts of men for taking care of their possibilities of life; in doing so I leave aside entirely the question of whether man ought to have these aspirations or not. If this starting point of mine is not illogical - something which Ross has not dared to assert - then his attempt to represent me as a metaphysician is hopeless.[50]

Stripped of its vituperation, this argument raises important issues. Lundstedt represented his neo-teleological model of social welfare as 'fact' based, but then Aquinas would have been astonished by a suggestion that the will of God might be anything other than fact, although he did, of course distinguish between things perceptible to human reason and those revealed by Divine grace. The question of whether or not people 'ought' to have the aspirations which they in 'fact' do, which Lundstedt set aside, leads inevitably to the question of the 'goodness' or otherwise of human nature and this must entail discussion of 'metaphysical' issues. A case may be made out that Ross was right to imply that Lundstedt's analysis did include a strong purposive element, notwithstanding the claim of value-neutrality made on its behalf. It may in this light be suggested that Lundstedt ventured to the very edge of Scandinavian Realist scepticism and gazed into vistas which his chosen school sought to eschew. This is, of course, only a criticism if the self-set definitional limitations of the School are taken to be inviolable.

The contribution of Petrazycki and the Scandinavian Realists to jurisprudence in general and to the theory of obligation in particular is at once both limited and highly significant. The basic thesis, that concepts such as validity and obligation operate on a psychological level is a valuable counter to excessive legal formalism and is obvious, once it has been stated. Clearly a concept such as obligation, like any other concept, operates upon a psychological level and, indeed, could operate upon no other. It is also the case that other factors, including physical coercion, play a role in the practical operation of law and this is not denied by Scandinavian Realists. Beyond this, the work of Olivecrona in particular is of great value in describing the psychological efficacy of law making in a stable society and, by extension, in accounting for the general unreflective bias in favour of conformity which is a general quality of such societies. Such an analysis does not, however, offer a satisfactory account of the limits of the psychological effectiveness of law. If a legislature, observing all the requisite constitutional formalities of enactment, were to establish a law requiring that the firstborn of all families in the country should be arbitrarily killed, it could hardly be expected that this demand would be 'psychologically effective'. It would be grossly unfair to attribute to Olivecrona the Pavlovian thinking which would be necessary to suggest the contrary, but the practical issue is effectively ignored. It may be suggested that such legislation would not only be psychologically ineffective but would produce swift and possibly violent constitutional change. Why? Because such legislation would run contrary to some very basic social and personal aspirations and feelings which may indeed be treated, in line with Lundstedt, as 'factual'. A second problem arises in the question of the generation and alteration of modes of establishing psychologically effective law-making mechanisms which is largely ignored in an analysis the primary focus of which lies in a stable political community. In fact the issue is partially addressed by Olivecrona. He argued in relation to revolutionary transfers of power that,

> New leaders step in and proclaim that they have 'assumed power', which is an empty phrase unless they are successful. They begin to issue laws ... To succeed they need ... a special ... psychological situation in the country. The ordinary source of strength for a government ... respect for the existing

constitution, is supplanted by a momentary gathering of diverse forces. But in actual fact, the revolutionaries make use of much of the foundations of the old power. ... People are ... familiar with the idea of ... [the necessity for] government ... . [Therefore] respect for the previous constitution may easily be transferred to the new one.[51]

There may be much to be said for this analysis of the revolutionary redirection of psychological efficacy but it still does not account for the origin of such efficacy. As with Kelsen's *grundnorm* as the foundation of a legal order one is ultimately left with a 'fact' which must be accepted as anterior to the analysis being advanced.

The limitation of Scandinavian Realist theory, for all its value, is further evidence of the defect of any legal theory which seizes upon an aspect of legal phenomena, however important, and treats it as a satisfactory account of the whole. Olivecrona himself makes the point in his comment that,

The surprising capacity of the will-theory to survive may be explained partly by our natural inclination to find single causes for complex phenomena. The idea of a will at the centre of a legal order satisfies this desire. The will ... invests the system with an apparent unity ... [but] innumerable difficulties arise as soon as more specific information is asked for.[52]

What is true of Austin's obsession with coercive sovereignty is also true of analyses in terms of psychological 'fact'.

The attempt of Scandinavian Realism to set limits to legal analysis by reference to psychological 'fact' is ultimately distorting even in its own terms. Part of the psychological response to a given legal order is inevitably found in human social aspiration and expectation, as Lundstedt concedes, and these are as much ideas having real effects as are the constitutional responses outlined by Olivecrona and the judicial behaviourism set out by Ross. To dismiss such thought as 'metaphysical' seems to tend towards dogmatism. Whether or not the expectations are believed to be, or indeed actually are, metaphysical in origin is unimportant in this context in comparison with the 'fact' that the ideas exist and have real effects in the life of the community concerned.

The relevance of Scandinavian Realist thought to the question of the obligation to obey law lies primarily in the area of formal obligations arising in a stable legal system. Psychological responses to formal stimuli are of clear importance in relation, e.g., to the efficacious functioning of contracts and to general acceptance of legal norms. They are not, however, a universal explanation for compliance and cannot, for example, take account of issues of force which also play a role in the working of law. The degree of obligation-scepticism of this school of thought may also be questioned. It is true that the objective 'reality' of obligation is denied, but the 'real' significance of ideas about obligation are not and this in the end may be suggested to be a matter of definition rather than of substance.

The Implications of American Realism

Quite a different approach is found in the work of the American Realists. The central thesis of this school was set out by Oliver Wendel Holmes, who suggested that law was best approached through assessment of the reactions of the 'bad man'. He stated that,

> if we take the view of ... the bad man, we shall find that he does not care [about] ... action or deduction, but that he does want to know what ... courts are likely to do in fact. I am much of his mind. The prophecies of what courts will do in fact and nothing more pretentious are what I mean by the law.[53]

As this basic statement of position suggests, the majority of American Realist thinkers were, like Holmes himself, practising lawyers and their emphasis was very much upon the importance of judicial action and its nature. They were highly sceptical of jurisprudential doctrines and saw in the 'fact' of judicial conduct and the question of its predictability the only real issues of legal theory. Broadly the school may be divided into 'rule sceptics', typified by Karl N. Llewellyn, and 'fact sceptics', typified by Jerome Frank. The former argued that legal 'rules' are greatly over-emphasized in traditional jurisprudence to the detriment of consideration of judicial behaviourism in legal decision making.[54] The latter argued that even the ascertainment of facts in litigation rests upon judicial action and that, therefore, the whole of jurisprudential enquiry is comprised within the study of judicial behaviour.[55] At a later stage of his thought Llewellyn advanced a 'law jobs' model of a legal system[56] in which he argued judicial 'craftsmanship' to be attuned to the performance of certain social tasks, including the avoidance or safe-channelling of disputes having the potential for serious social disruption.   This important suggestion has clear 'purposive' implications and, like the work of Lundstedt in a Scandinavian Realist context, moves to the boundaries of 'realist' scepticism.[57]

American Realist thought has had a very significant influence upon the development of Anglo-American jurisprudence and has served usefully to call into question the unqualified 'rules' model of law found in traditional common law thought.   It is not, however, of very great value in the analysis of the nature of an obligation to obey law.   The definitional limitations of a concept of law founded, in Holmes' terms, upon an external view by the 'bad man' of what courts will in practice do effectively precluded the school from any consideration of the association of moral or ethical obligation with positive law.   Even consideration of formal obligation is severely curtailed in any such 'external' view of law by virtue precisely of the exclusion of the 'internal' viewpoint the importance of which was rightly emphasized by H.L.A. Hart in the context of positivist theory.[58]   In this context there is a certain parallel to be drawn between the self-imposed limitations of American Realism and those of the Austinian 'command' theory.[59]   As with other 'external' models of law it is only in the rather dubious context of outright coercion that American Realism can be said to enter into debate upon the nature of an 'obligation' to obey law. Again, such comment is not in itself necessarily a criticism of American Realist theory, which as an analysis of law as judicial action has no necessary interest in issues of 'obligation' as such.   The source of error lies, as in the case of many other theories of law, in the claim to have found a single 'real' foundation of jurisprudence which in fact, and inevitably, excludes many phenomena which are relevant to law.   The 'scepticism' in this case may be more genuine but still appears to derive from the definitional limitations of a deliberately restricted analytical base.

The Critical Approach

Amongst modern approaches to legal theory the most radically sceptical is undoubtedly that offered by the Critical Legal Studies movement.   This movement arose from the same foundations as the more radical elements of American Realism, in conjunction with a search for a modern post-Marxist 'left' analysis of 'legal' phenomena.   Critical legal scholars are 'sceptical' of almost all other analyses of law, but most particularly of the claims and implications of a 'liberal' approach. This is represented as offering a view of law as rational and objective which conceals a reality of conflict and illegitimate power structures. The foundation of critical legal studies thus lies in a deconstructive endeavour to expose the hidden 'realities' and agenda of law and legal administration. An important part of this is found in the deconstruction of conventional 'liberal' legal discourse, including the discourse of 'obligation', which owes much to the later linguistic philosophy of Wittgenstein. In his later writing Wittgenstein advanced a 'games' model of language emphasizing *usage* rather than *meaning*, in place of his earlier analysis founded upon 'logical atomism'. In the context of legal theory such an approach has the obvious consequence of calling into question the seeming certainties of conventional legal discourse. Thus, a term such as 'contract' is conventionally taken to imply a bargain reached under the guidance of neutral norms, but this may also be seen as a distorted usage which conceals the real social and power relationships upon which legal phenomena 'in fact' rest. It is the perceived purpose of critical linguistic and 'literary' analysis to expose such covert agendas.[60] The conventional discourse of normative jurisprudence, whether founded upon formalist models or upon some external criterion of evaluation, is similarly considered by critical legal scholars to distort the real foundations of law in power relationships through their implicit claims of objectivity and/or autonomy.[61] This deconstructive approach has some evident affinities with Marxist analyses, but most critical legal scholars have distanced themselves from Marxist class instrumentalism and class determinism. Alan Hunt states that,

> critical theorists are agreed upon their rejection of Marxist instrumentalism ...
> [which posits] both a necessary and direct connection between class interests
> ... and either the content of legal rules or the outcome of the legal process. ...
> What underlies the critique of orthodox Marxism is better conceived as a
> critique of economism. ... [C]onstitutive theory [has] ... the major problem of
> finding the appropriate conceptual language to adequately explore the way in
> which law is imbricated in the social totality.[62]

Critical legal studies may thus be taken to reject not only the autonomy of law claimed by liberal theorists but also the substitution for it of an economo-centric model, preferring instead a more complex inter-relational model of social structures. In a seminal article Roberto Unger argues that most conventional legal orders represent 'frozen politics' in which habituated institutions embodying entrenched interests become highly resistant to change which therefore, upon a revolutionary or 'catastrophe' model, comes about finally only through a violent resolution of discontinuities.[63] In place of such an unsatisfactory condition Unger advances a concept of 'negative capability'. He argues that,

> Negative capability is the ... individual and collective empowerment made possible by the disentrenchment of normative structures ... [meaning] not permanent instability, but the making of structures that turn the occasions for their reproduction into opportunities for their correction. Disentrenchment therefore promises to liberate societies from their blind lurching between protracted stagnation and rare and risky revolution.[64]

This view represents a model of continuous development in contrast with the social 'catastrophe' theory of Marxism, but it does not seem to be obviously more than a theory of mechanism. Unger, however, argues that it implies a substantive social ideal in so far as it,

> describes the circumstances that permit an [increasing freedom from] ... the choice between isolation from other people and submission to them, and from the idolatrous identification of an established order with practical or moral necessity. It teaches the person to move within contexts with the dignity of context - transcending agents ... .[65]

This, however, seems to remain a supposition about the operation of mechanisms of change without any necessary conclusion about the substance of the change(s) thus to be wrought. A somewhat similar comment may be made upon the 'relational theory of law' proposed by Alan Hunt.[66] He argues for a 'reconceptualisation' of legal studies treating legal relations as a study of the interaction between 'legal' and other socio-political relations rather than focusing upon law as an autonomous phenomenon.

For the most part critical legal scholars seem to be concerned with the deconstruction, in particular, of 'liberal' analyses of law through related processes of 'trashing', 'delegitimation' and 'dereification'[67] all of which, in somewhat different ways seek to expose the 'real' objectives and agenda of law lying concealed behind a conventional rhetoric of impartiality and objectivity. Whether progress beyond deconstruction is a proper 'critical' objective is a matter for debate within the critical legal studies movement. Alan Hunt remarks that,

> [The roots of critical legal theory] lie in a deep sense of dissatisfaction with the existing state of legal scholarship. ... [Critical legal scholars] may not all share the same ... dissatisfaction but all are reacting against features of the prevailing orthodoxies ... [I]t is a movement in search of a theory, but at the same time it is a movement which has not agreed that such a theory is either possible or desirable.[68]

In this context it cannot be said that there is a 'critical' theory of obligation, nor is it clear whether there is even the potential for any such. Critical legal scholarship offers instead a deconstructive analysis which necessarily casts doubt upon conventional models of 'obligation'. Upon such an approach it is easy to see ideas of 'moral' obligation in relation to law as a myth supporting existing power structures and those of 'formal' obligation as a product of a distorting legal discourse without logical foundation.

The exposure of covert, and overt, power structures which may be accepted to have at least some role in the shaping of concepts of obligation may be an important contribution to understanding. One very important modern area of study in which this is a matter of vital significance may be seen in feminist critical legal studies. There is not, of course, only one feminist legal perspective, or even a single feminist critical legal analysis, but certain critical assumptions and methodologies nonetheless have particular significance in this area. From a feminist perspective the concealed power structure of law and legal administration is one of male dominance, not only in terms of overtly discriminatory rules and practices but also in terms of a 'male' mind set which does not necessarily relate to female experience. Joanne Conaghan and Louise Chudleigh, writing in the context of employment law, state that,

> From a feminist perspective the concept of equality is flawed because it constantly requires women to compare themselves with a male norm. Equality becomes 'sameness with men' and where women are clearly *not* the same as men, the concept of equality demands an eradication of the difference ... .[69]

This comment is made in the particular context of maternity provision, which exposes some of the discontinuities with particular clarity. In employment law this can be seen first in the assumption that the pregnancy of a worker is somehow an abnormality to be equated with 'illness' and, even where this is avoided, to endeavour to treat pregnancy as an 'interruption' in a 'normal' pattern rather than, e.g., creating workplace structures which take adequate account of both female and male parenthood. There is here both an inherited pattern of male dominance and a less overt substructure of 'male' assumption which acts to the detriment of women, and to some extent also of men.

This is a particular example of the marginalization of the female perspective in conventional legal discourse. The fundamental point is put briefly by Katherine T. Bartlett in her statement that,

> In law, asking the woman question means examining how the law fails to take into account the experiences and values that seem more typical of women than of men, for whatever reason, or how existing legal standards and concepts might disadvantage women.[70]

That such questions need to be asked at all is sufficient evidence of the necessity for feminist legal studies, including their 'critical' dimension.

The issue of gender distortion of law through patterns of 'male' assumption raises the general question of 'cultural' distortion in legal understanding. The evidence for this is manifest in gender studies, as well as in race and cultural studies where discrimination of both covert and unadmitted assumption can play as damaging a role as more overt forms of disadvantage. This can clearly have important implications for theories of obligation in so far as requirements are imposed upon people by reference to value systems and assumptions from whose remit they are essentially excluded. There is also, however, a danger of an equal and opposite distortion in suggesting extreme degrees of polarization which can seem as much to deny the validity of the inherently multi-dimensional nature of humanity and human experience(s) as the discriminatory assumptions originally objected to. There is, in short, a fundamental need for mutuality of affirmation in contrast with mere discriminatory selectivity - upon whatever basis this might be done. It is not infrequently suggested that the 'male' dynamic favours individualism and rights, whereas the 'female' dynamic favours community and consensus. In terms of gender experience, which may be culturally determined, there may be some degree of truth in this perception. It is, equally, not an absolute division in human experience and aspiration.   The perception of Aristotle that we are 'political animals' (*politikon zoon*)[71] underlines an essential point here.   We are, both men and women, individuals inclined to live in social groups, meaning that we have indeed individual aspirations and rights, but also the need of communality without which those very 'rights' have very little meaning. The point may be made by reference to another dichotomy which is sometimes advanced.   It is sometimes urged that there is a fundamental difference between 'western' and 'eastern' social traditions in that the former tends towards an anarchistic and uncaring individualism emphasizing 'rights', whilst the other tends towards a sometimes repressive communal cohesion emphasizing 'duties'.   There is, again, some truth in this perception, vast generalization though it clearly is, but in the end the two posited elements may be argued to be part of one social equation. Individuals who emphasize their own gratification to the exclusion of community demean an essential structure of human living to the detriment of all, including in the ultimate analysis themselves.   Communities which repress all individual expression in the name of conformity for its own sake fail fundamentally to nurture or sustain their members.   As individuals in community people have both individual and collective dimensions to their lives and the suppression of either may be argued to be a distortion.

In the immediate context of critical legal studies the deconstructive critical methodology has much to offer in exposing uncritically accepted conventional assumptions, including those which underlie some unreflective assertions of the claim of law to be obeyed.   At the same time it is necessary to take account of the critical 'agenda' itself.   The conclusions reached in a deconstructive analysis often depend upon the initial perception of the 'construct' which is to be analysed and this may in itself have a distorting effect.

Be that as it may, the varieties of deconstruction offered under the umbrella of critical legal studies suggests, in the absence of an agreed alternative 'constructive' agenda, that what is being offered is less a substantive critical 'theory' than a critical method.   In the case of 'obligation' the term has been used in a variety of ways and the process of demythologization which may result from a critical legal approach may have much to offer in the elucidation of both the concepts and their 'real' applications.   At a minimum such an approach must seem to support the essential contention here advanced that the ideas of a 'unitary' obligation to obey is a mirage.   Demythologization should not,   however,   in any context ignore the possibility, indeed the probability, that behind the myth there may lie a core of fact and truth. Once the false construct of a single and indivisible obligation to obey has been abandoned, there will remain, it is argued, distinct concepts of 'obligation' which, when properly appreciated, are much less open to deconstruction and demolition.[72]

Notes

1 M.B.E. Smith, 'Is There a *Prima Facie* Obligation to Obey the Law?' (1973) 82 *Yale Law Journal*, 950-976.
2 Ibid., p.950.
3 Ibid., p974.
4 Ibid.
5 See Chapter 2.
6 R. Cotterrell, *The Politics of Jurisprudence* (Butterworths, 1989), p.183.
7 See below.
8 F. Engels, 'The Condition of the Working Class in England', in *Collected Works* of Marx and Engels (Lawrence and Wishart, 1975), p.514.
9 H. Collins, *Marxism and Law* (Clarendon, Oxford, 1982), p.14.
10 See H. McCoubrey, 'The Reform of the Russian Legal System under Alexander II' (1980) XXIV *Renaissance and Modern Studies*, 115-130; also H. McCoubrey, 'Law Reform in Late Imperial Russia: A Legal History with Modern Implications?', *University of Nottingham Research Papers in Law*, November 1993.
11 An account of these and other cases will be found in S. Kucherov, *Courts, Lawyers and Trials under the Last Three Tsars* (New York, 1953), at pp.214-68. An instance of reactionary objection to the jury will be found in K.P. Pobedonostsev, 'Trial by Jury' in *Reflections of a Russian Statesman* (London, 1898, Ann Abor edn.), pp.59-89.
12 P.I. Stuchka, ed., *Entsiklopedia Gosudarstva I Prava* (Encyclopaedia of State and Law), Vol.III (Moscow, 1927), cited in translation by H.J. Berman, *Justice in the USSR*, 2 ed. (Harvard, 1963), p.26.
13 E.B. Pashukanis, *Law and Marxism: A General Theory*, available in English translation by B. Einhorn with an Introduction by C. Arthur (Ink Links, 1978), p.146.
14 Ibid., at pp.163-4.
15 See Chapter 3.
16 See Chapter 2.
17 For some radical suggestions along these lines see H. Collins, op.cit., ante.
18 *Sovietskaya Gosudarstvennoe Pravo* (Moscow, 1938), published in translation as *The Law of the Soviet State* (New York, 1963).

19   See H. Collins, op.cit., p.106.
20   H.J. Berman, op.cit., 2 ed. (Harvard, 1963), p.64.
21   W.E. Butler, *Soviet Law*, 2 ed. (Butterworths, 1988), p.37.
22   Op.cit., passim.
23   The *Ta Ch'ing Lu Li* of the (Manchu) Ch'ing Dynasty (1644-1911).
24   *The Analects of Confucius*, trans. A. Waley, 1938 (Unwin Hyman, 1988), XII:13.
25   See, e.g., an Imperial Edict of 17 August 1820 condemning the stirring up of litigation by 'litigation specialists', *Hsing-An Hui-Lan*, case 203,7,D., trans. and ed. D. Bodde and C. Morris, *Law in Imperial China: Exemplified by 190 Ch'ing Dynasty Cases* (University of Pennsylvania Press, by arrangement with the University of Harvard Press, 1973), p.416-7.
26   Professor Fei Hsiao Tung in *A Great Trial in Chinese History* (New World Press, Beijing, 1980), p.9.
27   *Main Documents of the Third Session of the Fifth National People's Congress of the People's Republic of China* (New World Press, Beijing, 1980), p.128.
28   J.P. Brady, *Justice and Politics in People's China* (Academic Press, Harcourt Brace Jovanovich, 1982), pp.246-7.
29   See Chapter 3.
30   E.B. Pashukanis, op.cit., pp.144-5.
31   See K. Renner, *Institutions of Private Law and their Social Functions*, in English translation (Routledge and Kegan Paul, 1949).
32   H. Collins, op.cit., p.146.
33   See Chapter 2. It must again be emphasized that Bentham made no such claim, he having been concerned with the limits of 'jurisprudence' as a discipline rather than with the absolute range of possible debate about, and influences upon, law.
34   A clear example of such 'fetishism' outside the area of law may be seen in the effect of Lysenkoism upon Soviet biological sciences.   Trofim Lysenko taught a doctrine of 'culturally' acquired features in distinction from genetic inheritance.   This was well adapted to Stalinism but without scientific basis and, ruthlessly imposed, it stifled Soviet genetic science for a generation.
35   See A. Hagerstrom, *Inquiries into the Nature of Law and Morals*, ed. K. Olivecrona, trans. C.D. Broad (Almqvist and Wiksell, 1953).
36   See review of L. Petrazycki, *Law and Morality*, by A.H. Campbell, 19 *Modern Law Review*, 436 at 439.
37   See L. Petrazycki, *Law and Morality*, with an Introduction by S. Timashev, trans. H.W. Babb, in the *20th Century Legal Philosophy* series (Harvard, 1956).
38   See Chapter 2.
39   See above.
40   K. Olivecrona, *Law as Fact*, 2 ed. (Stevens, 1971), p.71.

41 These psuedo-latinate terms were of Olivecrona's own devising.
42 K. Olivecrona, op.cit., p.124.
43 Ibid., p.90.
44 A. Ross, *Towards a Realistic Jurisprudence* (Einar Munkgaard, 1946), p.78.
45 A. Ross, *On Law and Justice* (Stevens, 1958), p.18.
46 Ibid., p.35.
47 H.L.A. Hart, 'Scandinavian Realism' (1959) *Cambridge Law Journal*, at p.233.
48 A.V. Lundstedt, *Legal Thinking Revised* (Almqvist and Wiksell, 1956), p.8.
49 Ibid., p.144.
50 Ibid., pp.174-5.
51 K. Olivecrona, op.cit., p.104.
52 Ibid., p.77.
53 O.W. Holmes, 'The Path of the Law' (1897) 10 *Harvard Law Review*, 457; also in *Collected Legal Papers* (Constable & Co., 1920), p.167.
54 Llewellyn somewhat qualified this in *The Common Law Tradition, Deciding Appeals* (Little, Brown and Co., 1960) emphasizing professional tradition and judicial 'situation sense' at least in the higher levels of US jurisdiction.
55 See, e.g., J. Frank, *Law and the Modern Mind* (Stevens, 1949); *Courts on Trial* (Princeton, 1949) and 'Cardozo and the Upper Court Myth' (1948) 13 *Law and Contemporary Problems*, 369.
56 See K.N. Llewellyn, 'The Normative, the Legal and the Law Jobs: The Problem of Juristic Method' (1939-40) *Yale Law Journal*, 1355.
57 Llewellyn's views on judicial predictability were strongly criticised by C.E. Clarke and D.M. Trabek in 'The Creative Role of the Judge: Restraint and Freedom in the Common Law' (1961-62) *Yale Law Journal*, 255.
58 See Chapter 2.
59 See ibid.
60 For discussion and application of deconstructive techniques of literary criticism in the context of legal materials see C. Douzinas and R. Warrington, 'On the Deconstruction of Jurisprudence: Fin(n)is Philosophiae', in P. Fitzpatrick and A. Hunt, eds., *Critical Legal Studies* (Blackwell, 1987), 33-46.
61 For discussion of the relation of discourse to theory see P. Goodrich, *Legal Discourse* (Macmillan, 1987); 'The Antimonies of Legal Theory: An Introductory Survey' (1983) 3 *Legal Studies*, 1 and 'The Rise of Legal Formalism or the Defects of Legal Faith' (1983) 3 *Legal Studies*, 248.
62 A. Hunt, 'The Theory of Critical Studies' 6 *Oxford Journal of Legal Studies*, 1 at 10. As examples of discussion of modern ideas of 'relative autonomy' Hunt cites Karl Klare, 'Law Making as Praxis' (1979) 40 *Telos*, 123 and Mark Tushnet, 'A Marxist Analysis of American Law' (1978) *Marxist Perspectives*, 96.

63   See R. Unger, 'The Critical Legal Studies Movement', 96 *Harvard Law Review*, 563.

64   Ibid., at 650.

65   Ibid., at 651.

66   See A. Hunt, 'The Critique of Law: What is "Critical" about Critical Legal Theory?' in P. Fitzpatrick and A. Hunt, eds., op.cit., p.5 at pp.16-18.

67   For brief discussion of this see H. McCoubrey and N.D. White, *Textbook on Jurisprudence* (Blackstone Press, 1993), pp.218-20.

68   A. Hunt., op.cit., at p.5.

69   J. Conaghan and L. Chudleigh, 'Women in Confinement: Can Law deliver the Goods?' in P. Fitzpatrick and A. Hunt, eds., op.cit., p.133 at p.139.

70   K.T. Bartlett, 'Feminist Legal Methods' [1970] 103 *Harvard Law Review*, 829 at 837.

71   See Chapter 3.

6 Superior Orders and Obligations

The existence of distinct forms of obligation in association with positive law clearly raises the possibility of conflict between them. In the case of a 'perfect' positive law, moral and formal obligation would coincide and coercion would be applied in support of them in cases of obdurate opposition. So perfect a concordance is in practice unlikely and there will in reality arise disparities in the relation of the various forms of 'obligation' to given propositions of positive law. These may range from minor divergences upon points of detail to, in the case of the greater iniquities, total opposition of claims. The resolution of the resulting conflicts is an evidently important aspect of any theory of legal obligation.

Three broad categories of situation require consideration. In the first place, conflict may arise within a given category of obligation where different substantive norms focus upon the same situation. This would most obviously arise where competing norms are imposed by different 'authorities', as in potential conflicts between secular and canon law. Secondly, conflict might arise between different categories of obligation. This may notably be the case as between formal and moral obligations, an issue which has been a staple of jurisprudence since at least the time of Plato's analysis in *The Last Days of Socrates*.[1] Finally, it may be asked to what extent coercion, which may generally be presumed to act in favour of some formal obligation, may 'weight' choices as between competing formal obligations or moderate the claim of a strong moral obligation over a contrary formal obligation.

These various questions arise in an analytically interesting form in the context of 'superior orders' as a defence or mitigating factor in relation to charges arising from alleged breaches by military personnel of the international laws of armed conflict. For the present purpose the jurisprudential claims of this area of public international law, or of such law in general, are not at issue.[2] It may, however, be remarked in passing that the exclusion of public international law by Austin from his category of laws 'properly so called' can be argued to have rested upon an institutional context which is now long out of date.   The question to be considered here is simply one of possibly competing *prima facie* obligations in a particular and extreme context.

The Relation of Laws and Orders

The basic issue was stated by H.A. Smith in a rather different context in remarking that,

> In such a case [i.e. an alleged 'war crime' committed pursuant to military orders] there is clearly a direct [conflict] ... between the defendant's duty of obedience ... and the obligation to obey the laws of war ... .[3]

This situation involves a potential conflict between the formal obligations imposed by municipal military law and those arising from the applicable norms of the *jus in bello*, that sector of the international laws of armed conflict governing the conduct of hostilities.[4]   In such cases there will also commonly be conflict with the moral imperatives underpinning the *jus in bello*.   At the same time strong immediate coercive pressures will be associated with municipal military law and the orders issued thereunder.

Military orders are uncompromisingly mandatory in form and perhaps approach closer than most other formal instructions to the Austinian model of a command backed by a sanction.   It is difficult to imagine a system of military law which would not require obedience to orders.   Both military discipline and, very possibly, survival in combat depend upon the presumption of obedience and the assumptions of mutual reliance associated with it.   Generally the matter will end there, but two substantial caveats require to be entered.   The extent of formal authority to issue orders will be determined by the hierarchic structure established under municipal military law and by the capacities set out within the terms of that hierarchy.   Certain 'orders', such as one to mutiny against an authority superior to that under which the 'order' was issued, would plainly be *ultra vires*.   In addition to this, an order which was manifestly contrary to the requirements of the *jus in bello* would be a contravention of public international law.   Much, although not all, of the *jus in bello* is considered to have the status of customary international law.[5]   Such law is a formal obligation binding upon all states according to international criteria of legal identification. Municipally the question of priority may be complicated by the view of the state in question as to whether a *monist* or *dualist* relation exists between its law and public international law.   In the former case international norms are considered automatically to form part of municipal law, calling into question the 'validity' of any contrary positive legal norms.[6]   A similar phenomenon may be observed in the relation of EU law to English law at the level of 'direct applicability'.   In the case of a *dualist* position the international norms will be binding upon the state *ab initio* in its international relations but will require further municipal enactment for internal effect.   Failure to do this will not, however, free the state from its international legal obligations or constitute a 'defence' in any international legal proceedings.   Any question of the formal legitimacy of an order will then turn upon the interaction between the relevant international and municipal legal norms.

The identification of the prevailing formal obligations where there are several possibilities is an issue central to the later positivist analyses, in particular to that of H.L.A. Hart, and also to the post-positivist theory of R.M. Dworkin.   *Prima facie* solutions may be sought in a 'rule of recognition' or in some appropriate lesser 'secondary rule' within the terms of Hart's theory.   In so far as interpretive shading of 'obligations' may arise, the non-regular 'principles' advanced by Dworkin may also have an obvious relevance.[7]   Neither of these approaches will, however, necessarily provide a complete solution to the fundamental question.

Competing Formal Authorities

This problem may be seen in one of its most acute forms in the treason trials of the English regicides following the 17th century Civil War and the restoration of Charles II in 1660.   The defendants ranged from the surviving signatories of the King's death warrant to the officer commanding the troops who kept order in Whitehall on the day of the execution in 1649, together with others charged merely upon the basis of having acted under Parliamentary or Protectorate authority.   Pleas of 'superior orders' were entered in defence upon the basis that the defendants had acted upon the authority of Parliament as *de facto*, although possibly not *de jure*, governing authority at the material times.   Constitutional discontinuities are problematic from a positivist viewpoint.   Upon a Benthamite or Austinian analysis the 'authority' of Parliament, or more accurately of the Parliamentary Army, was in 1649 undeniable.   The 'habit of obedience' of the people factually adhered to Parliament and the army, the trial of the King being in itself a convincing demonstration of this fact. The causes of the obedience, as between commitment and coercion, would not be of great significance in this form of analysis since it is the fact rather than the motive which is emphasized.   Much the same conclusion may, of this purpose, be reached upon a Kelsenian 'pure' theory analysis.   The test of 'effectiveness' which governs the practical identification of a substantive *grundnorm* would necessarily favour the 'authority' under which the defendants claimed to have acted in 1649.   The application of Hart's 'secondary rules' leads to much more ambiguous conclusions.   The model of union of primary and secondary rules assumes a stable legal order and is not well suited to the early stages of the establishment of a new regime following a revolutionary hiatus.

The defence of 'superior orders' was rejected by the courts after the 1660 Restoration which initially took a strictly 'legitimist' view. According to this view there was no constitutional hiatus.   Parliament had secured no sovereignty by detaining the King, an act treasonable in itself according to the 1351 Statute of Treason, and since Charles I neither abdicated nor recognized the Tribunal which tried him, the Prince of Wales automatically succeeded as Charles II at the moment of the King's death.[8] Thus, the orders issued to the defendants were treasonable, as was obedience to them.   In the case of the regicides themselves this was taken as an unequivocal case of high treason involving imagining and compassing the death of the Sovereign.   Indeed a plea relying essentially upon their own seizure of power could hardly succeed in altered circumstances, any more than his status as King had availed Charles I at his own trial. However, for lesser figures such as Colonel Axtell who commanded the troops at Whitehall on the fatal day in 1649,[9] the verdict can only seem harsh.   A sympathetic view of their position was expressed by Lord Campbell in his 'life' of Lord Clarendon in relation to the trial of Sir Harry Vane, who was not implicated in the regicide.   He remarked of this that,

No satisfactory answer could be given to the plea that the parliament was then *de facto* the supreme power of the state, and that it could be as little treason to act under its authority as under the authority of a usurper on the throne - which was expressly declared by the statute of Henry VII not to be treason.[10]

The latter point was also made earlier by Sir Matthew Hale in his *History of the Pleas of the Crown* in 1736, in which he state that,

A king *de facto* but not *de hure*, such as were H[enry] 4, H[enry] 5, H[enry] 6, R[ichard] 3, H[enry] 7, being in actual possession of the crown is a king ... so that compassing his death is treason ... .[11]

Hale cited *Bagot's case* in the reign of Edward IV[12] in support of this contention.   Bagot had been granted 'letters patent of denization', i.e. naturalisation, during the temporary resumption of the Crown by Henry VI in despite of Edward IV. It appears to have been decided by the court that the naturalization was valid because it had been granted by the actual occupant of the throne at the material time.

In the case of the 17th century lesser regicides it must seem reasonable that they should have relied upon the *de facto* governing authority.   It may be added that judicial recognition of a purported authority advanced by R.W.M. Dias as a criterion for the transference of sovereign power by reference to the case of *Madzimbamuto* v *Lardner-Burke*,[13] decided in what was then Southern Rhodesia (now Zimbabwe), is hardly a satisfactory test in this context.   Both Charles I and those who brought him to trial were at different times condemned by purported judicial authorities.   The final balance of formal rectitude was determined by the facts of the ineptitude of Richard Cromwell as successor Lord Protector and the, then, inevitable return of Charles II at the invitation of General Monk.[14]   The difficulties experienced by later positivist analyses of revolutionary transitions of authority may be taken by theorists sceptical of 'obligation' in relation to law[15] as supporting their position(s).   However, it may be argued that the point is one of appropriateness in context.   At this most stark interface between politics and law the factual power-based analyses advanced by Bentham and Austin perhaps afford the most viable 'solution'.   Such a view may be read into the determination in relation to those who acted under the authority of the Confederacy in the mid-19th century American Civil War that it had had *de facto* authority *pro tem* to issue binding commands to its subordinates.[16]

War Crimes and Conflicting Formal Authorities

Where orders issued under an established national military authority lead to the commission of acts which contravene applicable norms of the international *jus in bello* rather different questions arise. Here the conflict is not between authorities in competition at the same level but between the provision of formal authorities at differing levels.

An early precursor of modern 'war crimes' trials may be seen in the trial of Peter von Hagenbach in 1474.[17] The Archduke of Austria had pledged the city of Breisach to Charles the Bold, Duke of Burgundy, as security for a debt, subject to a guarantee of the traditional liberties of its citizens. Hagenbach was installed as the Burgundian governor of the city and instituted a reign of terror on Charles' behalf which shocked even late-medieval Europe. Upon repayment of the debt Charles refused to return the city to the Archduke and a war followed in which the city was retrieved and Charles himself killed. Hagenbach was captured and tried before a Tribunal constituted under the authority of the Holy Roman Empire but which may for most practical purposes be considered to have been 'international' in nature.[18]

Hagenbach's defence to charges which would now be expressed as 'crimes against humanity' was essentially one of 'superior orders'. His counsel, Hans Irmy, argued that,

> He had no right to question the orders which he was charged to carry out, and it was his duty to obey. Is it not known that soldiers owe absolute obedience to their superiors?[19]

The Tribunal rejected this defence, *inter alia* upon the ground that both the orders given by Charles the Bold and Hagenbach's implementation of them had been contrary to natural law deriving from the will of God and were therefore, in the strictest sense, *ultra vires*. This has *prima facie* the appearance of a moral rather than a formal evaluation, falling within naturalist rather than positivist legal theory. This appreciation must, however, be qualified upon closer examination. Although medieval legal theory was in many respects naturalist in focus, in the context of proceedings such as the *Hagenbach* trial the law of God was received in the highly institutionalized form of the law expressed by the western Church which could in principle transcend the contrary intentions of secular rulers under the Doctrine of the Two Powers.[20]   In this context Hagenbach's trial may reasonably be understood as an assessment of his formal obligation. Making due allowance for the differences between medieval and modern contexts, the *Hagenbach case* has clear elements of a conflict between 'national' and 'international' authorities with a decision in favour of the latter.

In most of the more modern jurisprudence of superior orders the basic proposition of the *Hagenbach case*, that such orders are not necessarily a defence to charges of alleged unlawful conduct, has essentially been maintained.   An important question has, however, arisen in relation to the degree of the patency of the unlawfulness of the order in question.   In this respect the comparison between English and Public International Law is instructive.

An early English case concerning this issue may be seen in *R* v *Thomas* in 1816.[21]   Thomas, a marine serving on board HMS *Achilles*, was under orders to keep boats away from his ship other than those which had been authorized to approach by an officer.   After repeated warnings to one persistently approaching but unauthorized boat he fired upon it killing one the occupants.   Thomas was subsequently convicted of murder but with a strong recommendation from the jury that he be pardoned.   The issue here was strictly one of ambiguity rather than authority of orders, but the recommendation of the jury in this case may be considered highly significant.   In *R* v *Smith* in 1900[22] during the Second Boer War, a civilian had refused to supply a bridle at the demand of a British officer.   Smith, a private soldier, had then obeyed the officer's order to shoot the civilian. He was subsequently acquitted upon a charge of murder before a special court in Cape Colony.   In judgment Solomon, J., said,

> if a soldier honestly believes he is doing his duty in obeying the commands of his superior and if the orders are not so manifestly illegal that he must or ought to have known they were unlawful, the private soldier would be protected by the orders of his superior officer ... .[23]

This 'ought to know' doctrine seems to represent the classical common law position and was generally accepted as such between 1900 and 1945. Similar views may be found expressed in United States jurisprudence[24] in cases such as *Riggs* v *State*.[25]   The same approach may be discerned in the few 'war crimes' trials conducted after the First World War.   These post-

1918 trials must be considered with some care in their very particular political and historical context. In 1918 a vengeful mood prevailed amongst Allied politicians and this was made manifest in the details of the Versailles settlement. The same spirit was shown in the desire of some for the trial upon criminal charges of very large numbers of German officers who had in many instances, objectively, little or no case to answer. The most prominent example was the ill-judged desire to try, and it was presupposed to convict and hang, the ex-Kaiser Wilhelm II. This plan was, in retrospect fortunately, aborted by the unwillingness of the neutral Netherlands authorities to produce the defendant from his retreat at Doorn. A number of lesser figures were tried *in absentia*, to little or no purpose. It was, however, agreed that some trials would be conducted in Germany and these are of some significance in the present context.

The most important of these several cases from the present viewpoint concerned the *prima facie* unlawful sinking of British hospital ships by U-boats of the Imperial German Navy. In the first of these, *Dover Castle case*,[26] the hospital ship *Dover Castle* was torpedoed and sunk by UC-67 commanded by Kapitan-Leutnant Karl Neuman in *prima facie* violation of the applicable laws of armed conflict at sea. Neuman argued before the German Supreme Court in Leipzig that he had acted upon orders predicated upon the supposition that British hospital ships, including the *Dover Castle*, were being used for the transport of fit troops and munitions and had, therefore forfeited their protected status. Such allegations are commonplaces of war-time propaganda and, in this case, the assertion seems clearly to have been false. This, however, is not here the essential point. The court acquitted Neuman upon the basis that he had acted pursuant to orders which he reasonably took to be lawful at the time of their receipt.

In the second case, the *Llandovery Castle case*,[27] after sinking the hospital ship the submarine, U-86, surfaced and opened fire upon the survivors in the water and the lifeboats, killing and injuring many of them. Irrespective of the status of the *Llandovery Castle* as a hospital ship this massacre of survivors was unequivocally a violation of the laws of armed conflict. The court found the responsible officers guilty of murder, including those acting 'under orders', relying upon article 47(2) of the German Military Code to the effect that 'superior orders' cannot be a defence for a subordinate charged with unlawful action if the illegality was patent. The distinction rests upon the question of whether or not those relying upon 'superior orders' had a reasonable belief in the lawfulness of the orders behind which they sought to shelter.

A superficially similar instance to the *Llandovery Castle case* after 1945 in the *Peleus case*,[28] involving the massacre of survivors from the freighter *Peleus* after its sinking by U-852 commanded by Kapitan-Leutnant Heinz Eck. It was at first thought that the commander had acted under the notorious *Laconia* order, which forbade U-boat officers to assist survivors from torpedoed ships under any circumstances, although it did not require that they be actively molested.[29] However, Kapitan-Leutnant Eck declined to advance such a 'defence' and no clear explanation of his actions emerged at his trial, although there was some suggestion that resentment over Allied air attacks may have formed part of his motive. Eck's junior officers did advance pleas of 'superior orders', but the defence failed because the orders upon which they sought to rely were so clearly unlawful.

The view of a defence of 'superior orders' taken after 1945 has *prima facie* been much more strict than that previously adopted. The Charter of the International Military Tribunal at Nuremberg provided that,

> [Superior] orders shall not free [a defendant] ... from responsibility, but may be considered in mitigation of punishment ... .[30]

On the face of it this provision can be read as a straightforward abolition of the 'defence' of 'superior orders' leaving in its place only a plea in mitigation. The practical jurisprudence of Nuremberg and Tokyo is, however, less clear cut when considered in its context. The cases actually before the two Tribunals generally involved outrageously unlawful decisions and actions to which 'superior orders' would have been most unlikely to afford a defence even under the 'ought to know' doctrine. A striking example can be seen in the *High Command case*.[31] Four very senior military officers were charged with having participated in a conspiracy to wage aggressive warfare in contravention of the 1928 Pact of Paris.[32] It was argued in their defence that from the time of a Fuehrer Conference in November 1937 the military defendants had acted upon the direct orders of the head of state, which they had no choice but to obey. This defence inevitably failed before the International Military Tribunal, but it could not have succeeded even in the absence of the Charter provision upon superior orders. A similar comment may also be made in relation to the conviction of the junior officers in the *Peleus case*. It would, nonetheless, seem that the post-1945 view of 'superior orders' is generally more restrictive than that previously taken.   The difference can be seen in the distinction between the statements made upon the subject by the 1944 and 1956 editions of the British Manual of Military Law.   The 1944 edition stated that,

> If the command were obviously illegal, the inferior would be justified in questioning, or even in refusing to execute it ... But so long as orders ... are not obviously [illegal] ... the duty of the soldier is to obey and (if he thinks fit) to make a formal complaint afterwards.[33]

In contrast, the 1956 edition of the Manual, issued after the Nuremberg trials stated that,

> If a person receives ... from his superior an order ... which is manifestly illegal he is under a legal duty to refuse to carry [it] out ... and if he does carry it out he will be criminally responsible. ... The better view appears to be ... that an order ... whether manifestly illegal or not, can never of itself excuse the recipient if he carries out the order, although it may give rise to a defence on other grounds ... .[34]

There is a clear change of view between these two statements, the latter asserting a simpler doctrine of *ignorantia non curat lex* in place of the earlier 'ought to know' doctrine.   It is also significant that the Statute of the Tribunal for former-Yugoslavia by article 7(4) repeats the 'Nuremberg' formulation upon superior orders without qualification, although it may again be wondered whether any 'ought to know' doctrine would in any event have much practical role to play in its proceedings.   In general, where the illegality of an order was unclear and in cases of technical violation it may still at the very least be taken that a superior order will act as a strong mitigating factor.   The practical difference between the status of a plea of 'superior' orders before and after 1945 may in fact be more apparent than real.   Much would depend upon the circumstances of the issue and receipt of the orders in question.

The issue arose peripherally in the court martial of *Lieutenant William L. Calley* in 1971.   Calley was tried and convicted under article 110 of the United States Uniform Code of Military Justice for his ordering of and participation in a massacre of civilians, including young children, at My Lai during the Vietnam War.   The case was more concerned with the issue of unlawful orders than with that of compliance with them, but there was also an investigation into the question of ambiguous instructions issued to Calley himself in a psychological atmosphere which tended to shift the onus of proof of non-combatancy onto the Vietnamese civilian population themselves. The unlawfulness of Calley's actions was so evident that such issues could not have affected the outcome of the court martial. It was, however, decided that his superior, General Westmoreland, had taken sufficient precautions in the issuing of orders to avoid culpability in the matter. In other circumstances it is possible for an officer to be held responsible for 'war crimes' committed pursuant to his or her unlawful orders. Such liability may stand even if subordinates successfully advance a plea of *respondeat superior* so far as their own liability is concerned.[35] There may also be liability where a superior officer fails to take adequate steps to avert the commission of war crimes even though s/he may not directly have ordered their commission.[36]

International Law and National Law

A different question arises in consideration of the relation between international and national law. Two broad opinions, with many variants in between, may be advanced and are conventionally termed *monism* and *dualism*. From the former perspective there is only one legal order and relevant norms, and obligations, of public international law must therefore *ex hypothesi* apply in any properly conceived national legal system. In contrast, the latter position treats international obligations as external considerations, albeit bindingly taken on by governments in their international relations, and made applicable in national law only through some formal process of deliberate incorporation. Hans Kelsen originally took a *dualist* view and, along with the classical positivists, felt considerable doubt about the claim of public international law to be 'law' at all. In his later writings, however, he reversed this view and presented international law not only as 'law' but as a foundation for general legal order with a *grundnorm* based upon the proposition that *pacta sunt servanda* - agreements are to be observed.[37] Such an analysis concords in part with one significant aspect of the jurisprudence of the International Military Tribunals at Nuremberg and Tokyo in so far as national failure to implement international norms in municipal military and civil law was held not in itself to constitute a defence against charges of crimes against peace, crimes against humanity and war crimes.[38]   A much more sceptical analysis can be found in the work of H.L.A. Hart.   Hart did not dismiss international law to an extra-legal sphere of 'positive morality' in the manner of Austin but concluded that whilst it has many 'legal' characteristics and may in some sense be considered proto-law it lacks the institutional structure to be termed 'law' *stricto sensu*.   This argument turns upon issues of formalism which perhaps rather miss the point in posing as a basic question the degree of similarity of public international law to municipal law.   There are inevitably very wide differences between the two, not least because the community represented by a nation state is very different in structure from the 'community of nations'.   If the question asked is one not of institutional similarity but of functional convergence a different and, it is suggested, more relevant answer is offered than those afforded by classical and later positivism or, indeed, by Kelsenian 'pure theory'.   In this context it may be seen that the task performed by international law in its context is close to that performed, differently, within a nation state by municipal law.   Where there is conflict between them the matter becomes one of competing formal prescriptions.   The norms of public international law must then bind the state upon the international level whatever 'national' attitude may be adopted; to plead failures of municipal enactment as a defence at the international level then becomes self-evidently problematic.[39]

Orders and Coercion

The necessarily mandatory nature of military orders has been referred to above and in any system of military law orders will be enforced, subject to questions of their inherent legality as part of the military system and possibly also in a wider context.   The immediate fact of actual or potential enforcement may, however, in the case of an unlawful order, raise questions of duress.   Attitudes towards such pleas have varied considerably.   French military law appears to have accorded considerable weight to pleas of 'superior orders' and it has thus been provided that,

Il n'y a ni crime lorsque l'homicide, les blessures, et les coups etaient ordonnes par la loi et commandes par l'autorite legitime.[40]

In the *Jaluit Atoll case*,[41] however, involving the unlawful shooting of prisoners of war by Japanese troops, it was made clear that the more general expectation of punishment for disobedience could not avail to condone manifestly unlawful actions. The point was emphatically reinforced by the decision in the *Zyklon B case*,[42] it was also stated strongly in the *Belsen case*.[43] As with pleas of duress in more general contexts, much will obviously depend upon the reality and the severity of the threat posed. In a case involving a gross violation of the *jus in bello* the answer would almost certainly be that even the prospect of relatively severe penalties would not suffice to exclude liability although it might, of course, operate as a strong mitigating factor. This question is fundamental to any analysis drawing upon a 'command' theory of law[44] and of more general importance as an issue in certain kinds of 'war crime' trial.

Discipline and Responsibility

In the present context the clear necessities of military discipline will have an obvious impact upon the understanding and operation of connects of obligation. Military discipline involves the clearest indication of the duty to obey for reasons referred to above. Effectiveness and even survival in combat depend to a significant degree upon disciplined obedience and mutual reliance. To express the point bluntly, the battlefield is neither the time nor the place for jurisprudential debate. An interesting analysis of superior orders in their practical setting has been advanced by J. Blackett, in the particular context of their role as a defence advanced by lower ranks in relation to actually or allegedly unlawful action carried out pursuant to them. In his conclusion he makes the point that,

> the law can recognise the military dilemma and grant the subordinate a defence in criminal proceedings in all cases where he acted in obedience to superior orders except those where the actions required of him were objectively manifestly illegal. In those cases the subordinate's training and background should be taken into account at least to mitigate his sentence ... .[45]

This is an important point of practical jurisprudence and it may, again, be emphasized that the question at issue is not the *existence* of liability for unlawful action but its proper placement.

Such basic considerations clearly need to be built into the formal appreciations of obligation or recognized as a 'moral factor', e.g., in mitigation of sentence in appropriate cases. They could not supportably be used as a form of 'dispensing power' in matters otherwise clearly covered by formal regulation. It is for this reason that, notwithstanding the restrictive 'Nuremberg' doctrine, an 'ought to know' doctrine such as that affirmed in the *Peleus case* after the Second World War appears still to have much to commend it. The context of this is usefully set out by 1949 Geneva Convention I, article 47 which provides that,

> The High Contracting Parties undertake, in time of peace as in time of war, to disseminate the text of the present Convention as widely as possible in their respective countries and, in particular, to include the study thereof in their programmes of military ... instruction, ...

The same requirement is stated by 1949 Geneva Convention II, article 48; 1949 Geneva Convention III, article 127 and 1949 Geneva Convention IV, article 144. In this context the necessities of discipline, the practical exigencies of military service and the formal norms of both the *jus in bello* and municipal military law may be maintained without conflict.

Internal Morality and Superior Orders

In its least dramatic impingement upon the assessment of obligation in the areas under consideration, moral obligation may contribute substantially to Dworkinian 'principles' which may be employed to clarify the 'grey areas' in positive provision. So far as the *jus in bello* is concerned an interesting example may be found in the 1982 Falklands Conflict between the United Kingdom and Argentina. Strict provision is made by the Third Geneva Convention of 1949 for the conditions in which prisoners of war are to be kept during internment. Article 22 of the Convention provides, *inter alia*, that, 'prisoners of war may be interned only in premises located on land' precluding the keeping of prisoners on board ships other than immediately after capture at sea and for purposes of necessary transport. This restriction derives essentially from the evil memory of the prison hulks of the Napoleonic Wars.   In the Falklands Conflict, however, the construction of shore-based prisoner of war facilities was hardly possible in adequate time in view of the large numbers of personnel involved following the recapture of Port Stanley.   The climate of the South Atlantic would anyway have caused serious difficulties in the creation of suitable accommodation.   In the circumstances the humane course of action was clearly to keep many prisoners in better conditions on shipboard for rapid repatriation.   This was done and no objection was raised by either Argentina or observers from the International Committee of the Red Cross.[46]   Taking humanitarianism as *ex hypothesi* the basic informing 'principle' of international humanitarian, or 'Geneva', law, this must appear to have been an entirely appropriate reaction to a situation not directly envisaged by the Convention.   This was not, of course, an instance of judicial determination but it might fairly be regarded in a general sense as a form of 'hard case' and the humanitarian solution adopted may readily be analysed as an analogy with the application of a Dworkinian principle in finding a solution coherent with the institutional moral structure in question.

As with Dworkinian 'principles', however, the focus is here upon an internalized morality found in the interstices of positive provision, in this case the Third Geneva Convention of 1949.   This is not to deny that the 1949 Geneva Conventions enshrine a more general humanitarian morality, but they are nonetheless in themselves positive legal provisions and as prone to inadequacy as any other such.   Beyond enshrined and formalized moralities there exists the further realm of moral obligation *stricto sensu*.   The interface of such morality with positive law is then the proper concern of 'naturalist' theories.

Moral Obligations and Superior Orders

Classical naturalist theories tended to address war in *jus ad bellum* rather than *jus in bello* terms.   Classical *bellum justum*, or 'just war', theory with which St. Augustine of Hippo, St. Thomas Aquinas, St. Raymond of Penaforte and Johannes Teutonicus are particularly associated,[47] was originally conceived and set out as a constraint upon military aggression.

Unfortunately it swiftly degenerated into a 'licensing' system with a vast and largely realized potential for abuse. Of the doctrine in its ultimate and debased form Jean Pictet remarks that it 'did nothing less than provide believers with a justification for war in all its infamy'.[48] In the present context it also tended to increase the barbarity of response to enemies who were perceived as 'unjust'. This occurred despite the specific teaching of St. Augustine of Hippo, adopted by St. Thomas Aquinas, that even a 'just' cause may be rendered 'unjust' by excessive or cruel pursuit.[49]

The lack of *jus in bello* address in Scholastic legal theory was partly filled in medieval thought by the *jus armorum*, described by Philippe Contamine as,

> [a] simple codification of the chivalric ideal ... in moral imperatives governing the behaviour of soldiers, by rules of military discipline, and by a system of usages, customs and rites proper to the world of soldiers ... .[50]

The practice was in many ways less exalted than the theory. The massacre of prisoners ordered by Henry V at the battle of Agincourt in 1415 was considered shocking at the time but was by no means a unique aberration.[51] In this context the naturalist analysis of the obligation arising from an 'immoral' order arises as a pointed issue.

Aquinas himself gives one example of a justification for disobedience in relation to a specifically 'military' order, that of the closure of the gates of a city under siege. He argued that such an order might be disobeyed in order to admit a body of citizens in flight from the enemy. Obviously some serious practical issues might arise here, such as how closely the enemy were following behind, but the matter is represented as essentially one of *necessity* in the comment that,

> Si vero sit subitum periculum, non patiens tantam moram ut ad superiorem recurri possit, ipsa necessitas dispensationem habet annexam, quia necessitas non subditur legi.[52]

That is to say that in a case of immediate danger which allows no time for recourse to higher authority, necessity may act as a dispensation from the obligation to obey because necessity knows no law. This, however, is a case of an ordinance which is 'good' in principle but inappropriate in a given specific circumstance. As a 'principled' but variant interpretation of a rule which is 'good' in itself, the 'principle' being the protection of citizens from the besieging army, the case is arguably more Dworkinian than strictly naturalist in its implications.

More difficult questions arise in the context of the central 'naturalist' case of direct conflict between the requirements of moral and clearly expressed formal (positive) norms. In the present context of an 'immoral' military order which does not contravene positive public international legal norms, the issue is not much different in principle from that already considered in relation to general conflict between moral and formal obligations.[53]

For reasons which have already been considered in the context of the practical exigencies of military discipline, any idea of a moral override upon the obligation to obey an order must be approached with extreme caution. It may, indeed, be argued that most such instances in the event of armed conflict would anyway involve a contravention of the applicable norms of the *jus in bello*. The reported refusal of some senior Russian officers to engage in apparently indiscriminate bombardment of the city of Grozny during action against the separatist Chechen Republic in December 1994 might be an example. Technically, of course, the delicate question of the status of this conflict and, therefore, the applicable positive norms would require prior consideration from a positivist viewpoint.

In a hypothetical situation of a simple conflict arising between clear formal and moral obligations the same considerations would require to be balanced in the case of a military order as in any other context.[54] That is to say, that the relative harms likely to result on the one hand from obedience and on the other from disobedience would require to be weighed, taking into account the Thomist *prima facie* 'weighting' in favour of obedience in terms of the, not unlimited, 'price' in 'bad' law to be paid for social, including military, order. If, in an extreme case, the ultimate conclusion is in favour of disobedience this would not, of course, afford a defence to charges of insubordination or mutiny at the formal level. The question must then return to the issues set out by Plato in the *Crito* dialogue in *The Last Days of Socrates*. In some cases it is possible that a principled preference of a moral over a formal norm might retrospectively be judged to have been 'right'.[55] The position of Count von Stauffenberg and the other 'July plotters' who conspired unsuccessfully to assassinate Hitler and bring down the Nazi Third Reich regime raises interesting questions in this context, albeit not directly in relation to superior orders as such. Albert Speer's attempts to minimize the destructive impact of Hitler's sweeping *gotterdamerung* instructions for the destruction of Germany's industry and infrastructure towards the end of the Second World War may be more directly in point in the present context.

One matter must here be re-emphasized. The misconceived argument once grafted onto classical 'just war' theory that a moral end may justify immoral means must be rejected. Use of *jus ad bellum* considerations as a dispensing power in relation to *jus in bello* constraints is excluded as a matter of positive law by both the 1949 Geneva Conventions and by 1977 Additional Protocol I thereto.[56] It may readily be argued that the same conclusion can be supported in moral argument. An immoral infliction, in whatever cause, remains an immoral infliction upon its victims, who are rarely the same people who perpetrated the original injustice. This is a separate consideration from the question of resort to armed force in the first place, which raises complex but quite distinct moral and ethical issues.

The association of moral and formal obligations in the present context of superior orders is not different in principle from that arising in other legal sectors, albeit typically presented in more extreme conditions. The interest of the decision-making parameters arises not so much from the substance of their foci of concern but rather from the exposition of general questions in an unusually sharpened form.

Conclusions

The extreme circumstances in which the question of the level and nature of the 'obligations' imposed by superior orders may require to be considered afford a clear demonstration of the conflicts which may potentially arise between and within the various suggested categories of 'obligation'. Within both the formal and the moral categories there may be conflicting apparent 'obligations', as, for example, between norms of municipal and public international law within the formal classification. Such 'internal' conflicts fall to be resolved according to the criteria of identification found in the formal sector or the adopted substantive canons found in the moral sector. There may then be conflict between the respective moral and formal obligations which emerge.

The question of primacy as between the categories of 'obligations' will be determined according to the moral/ethical arguments advanced from the time of Plato onwards and considered above.[57]   The factor of coercive force is argued not strictly to relate to direct comparison between the forms of obligation strictly so called.   The erroneousness of an identification of either 'law' or 'obligation' with a simple *potestas coactiva*, whether in the form of Augustinism, Benthamism or Marxism, has been addressed above.[58]   The attachment of coercive force to positive legal provisions is, however, a common factual element and was correctly so identified by Bentham and Austin.   It is, nonetheless, not a necessary diagnostic factor in the assessment of 'legal' quality, nor is it an independent generator of obligation, as H.L.A. Hart convincingly demonstrated in a positivist context.   It may, at most, either reinforce a decision made upon the direction of 'obligation' or provide a mitigatory explanation for non-compliance with an identified obligation.

The instance of 'superior orders' may be put forward as a model of the relation of 'obligation' to a 'complete law' in the broad Thomist sense of a 'law' as '*rationis ordinatio ad bonum commune ab eo qui communitatis habet, promulgata.*[59] involving rationality, public benefit, sovereign authority and promulgation.   A military order which is issued in accordance with formally identified authority and which does not conflict with any hierarchically superior positive norms, such as those of the international *jus in bello*, will impose a clear formal obligation upon those subject to it.   Such an obligation will almost certainly be backed by the factual potential for coercive enforcement, which, however, neither adds to nor detracts from the quality of the formal obligation as such.   Such an order which also concords with the purposive moral/ethical framework to which the context in which it is issued relates may be taken to carry moral, as well as formal, obligations of compliance.   Where a superior order thus carries both formal and moral obligation, supported by any relevant potential for coercive enforcement, it may be considered 'complete' in the Thomist sense.   Where one or more of these elements is missing in whole or in part, the order will be to a greater or lesser extent defective in the degree of suasion which it will exercise.

The extent and effects of any such deficiency will vary across a broad range, according to the circumstances.   At one extreme may be placed an order to undertake an 'immoral' action which is issued without authority, e.g. one uttered by an impostor, which will impose neither formal nor moral obligation, although it may in the very short term be backed by implicit or even actual coercive force.   At the other extreme would be a marginally 'immoral' order issued with full formal authority and coercive backing, which might indeed, depending upon the degree of the marginality of its 'immoral' quality, carry both formal and moral obligation even if the latter may be slightly impaired.

In practice no law or order is likely to achieve perfect 'completeness'. In most if not all cases, therefore, the final balance of obligations will be determined by the complex interaction between the various categories of 'obligation', together with the external factor of coercive pressure. The conclusion reached will ultimately be determined by the balance between these factors, bearing in mind, as Aquinas and many others have counselled, that there will generally be a strong 'weighting' in favour of obedience even if this is not always automatically to be presumed. In a military context both discipline and the, literally, vital need for mutual confidence and reliance in combat will mean that this general 'weighting' is presented in an especially powerful form. This does not, however, mean that every action of all armed forces can gain an unlimited licence upon this basis. It was for this reason that the International Military Tribunal at Nuremberg adopted, in its immediate context of consideration, an extremely restrictive view of a 'defence' of superior orders. In less extreme or more ambiguous circumstances a more subtle approach might be encouraged but the basic 'Nuremberg' reasoning upon this matter will still underline a most important consideration in this context.

Beyond these questions in both their general and specific foci there lies the question of the relation between the concepts of 'obligation' and 'validity'. Is a valid law necessarily 'complete' in a Thomist sense or does the concept of validity relate only to a particular form of obligation? This is a question distinct from that of the relation between differing forms of obligation and one which demands separate consideration.

Notes

1 See Chapter 3.
2 For discussion see H. McCoubrey and N.D. White, *International Law and Armed Conflict* (Dartmouth, 1992), Ch.1.
3 H.A. Smith, *The Law and Custom of the Sea* (Stevens, 1954), p.174.
4 For discussion of structure see H. McCoubrey and N.D. White, op.cit., Ch.13.
5 For discussion in relation to major modern developments see C. Greenwood, 'Customary Law Status of the 1977 Additional Protocols' in A.J.M. Delissen

and G.J. Tanja, eds., *Humanitarian Law of Armed Conflict: Challenges Ahead (Essays in Honour of Frits Kalshoven)* (Martinus Nijhoff, 1991), pp.93-114.

6 For discussion of the question of 'validity' and its relation to obligation see Chapter 7.

7 See Chapter 4.

8 The only constitutionally admitted interregnum was that between the deemed 'abdication' of James II in 1688 and the joint accession of William III and Mary II. See S.A.de Smith and R. Brazier, *Constitutional and Administrative Law*, 6 ed. (Penguin, 1989), pp.8-9. For all official purposes the reign of Charles II is dated from 1649 and not from 1660, the date of the Restoration. All such analyses rest upon *realpolitik*, Charles II was restored whereas James II was not.

9 For discussion of Colonel Axtell's case see A. Roberts, 'Obeying the Law of War' *The Independent* (London), 29 February, 1988.

10 Lord Campbell, *Lives of the Lord Chancellors* (John Murray, 1846), Vol.III, p.195.

11 Sir Matthew Hale, *Historia Placitorum Coronae* (London, 1736), republished in the *Classic English Law Texts* series, ed. P. Glazebrook (Professional Books, 1971), p.101-2.

12 9 Edward IV 16, cited by Hale, op.cit., at p.101, note 3.

13 (1968)(2) SA 284; on appeal to the Privy Council [1969] 1 AC 645.

14 For further discussion of treason trials in the context of civil war see H. McCoubrey and N.D. White, *International Organizations and Civil Wars* (Dartmouth, 1995), at pp.256-9.

15 See Chapter 5.

16 For discussion see Y. Dinstein, *The Defence of 'Superior Orders' in International Law* (A.W. Sijthoff, 1965), passim.

17 A detailed account may be found in G. Schwarzenberger, *International Law, Vol.II, Armed Conflict* (Stevens, 1965), pp.462-6.

18 Technically the status of the Tribunal would turn upon the status of Switzerland in relation to the Holy Roman Empire at the relevant time, see ibid., at pp.463-4.

19 Ibid., at p.465.

20 See Chapter 3.

21 (1816) 4 M&S 41.

22 [1900] 17 SCR 561.

23 Ibid.

24 See L.C. Green, *Superior Orders in National and International Law* (A.W. Sijthoff, 1976), pp.122-3.

25 (1866) 43 Tenn. 85; see also L.C. Green, op.cit., at p.123.

26 (1922) 16 *American Journal of International Law*, 704.

27 Ibid., at p. 705.

28   See *The Peleus Trial*, Vol.I, *War Crimes Trials* (William Hocky and Co., 1948).
29   The *Laconia* Order was issued by Grand Admiral Doenitz as a result of Hitler's anger upon hearing of the exemplary humanitarian endeavours of the commander of the U-Boat which sank the troopship *Laconia* in the Mediterranean.   The U-Boat had been attacked whilst gathering the lifeboats together and in so far as the order forbade commanders to place their submarines at unacceptable risk it must be considered to have been lawful.   Its unlawfulness arose from the instruction that U-Boats should *in no circumstances* engage in humanitarian rescue work.
30   Charter of the International Military Tribunal, article 8.
31   See *Trials of War Criminals* (USGPO, 1950) Vol.XI, p.310 and 462 ff.
32   The indictment was found under article 6 of the Charter of the International Military Tribunal relating to crimes against peace.
33   1944 *Manual of Military Law*, para.13.
34   1956 *Manual of Military Law*, para. 24.
35   See L. Friedman, op.cit., Vol.II, p.1705.
36   *Re Yamashita*, US. 1945, 672.   See now 1977 Protocol I Additional to the 1949 Geneva Conventions, article 86(2).   For discussion see W.H. Parks, 'Command Responsibility for War Crimes', 62 *Military Law Review*, 1963.
37   See H. Kelsen, *General Theory of Law and State*, trans. A. Wedberg (Harvard, 1949), pp.369-70.   For criticism of the basic idea of such a unified system J. Raz, *The Concept of a Legal System* (Oxford, 1970), pp.100-109.   For an alternative view see A. Wilson, 'The Concept of a Legal Order' (1982) 27 *American Journal of Jurisprudence*, 64.
38   This later Kelsenian analysis sits markedly less comfortably with the selectivity of Nuremberg jurisprudence against war criminals on the defeated side.
39   The discussion will be found in H.L.A. Hart, *The Concept of Law* (Clarendon, Oxford, 1961/94), Ch.X.
40   French Penal Code, article 327.
41   *Law Reports Trials of War Criminals* (HMSO, 1947), Vol.I, p.93: see also L. Friedman, op.cit., Vol.II, p.1487.
42   *Law Reports Trials of War Criminals* (HMSO, 1947), Vol.I, p.93; see also L. Friedman, op.cit., Vol.II, p.1487.
43   *War Crimes Trials* (William Hocky & Co., 1949), Vol.II.
44   See Chapter 2.
45   J. Blackett, 'Superior Orders - The Military Dilemma', *Royal United Services Institute Journal*, February 1994, p.12 at p.17.
46   See S-S. Junod, *Protection of the Victims of Armed Conflict Falkland-Malvinas Islands (1982)*, 2 ed. (International Committee of the Red Cross, 1985), pp.30-31.

47 For discussion of the origin and development of the classical doctrine from the Roman *Jus Fetiale* see G.I.A.D. Draper, 'The Origins of the Just War Doctrine' (1964) 46 *New Blackfriars*, 82. See also P. Contamine, trans. M. Jones, *War in the Middle Ages* (Basil Blackwell, 1984; first published as *La Guerre au Moyen Age*, Presses Universitaires de France, 1980), pp.282-292.

48 J. Pictet, *Development and Principles of International Humanitarian Law* (Martinus Nijhoff, 1985), p.13.

49 St. Thomas Aquinas, *Summa Theologica*, 2a2ae.40, citing St. Augustine of Hippo, *Contra Faustem* LXXIV.

50 P. Contamine, trans. M. Jones, op.cit., p.290.

51 See M. Walzer, *Just and Unjust Wars* (Allen Lane, 1978), pp.17-19.

52 St. Thomas Aquinas, *Summa Theologica*, 1a2ae.96,6.

53 See Chapter 3.

54 Ibid.

55 The question of retrospective invalidation of 'immoral' positive provisions was debated at length in the aftermath of the Second World War, see Chapter 7.

56 See article 1 common to the four 1949 Geneva Conventions, also the Preamble to and article 1(1) of 1977 Additional Protocol I.

57 See Chapter 3.

58 See Chapters 2, 3 and 5.

59 St. Thomas Aquinas, *Summa Theologica*, 1a2ae.90,4.

7 Validity and Obligation

It has been argued in the preceding chapters that there are at least three usages of the term 'obligation' in the context of obedience to law in jurisprudential discourse, relating respectively to coercive, formal and moral factors. It has also been argued that conventional failure to make adequate distinctions between these categories of obligation has led to much confusion and misdirection of argument. Does it therefore follow that a 'valid' law imposes 'obligation' whilst a law which is in some sense defective in its imposition of obligation must be 'invalid'? A summary of the starting positions was set out by Roscoe E. Hill in the comment that,

> According to ... positivists ... so long as the unjust law is a valid law, one has a legal obligation to obey it ... [according to the naturalists] since an unjust law is not truly a valid law one clearly has no obligation (legal or moral) to obey it.[1]

This is a fair representation of conventional jurisprudential perceptions, but the propositions represented actually rather over-simplify the position of the various schools of thought. It would be tempting to resolve the apparent problem by taking 'validity' to be a term of multiple jurisprudential usage in parallel with, at least, the formal and moral usages of the term 'obligation'. This *prima facie* rather attractive symmetry would, however, be without any firm foundation.

The nature of the relationship between validity and obligation is best examined in the context of a positive provision or system of government which may be agreed to have been 'iniquitous'. Examples of laws which might to a greater or lesser degree be so regarded are, sadly, not difficult to find, but the most obvious example for the present purpose is the misuse of law in the Third Reich. Since 1945 there has developed a comforting but dangerous illusion that the, very real, abominations of the Nazi era were a unique phenomenon quite unrelated to 'normal' conditions. In fact they may be seen as extreme and appalling examples of phenomena which were not unique in their own time and have been repeated more recently at various times and in various places. The closing period of *glasnost* and *perestroika* in the former USSR and currently in the former Soviet Republics revealed further details of the extent of mass killing by the Stalin dictatorship. Much more recently the horrors experienced under the Khmer Rouge regime in Cambodia (then Kampuchea) and some aspects of the armed conflict(s) in former-Yugoslavia warn against complacency in this regard. The Third Reich remains, however, a prime example both by reason of the extent of its enormities and because, through the exigencies of military defeat, it is peculiarly well documented.

The Condition of Law in the Third Reich

The peculiarity of Nazi abuse of law lay in the maintenance of the outward forms of a *rechtstaat* coupled with the subversion of its substance. As a political doctrine Nazism had a distant and twisted relationship with the thought of Hegel and Nietzsche, notably in its glorification of the state and the *ubermensch*, but it was more practically and immediately a German development of the Fascist doctrines which took root somewhat earlier in Italy. Fascism was founded upon the submersion of the individual in a hierarchy of authoritarian corporate structures culminating in a state dominated by a 'Leader'. Italian Fascists emphasized a bellicose nationalism founded upon bogus claims to succession to the Roman Imperium. Hitler and the Nazis added to German nationalism a racism which was extremely, but not exclusively, anti-semitic. The Nazi state was organized upon the basis of a *Fuehrerprinzip*, or Leadership principle, in which each level was 'led' by the next above it and the whole was 'led' by the Fuehrer himself. No institutional constraints upon the will of the leadership were admitted and, in the words of an Italian political theorist, 'supremacy of ends, supremacy of force ... sum up the idea of the Fascist State'.[2] Law in such a system was seen merely as an instrument for the application of the will of the party and the leader, certainly not as a Diceyan limitation upon state action. The Nazis did, however, continue to enact laws throughout their era of rule, some of which were morally abhorrent, others of which were not necessarily so. It must then be asked whether the laws made by the Nazi regime between 1933 and 1945 were 'valid'.   A historical analysis indicates a clear, if tenuous, positivist pedigree for law making in the Third Reich.   In 1933 Adolf Hitler was elected *Reichskanzler* in accordance with the post-1918 Weimar Constitution, even if the election was marred by significant 'brown shirt' intimidation by the SA.[3]   Hitler's later dictatorial powers were not, strictly speaking, founded upon the constitutional discontinuity of a coup d'etat.   On 28 February 1933 the ageing and ill President von Hindenberg was persuaded by Hitler to exercise emergency powers under the Weimar Constitution to grant him extraordinary powers in a 'national emergency'.   This decree was secured by means of a misrepresentation that the country faced imminent communist revolt.   This was facilitated by the burning of the *Reichstag* building in Berlin on 27 February, an event which continues to stir debate but which was certainly convenient to the Nazis whether or not they were actually involved in it.   President von Hindenberg certainly had the constitutional power to issue the decree, even if he was misled as to the need for it.   The sweeping powers thus granted to Hitler in February 1933 were consolidated by a *Reichstag* enactment of 24 March in the same year which conferred upon him powers of legislation by decree renewable by *Reichstag* votes at four year intervals.   There was, of course, no uncertainty about the passage of these votes in the 'brown' *Reichstag* between 1933 and 1945.   Upon the basis of this history it is possible to argue that, despite the gross subversion of Weimar constitutional processes, there was, just, a formal continuity of pedigree from the legislation of the Weimar Republic to that of the Third Reich.

In the same way, the outward form of the judicial institutions inherited by the Third Reich from the Weimar Republic, and ultimately from Wilhelmine Germany, were just about retained but adapted to meet the requirements of the *Fuehrerprinzip*.   The ordinary courts were subjected to a marked degree of political pressure in their decision making, but they were in the end not so much subverted as sidestepped.   This can be seen most strikingly in the creation through a law of 21 March 1933 of special political courts (*sondergericht*) and, on 24 April 1934, of the Supreme Political Court (*Volksgerichtshof*).[4]   In a *Sondergericht* an outward show of due process was maintained, but the three judges presiding over a case were checked by the Nazi authorities for their 'reliability' as were counsel appearing before the court.   Defence counsel were not expected to exert themselves unduly on their clients' behalf and to bring action against the state in such courts was supremely ill-advised.   When the widow of Dr.

Klausener, the leader of the Catholic Action Party who was murdered by the Nazis, brought an action against the state for damages in respect of the killing her lawyers were incarcerated in the Sachsenhausen concentration camp until they agreed to withdraw the case.[5]   Cases before the *Volksgerichtshof* were heard by two professional judges, again approved by the Nazis, sitting with five more drawn from the army, the SS and the Party. The President of the Court, Roland Friesler, was noted for his bias and vituperation in the conduct of cases.   William L. Shirer remarks of proceedings before this court, which he witnessed as an American journalist, that,

> [They resembled more] a drumhead court-martial than a civil-court trial. The proceedings were finished in a day, there was practically no opportunity to present defence witnesses ... and the argument of the defence lawyers, who were 'qualified' Nazis, seemed weak to the point of ludicrousness.[6]

The reference to courts martial, in general, may be considered unfair, but the point being made is obvious.   In this context findings of guilt were inevitable and capital sentences commonplace.[7]

Even before the ordinary courts proceedings were at all times liable to arbitrary political interference.   The Nazi Party made no secret of the fact that they did not consider themselves to be bound by legal niceties, indeed any such concept would have been in clear conflict with the *Fuehrerprinzip*. If any doubt remained upon this point it was resolved by the Gestapo Law of 10 February 1936 which stated explicitly that the security police were not subject to legal limitations in their operations.   The point was made bluntly by Dr. Werner Best, deputy of the *Reichsfuehrer SS*, Heinrich Himmler, in his comment that, 'so long as the police is carrying out the will of the leadership, it is acting legally'.[8]   Exactly what was meant by this in practice was shown, *inter alia*, in the case of Pastor Niemoller.   Niemoller had a distinguished record as a U-boat commander in the Imperial German Navy during the First World War. After the War he had become a noted Lutheran Pastor, at the Church of Christ in the Berlin suburb of Dahlem, and in that capacity he preached courageous sermons against Nazi outrages which led to his being arrested and charged with sedition.   Astonishingly, and much to its credit, the court before which he first appeared dared to acquit him upon all but a minor and technical charge.   However, as he left the court he was seized by Gestapo agents and   detained without   further legal process in concentration camps in which he managed to survive until he was liberated in 1945.   In addition to such *ex post facto* interventions Hitler made a habit of ordering both the commencement and termination of proceedings in accordance with political convenience.[9]

The Jurisprudential Questions

In general the evidence of legal practice in the Third Reich strongly supports the conclusion advanced elsewhere that the Nazi regime represented,

> A state in which the bare shell of legality was maintained while the reality involved naked political interventions at every level ... .[10]

Is it then possible to say that Nazi law was 'valid' and, if so, what level of obligation attached to it ?   Several questions are in fact raised here and it is unfortunate that the principal academic debate in the area, between H.L.A. Hart and Lon L. Fuller, was founded upon an erroneous factual report. Three quite distinct issues may be discerned.   First, the standing of Nazi law according to formal, positivist, criteria;   second the propriety of its application in particular cases;   and third its moral and ethical claims. Upon the first issue it must seem that there was a sufficient 'rule of recognition' in Nazi Germany to satisfy the test set by H.L.A. Hart[11] and even that there was a continuity of pedigree from the Weimar Republic into the Third Reich.   Whether the Third Reich can be considered to satisfy the requirements of Fuller's 'procedural natural law'[12] is a more complex issue which is considered below.   Assuming that there were 'laws' in the Third Reich, the question of application arises.   A 'valid' law may, of course, be 'invalidly' applied, for example if a judge accepts a bribe to determine the interpretation of a rule.   In this sense proceedings before a *Sondergericht* or the *Volksgerichtshof*, as well as many other Nazi tribunals, must be considered to have been at the least profoundly questionable.   The final issue, that of the moral and ethical standing of Nazi enactments, represents a different order of difficulty.   The knowledge of Nazi iniquity encourages a response in   absolute terms that the law of the Third Reich must have been devoid of moral   claim.   This,   however, can   hardly   be   considered an adequate response. Many laws made by the Third Reich were morally neutral and even useful, such as those dealing with general traffic regulation which differed little from those found in other places and times. Even some provisions which were highly objectionable, such as the racist 'aryan' marriage laws, cannot simply be swept aside. To claim that all people married in Germany under these laws did so under a disqualifying moral defect would entail consequences as morally dubious as the racist frustration of some marriages under their terms. Some Third Reich enactments, especially those directly concerned with the implementation of the policies of genocide, can, of course, be dismissed as abominations having no moral claim whatever. Such questions of moral standing are essentially those at the centre of naturalist theory[13] and a response may usefully be sought in the Thomist analysis of the 'price' in 'bad' law which may be expected to be paid for social stability and its limits.

Post-War Judicial Consideration of Nazi Law

Post-war courts, both within and outside Germany, were confronted with considerable difficulties in coping with the aftermath of Nazi abuse of law. It was necessary to find some means of distinguishing between law and non-law whilst, in any event, undoing so far as was possible the continuing effects of Nazi wrongdoing. Four somewhat contrasting cases, two before the courts of the former Federal Republic of West Germany, one in the United States and one in the United Kingdom, usefully illustrate the variety of approaches adopted.

The two German instances were examples of 'grudge informer' cases in which, prior to 1945, persons had made use of repressive provisions for the satisfaction of personal malice. The facts of the two cases were sufficiently similar to admit joint summary. In each case a German soldier home on leave made derogatory remarks about Hitler and the regime to his wife in private and she, having tired of him, then reported these to the Nazi authorities with a view to ridding herself of him. In each case charges were brought against the husband under a law of 20 December 1934 which prohibited the making of statements inimical to the regime and a law of 17 August 1938 which prohibited all actions, *inter alia*, inimical to military morale. The wives insisted upon giving evidence, in the absence of which

- even in the Third Reich - the cases could not have proceeded, despite in one of the cases having been strongly urged not to do so. In each case the husband was convicted and sentenced to death but then 'reprieved' and sent to serve on the Eastern Front, which was by then seen essentially as an alternative form of death sentence. In each case he in fact survived and after the war sought redress against both his spouse and the judges who had condemned him.

In the first of these cases[14] the action was brought under paragraph 239 of the German Penal Code of 1871 relating to unlawful deprivation of liberty. The post-war court did not address the issue of 'validity' directly, it found, however, that the Nazi provisions concerned had generally been regarded as repressive and that the use of them by 'grudge informers' had at all relevant times been considered an abuse. Faced with a dichotomy between positive law and revulsion of moral and popular sentiment, the court reached a conceptually awkward compromise. It concluded that the judges had applied the law, however harsh, as they found it and had therefore committed no offence. The wife, in contrast, was found to have used a repressive law for the satisfaction of personal malice and, therefore, through abuse of process, to have committed an offence. The court in effect decided that the decision had been lawful, if harsh, so that there had been no *actus reus*, but the wife in using the law for her own ends had had *mens rea* - in other words she had committed a crime of pure intention.

The conclusion of this court seems unsatisfactory upon whatever level it is approached. If the laws were valid, though harsh, the judges clearly committed no offence in applying them under the then prevailing laws of Germany. If that were the case, what offence had the woman committed ? Is it being suggested that her motive, of personal malice, rendered her guilty of an offence which she would not have committed had she been motivated by Nazi fanaticism?   There is also the question of the retrospective criminalization of acts lawful, indeed encouraged, at the time of their commission.   To raise these questions is not, of course, to express approbation of the conduct of the original Nazi proceedings.

A much more rationally consistent decision was reached by the (West) German Federal Supreme Court in the second of these cases in 1952.[15]   In this case charges of unlawful deprivation of liberty and attempted murder had been dismissed by the Provincial Court of Wurzburg.   The Federal Supreme Court then determined that any finding of guilt in respect of the spouse must necessarily entail guilt on the part of the judges.   The court avoided the issue of validity as such but decided instead that the proper approach lay in a strict consideration of the formal rectitude of the conduct of the original proceedings. Not surprisingly, in the context, serious flaws were readily found. The offence created by the Nazi decree involved the public dissemination of seditious opinions and it must be supposed that the 'public' element of the offence was intended to make a distinction from some 'private' sphere. If this was so, it is difficult to imagine a more 'private' context of communication than that between spouses. It was therefore concluded that upon the wording of the decree the criticism expressed by the husband had not been an offence, in which case the conduct of both the informing wife and the judges could be held culpable. Even should that view prove erroneous, it was held that the existence of a scale of penalties under the decree, ranging from the relatively minor to capital sentences, indicated a gradation of culpability in which, upon any objective analysis, the act in question must have been amongst the slightest. This being so, the passing of a capital sentence - including the so-called 'reprieve' - was held to amount to a culpable failure to exercise judicial discretion in sentencing which had been anticipated and intended by the informing spouse. Consequently, the Federal Supreme Court referred the case for reconsideration upon the basis of a finding of unlawful deprivation of liberty up to the time of the passing of the sentence and of attempted murder thereafter upon the part of both the informing spouse and the judges.

These post-war German cases represent an essentially positivist approach to the problems of Nazi law. When applied with sufficient subtlety such an approach is well calculated to resolve many of the difficulties, especially in the light of the gaping lacunae in the procedural proprieties of the Third Reich. It avoids the issue of validity but assumes that the state is capable of making such laws as it may think fit, preferring to afford later redress by reference to, all too readily found, procedural abuses. There remains, however, the potential problem of procedurally 'correct' outrages. An interesting response can be found in the American case of *Leidmann* v *Reisenthal*.[16] The plaintiffs had sought to escape from anti-semitic persecution in Vichy France and had paid over money and valuable jewellery to the defendant who had promised to take them to safety. In fact he simply abandoned them and they ultimately succeeded in escaping by other means. In an action for money had and received brought by the victims after the end of the Second World War in New

York where the plaintiffs later encountered their plunderer, the defendant claimed that under the relevant local law, that of Vichy France, the contract to aid the escape had been illegal and that the New York court therefore had no jurisdiction to order recovery. Hooley, J., held that in circumstances such as these, in which the plaintiffs had been driven to act *in terrorem*, the formal illegality of the original contract could not be permitted to act as a bar to an action for restitution. The validity of the Vichy law was not directly questioned but the attempt to use it as a bar to proceedings for redress brought in the United States was rejected as, in effect, an abuse of process. This is again an essentially positivist approach which avoids the question of validity as such, but which also avoids the continuing effect of iniquitous laws through formal analysis, for which in this instance the *in terrorem* element sufficed.

A very different, and much more problematic, response can be seen in the English decision in *Oppenheimer* v *Cattermole*, conjoined with *Nothmann* v *Cooper*,[17] decided in 1975. The cases were closely similar and the facts of *Oppenheimer* v *Cattermole* will suffice for purposes of exposition. Oppenheimer had been born a German citizen and until 1933 he had worked as a teacher in a Jewish orphanage. He was for a time imprisoned by the Nazis but was then permitted to flee abroad but not to remove his property from Germany. His assets were expropriated under a decree of 25 November 1941 which stripped non-resident German Jews of their citizenship and property. In 1948 he became a British citizen by naturalization and in 1953 the former Federal Republic of West Germany granted him a reparationary pension. The case concerned his liability to taxation in respect of this pension which, under double taxation conventions of 1954 and 1964, was assessable for purposes of United Kingdom income tax if the recipient had only UK citizenship, but not if he had both British and German citizenship.

The case turned upon German nationality law, in particular the German Nationality Law of 1913, the 1941 Nazi Decree and the 1949 Basic Law of the former Federal Republic of West Germany. The 1913 law provided that a German citizen resident abroad would lose citizenship upon acquisition of a foreign citizenship without the consent of the German government. According to this Oppenheimer would have lost his German citizenship upon acquiring that of the United Kingdom in 1948 even if he had not already done so by virtue of the 1941 decree. The 1949 Basic Law provided by article 116(2) that persons who had been stripped of German citizenship upon racial grounds by the Nazis were entitled to the restoration of (West) German citizenship upon application.   It was apparently felt that automatic restoration might be found offensive by former victims of Nazi persecution in Germany.   Oppenheimer has made no such application and it was ultimately held that he had only United Kingdom citizenship and was therefore liable to UK taxation upon his pension.   In the course of the proceedings Opppenheimer had pleaded, *inter alia* that the 1941 decree was inherently invalid and of no effect.   Upon this question the House of Lords made highly significant comment *obiter dicta*.   It was common ground amongst the majority of the court[18] that the 1941 decree was so contrary to basic human rights norms as to be incapable of recognition or effectuation by an English court, notwithstanding the general expectation that the internal competence of other states should be recognized as an aspect of the comity of nations.[19]   The basic conclusion of the majority was set out by Lord Cross of Chelsea thus,

> legislation which takes away without compensation from a section of the citizen body, singled out on racial grounds, all their property ... [and] deprives them of their citizenship ... constitutes so grave and infringement of human rights that the courts of this country ought to refuse to recognise it as law at all.[20]

This broad conclusion was, however, reached through two quite different forms of argument.   On the one hand it was suggested that the 1941 decree was nullified by its contravention of human rights norms of public international law.[21]   On the other hand it was also suggested that the decree was invalidated simply by the virtue of its moral turpitude.[22]   The first argument is much less startling than the second and turns essentially upon the relationship between public international and municipal law.[23]   It may be noted in parenthesis that it has been held, in *Trendtex* v *Central Bank of Nigeria*,[24] that public international law is 'incorporated' into English law at least to the extent that an English court may consider the current state of such law in preference to earlier formulations enshrined in precedent.

   The second argument appears at first sight to have been a rather literal application of the maxim of St. Augustine of Hippo that *lex iniusta non est lex*.   The court having taken the words not in the general moral sense which St. Augustine actually intended, but rather in that of the now traditional positivist misunderstanding of the statement implying that an unjust law is formally ineffective.[25]   The unease of the majority of the court with what might seem to be implied was emphasized by their insistence upon the point that the 1941 decree was the former law of a defeated enemy and not the current law of a foreign state.   Lord Salmon remarked that,

> England was [engaged in a] ... war with Germany in 1941 [which] ... was presented in its later stages as a crusade against the barbarities of the Nazi regime ... .[26]

Whether a similar view of Nazi legislation would have been taken by an English court in, say, 1936, must be considered at best doubtful.

It must be stressed that the point at issue here is the formal *validity* of the 1941 decree.   The willingness of an English court to give effect to its substantive provisions in a case arising outside Germany is an entirely different matter.   As it has been suggested above good formal reasons may readily be found for avoiding such an outcome, including incongruance with international legal norms and, as Lord Salmon may have been suggesting, grounds of public policy.   Elements of this latter may be suggested also in *Leidmann* v *Reisenthal* in the United States.

In only one of the four cases here outlined was the question of validity raised directly.   One is left to ask whether the formal 'validity' assumed in the two 'grudge informer' cases differed from the moral validity in part considered in *Oppenheimer* v *Cattermole*.   The principal academic debate upon this issue was conducted between H.L.A. Hart and Lon L. Fuller in the context of the first of the 'grudge informer' cases referred to above. Unfortunately, as it has already been indicated, the discussion was founded upon an early and erroneous description of the case which suggested, wrongly, that the post-war German court had founded its decision upon a basis of moral invalidation.[27]   Despite this, the debate did raise a number of illuminating issues upon the question of validity in general.

The Hart/Fuller Debate

H.L.A. Hart argued that a court faced with the task of applying positive law does not have the luxury of making a moral choice amongst the laws which it will apply but must recognize all those, but only those, which satisfy the formal criteria set out by the system under consideration. Obedience or disobedience in response to an iniquitous demand is then represented as an individual choice which is not relevant to the status of law as *recht*.[28] Fuller, in contrast, took the view that some forms of iniquity may subvert the 'legal' claim to obedience exerted by a positive provision, although not the ability of the state to enforce it against its victims.[29] Although presented as an argument upon 'validity' this 'debate' was not in fact so. It concerned a traditionally misconceived divergence of opinion upon the 'obligation' to obey law, informed by an assumption that 'validity' is more or less synonymous with the imposition of 'obligation'.

The True Relation of Validity and Obligation

Once it has been accepted that the obligation(s) to obey law may exist at differing levels and in widely different forms the relation between validity and obligation necessarily becomes diffuse. The concepts are in fact fundamentally different in nature. Validity is essentially a matter of concern in formal legal application and specifically to courts. A court to which a provision is cited as purporting to be positive law is faced with an absolute choice: it cannot, unlike the curate's egg in the 19th century *Punch* cartoon, be 'excellent in parts', it either satisfies the applicable formal criteria of identification or it does not. This is so across the range of positivist theories and is arguably no less the case within the context of Kelsen's 'pure theory'.

    Is there then some differently conceived and applied phenomenon of 'moral validity'? It is suggested that there is not. Minimum moral requirements for proper law making may be suggested, this indeed is a substantial part of the endeavour of mainstream naturalist legal theory. It is even possible for courts to take account of such matters in the fine tuning of their application of laws recognized to be formally valid. This includes, but is not limited to, the institutional morality of the 'constitutional' principles advanced by Dworkin in his analysis of 'hard case' adjudication.[30] In this general context Roscoe E. Hill argues that,

> the concept of being legally obliged ... simply involves the (value free) recognition that the law in question is valid, i.e. that [it satisfies] ... the rule of

recognition and will be enforced. ... [T]he concept of legal obligation ... involves the (value charged) recognition that the law conforms to the 'true' principle of justice and morality, that it serves the public interest ... .[31]

In a discussion which is close to Dworkin's position, and similarly founded in the constitutional practice of the United States, he then addresses the account taken of 'non-rule' moral factors in the application of laws. This does not, however, go to the root of legal validity as it is here conceived. The willingness of a court to mitigate or even to waive the effects of positive legal provision in a given case had noting to do with its validity. If the provision is invalid it can, *ex hypothesi*, not be applied at all. It is true that interpretation can have dramatic effects upon the application of law. A classic case of innovation founded upon ethical considerations may be seen in the decision in *Donoghue* v *Stevenson*.[32] In that case it was held that a victim of negligently contaminated ginger beer should not be denied a remedy because of the technicality of a lack of contractual nexus with the person responsible. This was not, however, an issue involving the status of law as *recht*. Only in rare instances such as *Oppenheimer* v *Cattermole* has the suggestion tentatively been made that moral or ethical consideration might operate formally to 'invalidate' a purported law. An analysis of the implications of such a position immediately suggests its untenability as a model of 'validity'.

Returning to the definition of a complete law offered by St. Thomas Aquinas, *rationis ordinatio ad bonum commune, ab eo qui curam communitatis habet, promulgata*,[33] a rational ordinance made for the good of the community by those who have the charge of it and promulgated, the distinction between the moral and formal elements of the analysis again become highly significant. Whether the provision is made by, in effect, the sovereign and promulgated are matters which are in most cases open to clear answers. Whether the provisional is 'rational' or conducive to the public good are issues much less open to simple answers. Except in extreme cases, such as the Nazi provisions for the commission of genocide - which were not, of course, phrased in quite that way - the moral quality of most laws will have to be ascertained upon a scale of values and consequences rather than being susceptible to precise formal evaluation.

This suggests that 'validity' is a formal rather than a moral or ethical concept. If this is the case it relates only to the formal category of obligation associated with law and not to any moral obligation to comply, except in so far as the question of 'legal' obligation could not arise in any form in relation to a thing which is not law.   The same may be said in relation to coercive enforcement which is, usually, predicated upon an assumption of the validity of the provision to be enforced.   If validity thus relates only to the formal dimension it would follow that a provision might in an extreme case be both valid and devoid of moral claim.   This proposition affords a solution to the problem of the iniquitous but formally 'correct' positive provision and resolves at least some of the infelicities of the Hart/Fuller debate in this area.

To return to the 'grudge informer' cases, a starting point might then be that Nazi law making had a thin but clear formal pedigree and that the laws in question were recognizably an exercise of legislative power by a government for the time being, however deplorable.   Such a recognition does not legitimate the gross procedural abuses perpetrated in the implementation of these laws and this, without going beyond a formal level of analysis, is sufficient to resolve the issues of the 'grudge informer' cases.   Turning to *Oppenheimer* v *Cattermole*, to conclude that the 1941 decree was 'valid' is to say no more than that it was the product of a formally recognized process.   This is not to say that it should therefore uncritically be applied.   In a modern context its effects may be attacked, with far greater strength than in 1941, upon the basis of the human rights norms of public international law which may indeed be concluded formally. It is also open to later Tribunals to place severely restrictive interpretations upon it, broadly upon moral or policy grounds.

Validity and Procedurally 'Correct' Iniquity

In a rather thinly disguised analysis of the legal aftermath of Nazism Lon L. Fuller suggested a number of possible responses in a context of 'procedural natural law'[34] but, as it has been suggested above, such an approach necessarily leaves open the question of the 'valid', in the sense here adopted, but iniquitous law.   In this respect at least H.L.A. Hart was surely correct in arguing in his 'debate' with Fuller that the question of retrospective criminalization must be squarely faced.[35]   Retrospective criminalization of acts legal at the time of commission is in general profoundly objectionable, indeed this is one of the failings listed in Fuller's procedural natural law and was one of the objectionable features of Nazi law itself.   Can it therefore be acceptable to redress the wrongs perpetrated by an iniquitous regime by employing its own objectionable methods? This is not actually a necessary part of the process: many of the abuses of the Nazi regime were already criminal in either or both of German and international law. The claim that, e.g., the prosecutions at Nuremberg involved retrospective criminalization is largely a claim founded upon the question of *individual* responsibility in international law. The norms of positive public international law, including the 1928 Pact of Paris and the Hague and Geneva Conventions, which Third Reich political and military policies were at least as much formally valid as the internal laws and directives of the Reich. To allow 'act of state' to be pleaded in effect by those who had had the direction of the Reich government and armed forces at the material times would have been to allow a defence of infinite regression. The calling to account of individuals at Nuremberg may in many ways be compared with the 'piercing of the corporate veil' in English company law where corporate legal personality is believed to have been used as a screen for wrongdoing. Ultimately, a paper thin formal 'pedigree' could not be used to 'justify' iniquities when when abuse of the legal system which it supported lay at the heart of the problem.

Conclusion

Validity in a jurisprudential context is argued to be essentially a formal concept symbolising the satisfaction of strictly 'positivist' formal criteria of identification. By its nature validity is an absolute quality with which any given positive provision is either vested or not, whatever the subtleties of its practical interpretation and application may be. The effect of the claim to 'validity' is broadly to label the provision concerned as one imposing a formal obligation to obey, subject to decisions of interpretation and application.

If this view is accepted it must also be taken that there is no equivalent concept of 'moral validity'. The moral obligation attached to law is subject to variant shadings and not a property which a positive provision can, in other than extreme circumstances, be said absolutely to possess or not to possess. Still less may 'validity' be associated directly with the potential or actual application of coercive force. No doubt a state will support its law with force where it considers it necessary, but this is no more than an exercise of factual power, which may or may not concord with either or both of the operative formal and moral norms. Coercion as such is not necessarily a badge of validity in the sense here suggested or even symptomatic of it.

Validity is thus an important but rather limited jurisprudential concept. A 'complete law' in the Thomist sense will clearly be formally valid according to formal criteria of identification but will also possess qualities going beyond, and essentially distinct from, formal 'validity'. These include moral and ethical qualities and may also include the willingness of the state to maintain the provision, *inter alia* through mechanisms of coercive enforcement. Such additional qualities are also of great practical importance but are not in themselves susceptible to analysis in terms of formal validity. Validity is left as a formal statement of recognition which is relevant only to one, the formal, category of the obligation of the obligations to comply associated with law. Its primary importance is that of a 'bracketing' concept which identifies the cumulative effect of the application of formal criteria of identification, most obviously - but not only - by the courts.

Notes

1   R.E. Hill, 'Legal Validity and Legal Obligation' (1970) 80 *Yale Law Journal*, 47.
2   A. Rocco, *La Transformazione della Stato*, cited in translation by A.H. Campbell in 'Fascism and Legality' (1946) 62 *Law Quarterly Review*, 141.
3   *Sturm Abteilung*. The leaders of this organization were later killed upon Hitler's orders and their role was to a large extent assumed by Himmler's SS (*Schutzstaffe*).
4   For discussion of these courts see H.W. Koch, *In the Name of the Volk: Political Justice in Hitler's Germany* (J.B. Tauris & Co., 1989).
5   W.L. Shirer, *The Rise and Fall of the Third Reich* (Pan edn., 1964), p.335.
6   Ibid.
7   According to W.L. Shirer, op.cit., p.335, Friesler claimed that there was 'only' a 4% rate of capital sentences, but this seems to have been a vast understatement. H.W. Koch, op.cit., indicates that between 1934 and 1938 the proportion of capital sentences was indeed relatively low but in later years the proportion grew rapidly, so that in 1943 1,662 persons out of 3,338 accused and in 1944 2,079 persons out of 4,379 accused were condemned to death. (See H.W. Koch, op.cit., p.132. Figures derived from Friesler's own reports.)

8   Quoted in translation by W.L. Shirer, op.cit., p.337.
9   As in the case of the long protection of Julius Streicher, *Gauleiter* of
    Franconia, whose conduct was gross even by Nazi standards.   He was
    eventually condemned to death by the International Military Tribunal at
    Nuremberg.   See A. Neave, *Nuremberg* (Hodder and Stoughton, 1978;
    Coronet edn., 1980), pp.90 ff.
10 H. McCoubrey, *The Development of Naturalist Legal Theory* (Croom Helm,
    1987), p.135.
11 See Chapter 2.
12 See Chapter 4.
13 See Chapter 3.
14 See H.O. Pappe, 'On the Validity of Judicial Decisions in the Nazi Era' 23
    Modern Law Review, 260.
15 See ibid., at 264 ff.
16 57 New York St. Reps. (2d), 875.
17 [1975] 1 All ER 538.
18 Lords Cross of Chelsea, Hodson and Salmon;   Lords Hailsham of St,
    Marylebone and Pearson dissenting.
19 As to the treatment of municipal law in the context of public international law
    see I.A. Shearer, *Starke's International Law*, 11 ed. (Butterworths, 1994),
    Ch.4.
20 [1975] 1 All ER at 567.
21 See, e.g., Lord Salmon at pp.571-2.
22 See, e.g., Lord Hodson at p.557.
23 See above and Chapter 6.
24 [1977] 2 WLR 356.
25 See Chapter 3.
26 [1975] 1 All ER at 571.
27 (1950-51) 64 *Harvard Law Review*, 1005.
28 See H.L.A. Hart, 'Positivism and the Separation of Laws and Morals' (1958)
    71 *Modern Law Review*, 593.
29 See Lon L. Fuller, 'Positivism and Fidelity to Law' (1958) 71 *Modern Law
    Review*, 630.
30 See Chapter 4.
31 R.E. Hill, op.cit., at p.70.
32 [1932] AC 562.
33 St. Thomas Aquinas, *Summa Theologica*, 1a2ae. 90,4.
34 See Chapter 4.
35 H.L.A. Hart, op.cit., passim.

8 A Theory of Legal Obligation

The starting point for the present analysis was the proposition of H.L.A. Hart that, 'where there is law, ... human conduct is made in some sense non-optional or obligatory'.[1] Whilst 'obligation' manifestly operates across a far wider sphere than that of positive law, it may still be said, with Hart, that the attachment of an obligatory quality to defined patterns of human conduct is an important characteristic of law. Its significance is recognized in one way or another over a broad spectrum of legal theories, but there is very little apparent agreement as to its nature and impact. It is not the purpose of this concluding chapter to advance yet another 'new' theory of legal obligation.

It has been an unfortunate characteristic of the development of legal theory that new or altered perceptions have commonly been claimed to supersede earlier theories which were then claimed to have been in some sense misconceived or 'wrong'. One clear instance can be seen in the iconoclastic elements of the arguments of Bentham and Austin,[2] which derived, significantly, from a misunderstanding of the true nature of classical naturalist argument.[3] The same tendency can be seen in more recent developments and it has had an unhelpful effect upon the development of the understanding of the nature of the obligation(s) to obey positive law. It has been contended in earlier chapters that the proper understanding of the obligation to obey law rests upon acceptance of the diverse nature of the phenomenon, in fact of a theory of obligations rather than one of obligation.

Obligation in Jurisprudential Discourse

It may be considered a misfortune that the various aspects of the 'obligatory' characteristic of law are subsumed within the single term 'obligation'. This usage has led to the treatment of the phenomenon in legal theory as essentially unitary. Such an attribution of a singular 'meaning' to a term represented a now largely discredited and abandoned linguistic philosophy. The 'logical atomism' based upon a 'picture model' of language found in the earlier linguistic philosophy of Wittgenstein was abandoned in his later work in favour of a 'games model' based upon usage rather than 'meaning'.[4] Such a view does not necessarily lead to an anarchic theory of language in which the concept of 'meaning' is wholly denied. The implication is rather that the intended 'meaning' of a term depends upon the context in which it is used and may well vary quite considerably. This may now be argued to be very much the case for the term 'obligation' in relation to compliance with positive law. If it is accepted that the term is one of multiple usage within a broadly conceived 'province of jurisprudence', the task of a modern theory of legal obligation becomes evidently twofold in nature. First it is necessary to identify the various uses of the term 'obligation' in jurisprudence and second to analyse their relationship in the operation of a 'complete law'.

The Categories of Obligation to Obey Law

In the foregoing discussion three categories of obligation to obey law have been advanced, coercive enforcement, formal duty and moral obligation. It is not contended that this is an exhaustive list of the jurisprudential usages of the term 'obligation', it is, however, advanced as a reasonable statement of the broad categories of usage. An obvious preliminary question is that of whether it would be preferable to abandon the misleading appearance of unity associated with the term 'obligation' in favour of a more appropriate variety of terms. Tempting as such an approach might be, there would in practice be severe and probably insuperable obstacles in the way of its pursuit. The selection of appropriate terms would be difficult in itself, since there could be no guarantee that any such terms would themselves be free from a misleading burden of assumed 'meaning'. Even in the unlikely event of a suitably 'pure' terminology being found, to establish it in usage would present immense difficulties. The approach here adopted of retaining the term 'obligation' but qualifying it appropriately to clarify its usage in each given context would therefore seem to be preferable. This approach may not necessarily supply a very elegant solution to the linguistic difficulty but it may be claimed to have the merit of practicality.

Law, as a structure of norms, is imbued with a spirit of 'oughtness'. It is never suggestive in form. Even in the case of a provision such as the Wills Act 1837 which may be seen as facilitative in function, the law is presented as the only permissible way of performing the act in question. It is not necessary to enter into the more distorting realms of Austinian imperatives to perceive law as a structure of provisions intended to induce obedience, not casually or from choice but by reference to a spirit of normativity or 'obligation'. The central contention of the argument so far advanced has been that the operation and attachment of 'obligation' to law varies at differing levels of analysis. The three broad forms of 'obligation' here suggested may be summarized briefly.

Coercive Force

The classical positivist analyses of Bentham and Austin identified 'sanctions', in association with sovereign imperation, as one of the principal definitive characteristics of positive law. Even making allowance for Bentham's concession of positive sanctions, this principally meant the actual or potential application of coercive force. If Karl N. Llewellyn's 'law jobs' theory[5] is accepted, the extent to which coercive force can be accepted as a basic incident of positive law may be questioned. Modern legal anthropology tends to emphasize the persuasiveness of customary norms in so-called 'primitive' societies which lack the capacity for extensive organized coercion of the refractory.[6] Whether such a situation is regarded as pre-legal in a Hartian sense or as a particular social form of 'legal' organization is not relevant to the present argument. The essential point is that in most forms of social organization there will be institutions capable of applying coercive force. From a standpoint of brute fact, such as that of Oliver Wendel Holmes' 'bad man', coercive force will become an important attribute of the working of law in significant aspects of its operation. It was as such correctly identified by Bentham and Austin and recognized, if deplored, by naturalists such as St. Augustine of Hippo.

The dangers of the identification of law with a simple *potestas coactiva* were rightly identified by H.L.A. Hart in his distinction between 'being obliged' and 'being under [formal] obligation' in the example of the bank robber.[7] A similar point in relation to moral obligation was made by St.

Augustine, citing Cicero, in relation to a confrontation between a captured pirate and Alexander the Great.[8]   At no level may the potential or actual application of coercive force be taken as necessarily indicative of legitimacy.

It is a nice point whether coercive force may properly be brought under the conceptual umbrella of 'obligation'.   It is not directly related to any of the senses of normativity which underlie most usages of the term 'obligation'.   To be forced to act in a specified fashion is not by any means necessarily to feel oneself to be under a duty so to act.   To emphasize the distinction the term 'coercive force' is here used in preference to, e.g., 'coercive obliging'.   The factor of coercive force is however so commonly employed in close association with the various 'genuine' forms of 'obligation' that it has an inevitable place in a complete analysis of the obligation to obey law.

Formal Obligations

The distinction between coercive force and formal obligation is essentially that drawn by H.L.A. Hart between 'being obliged' and 'being under obligation'.[9]   Whereas coercive force is an external applied factor having no direct relevance to attitude, beyond the fears of Holmes' 'bad man', formal obligation is generated by the 'internal' operation of a legal system, in Hart's terms, upon the assumption of the 'rightness' of legal provision as a critical reflective standard.   Such obligations are the product of the formal operation of a legal system and this is the usage of the term 'obligation' most typically found in technical legal discourse.   They are distinct not only from the consequences of the application of coercive force but also from moral obligations.   A contractual obligation to perform an immoral, but not illegal, action will be enforced by a court of law.

The definitive characteristic of formal obligation is its 'internal' nature, as Hart identified it.   It arises from recognition in accordance with formal criteria of identification.   The American Realist view that law consists of predictions of what courts will do becomes ridiculous when pursued to its logical extremities, but the potential for recognition by a court, should a dispute arise, is indeed a practical touchstone for the identification of formal obligations.   The consequences of this are important.   First, there is the close relationship between formal obligation and validity which has been considered above.[10]   Only a provision which satisfies intra-systemic criteria of validity can generate formal obligation in this context.   Whether in a given case such obligations actually have arisen will of course be a matter for interpretation, taking into account where appropriate the various non-rule factors in decision making emphasized by Dworkin.   It must again be stressed, however, that these factors do not blur the distinction between formal and moral obligations because these represent a 'formal' and internalized morality which is itself part and parcel of the legal system.

The evident importance of 'recognition' in the assessment of formal obligations has led some writers to the opinion that the opinion of officials is of especial importance in the evaluation of law.   This is notably the case for Kelsen's 'pure theory' but is also at least strongly implicit in H.L.A. Hart's analysis.   A variation upon this theme can be seen in Olivecrona's approach, founded upon the methodological difficulty of establishing a general, as compared with an official, psychology of law.   That the lawyer's view of law should be more detailed and, possibly, more sophisticated than that of the lay person is hardly surprising.   To deduce from this that law is, therefore, primarily addressed to officials is to draw an extreme and ultimately problematic conclusion.   Positive law functions within society as a whole and mostly operates without any direct reference to officials or to lawyers.   The average citizen may not have a detailed acquaintance with the technical details of the law of contract, but in daily shopping the average person successfully operates the system in practice without, in the overwhelming majority of situations, having recourse to lawyers.   If it were otherwise the law of contract as a commercial code could hardly operate and would, from the viewpoint of most of the people affected, become an 'external' and largely inefficacious phenomenon.   The only theories which actually assert the externality of formal obligations are those such as classical Marxism or the more extreme forms of American Realism which have here been categorized as 'sceptical'.   These schools of thought have been argued to be founded upon severely limited models of 'law' which are distorting in their effects when extended into wider analytical spectra.[11]

The most jurisprudentially interesting question to be asked in the context of formal obligation is perhaps that of its efficacy.   Hart's concept of 'recognition' affords a useful analysis of the phenomenon but does not account for its origin or the reasons for its acceptance.   In so far as Hart's legal anthropology suggests an origin in simple coercion this seems to be wholly inadequate.[12]   The efficacy of formal obligations may be suggested in fact to rest upon a complex interaction of moral, political and psychological factors, which many theoretical constructs attempt ill-advisedly to treat in isolation.   Formal obligation in a legal context may be suggested to be characterized by its 'internal' and intra-systemic nature, its practical operation in any given instance resting upon the operation of a variety of factors which are 'impure' in a Kelsenian sense in not forming part of the 'legal' structure *stricto sensu*.

Moral Obligation

It has been contended in the foregoing argument that a failure properly to distinguish between the categories of formal and moral obligation has historically been a principal cause of misdirection in the development of legal theory.[13]   In both its substance and its effects moral obligation is an entirely different phenomenon from its formal counterpart and the existence of the one in relation to a given proposition by no means guarantees the attachment of the other.   The attachment of moral obligation to provisions of positive law is related to the role of law as a statement of the minimum norms of a social and 'political' order.   This element is found in most mainstream naturalist thinking, even in that of St. Augustine of Hippo who adopted a very limited view of law as a *potestas coactiva* necessitated only by the evils of a fallen social order.   The point is brought out much more strongly in the various theories related to the Aristotelian view of human beings as *politikon zoon*, political or social creatures.   In varying fashions this can be seen in the work of St. Thomas Aquinas, the 17th and 18th century Social Contractarians and modern writers such as Finnis.   The central theme may be described as purposive analysis of law and its evaluation in terms of its tendency to facilitate or to frustrate the attainment of the teleological 'good' of its subjects.   Such 'good' may be said to require, at the least, the appropriate balancing of both the individual aspirations and the collective mutuality of human beings in society.

The issue most obscured by conventional jurisprudence in this area has, inevitably, been the relationship between moral and other obligations.   It must again be emphasized that moral obligation is not at all a definitive characteristic of positive law as such. It is, on the contrary, a product of a specifically external evaluation of positive provisions by reference to their purposive qualities. Moral obligation is not a factor which is directly taken into account by courts, except in the rather distant context of Dworkinian 'standards'. In the original stages of legal activity, those vested with legislative power can and should consider moral obligations in their deliberations and the consequences of their doing so, or failing so to do, will be an element in a 'naturalist' analysis of the resulting provision. The product will, however, in any event be a 'law' from a formal viewpoint if the required legislative processes were performed. Moral obligation, in short, is neither a synonym for nor an adjunct of formal obligation, and still less of coercive force. That it should ever have been so considered, even by implication, seems most likely to have been a product of the necessary 'internal' assumption of the 'rightness' or legal provisions distorted and extended to an absurd degree. Moral obligation in legal theory is the product of an external evaluation of positive law which may coincide with formal obligation but can by no means automatically be assumed to do so.

The Tripartite Categorization of Obligation(s)

The tripartite categorization of the elements contributing to the obligatory characteristic of positive law into coercive force and the formal and moral types of obligation is not, of course, exhaustive. Many detailed sub-divisions might be set out within each category. This broad tripartite division may, however, usefully be taken to delineate the major boundaries upon the map of legal obligation(s). The basic categories have long been represented by the typical concerns of a multiplicity of theories bearing upon the obligation to obey law. Indeed, specific recognition of the boundaries between the categories is not hard to find, as in the division between 'being obliged' and 'being under obligation' drawn by H.L.A. Hart, which is essentially that between coercive force and formal obligation. At this level there is no requirement for a 'new' theory of legal obligation, those presently established might be considered to represent a more than ample sufficiency. The requirement is rather for a schematic concordance based upon a sound analysis of the historical and current usages of the term 'obligation' in legal theory. Based upon such an approach a re-examination of the relevant theory may be hoped to resolve many of the apparent inconsistencies and antagonisms found in conventional presentations. It is suggested that the basic tripartite categorization here advanced is the foundation for such a concordance. It is not, of course, to be imagined that all disagreement in this area could be shown to be illusory, there is much scope for genuine and fruitful debate between differing perspectives. Such an approach may, however, be hoped to go some considerable way towards purging theory of the illusory differences which have, for the past century and a half, been a material bar to progress in the analysis of legal obligation.

Categorization of the various forms of obligation is for this purpose an important preliminary step but it is not in itself sufficient. It is also essential to develop a theoretical model of the relationship of the various forms of obligation when focused upon a given provision of positive law. The practical importance and complexity of these relationships has been examined from the particular viewpoint of a 'defence' of *respondeat superior* in relation to the laws of armed conflict.[14] Unfortunately the conventional analyses of these relationships have proved a most fertile source of misdirection and confusion. The recognition of a properly multipartite analysis of obligation, however, suggests a more satisfactory way forward.

The Non-Convergence of the Forms of Obligation

Much academic effort has been devoted to variously explicit and implicit searches for the jurisprudential equivalent of the alchemical 'philosophers' stone' in the shape of a 'definition of law'. These endeavours have led to definitions of aspects of law and its operation which, although satisfactory to varying degrees in their original contexts, have produced manifest distortions when sought to be endowed with wider or comprehensive significance. This is particularly evident in the case of the 'imperative' theories advanced by Bentham and Austin, but it is also much more widely the case. One of the foundational elements underlying this, arguably, very largely misdirected search for a comprehensive 'definition' of law would seem to have been a generally implicit belief in the essentially unitary nature of the obligatory characteristic of law, which is here strongly denied.

It is clear that all three of the categories of 'obligation' here advanced are in their various ways incidents of positive law, but also that the nature of their incidence varies as do the consequences of their respective strength or weakness in any given situation   Neither moral obligation nor coercive force are uniquely related to law, even though commonly associated with it. Formal obligation, in contrast, is the specific creation of a legal system.   Its presence is more evident where a condition of Hartian dynamism exists with an infrastructure vested with powers of enactment and formal interpretation, but it also exists in other types of legal order, including the purely customary.   The conclusion that the capacity to impose formal obligation is central to the identity of positive law seems to be inescapable. This centrality does not, however, mean that formal obligation is necessarily the pre-eminent, and still less the only, form of obligation associated with law.   It is an 'internal', in Hart's sense, assertion of the obligatory character of law, but any attempt to consider it in isolation leads to a model of legal autonomy which ignores the social, moral and political context in which it operates and which can be accepted only for the very limited purposes of 'professional' legal discourse.   Formal obligation exists in relation with other factors which can only be ignored at the peril of creating a circular argument in which law generates formal obligation and is therefore obligatory.   Subject to his rather unsatisfactory 'minimum content of natural law', H.L.A. Hart's analysis approaches dangerously close to such circularity.   The union of primary and secondary rules provides, making due allowance for a role to be played by Dworkinian 'standards', an account of the 'internal' generation of obligation within a legal system, but it provides little useful explanation of other highly significant factors bearing upon the obligatory character of law.

Formal obligation may be seen as an analogy with moral obligation which is adopted by a system which, necessarily, assumes its own 'rightness'. Moral obligation as such, however, covers a much wider range than formal obligation even though the two may be hoped ideally to coincide where the same subject is addressed.   The evident fallacy of any notion that provisions of positive law should be regarded as inherently 'good' was made plain by the classical positivists, even as it is so in the work of the mainstream naturalists when properly understood.   Positive law is nonetheless a structure of norms which, within the generating system, endows propositions with an obligatory character. From a moral-purposive viewpoint such propositions derive their normativity from concordance with a higher order, whether founded ultimately upon the Divine will or upon observation of the nature of human beings living as social creatures, not that these should necessarily be seen as either alternatives or in opposition one to the other.   This combination leads in the end to the complex moral-purposive analysis exemplified in the Thomist model of a complete law, which includes as a factor the normative value of social organization as such.   Moral obligation, therefore, is both the 'external' analogy for formal obligation and the extra-systemic base of the 'authority' of positive legal propositions which are purposively appropriate.

The role of coercive force requires little further comment.   It is distinguished both from formal and moral obligations by its factual nature, no process of evaluation is required for the determination of its existence. It cannot be regarded as a criterion for the existence of a 'legal' order, as is made clear in different ways through St. Augustine's pirate and H.L.A. Hart's bank robber.   Nonetheless, as Bentham correctly perceived, actual or potential coercive force is in most systems a common concomitant of 'law' and legal activity.

The Relationship of the Categories of Obligation to Obey Law

The relationship between the three broad categories of obligation may now be set out.   Essentially it is suggested that the three forms of obligation associated with law may be seen as three zones which partially overlap.   In the zone of total overlap there may be seen the Thomist complete law which carries both formal and moral obligation and is supported where necessary by coercive enforcement.   In lesser zones of overlap there may be provisions which are associated with two of the forms of obligation but not the third, for example a law which is formally valid and coercively enforced but immoral.   This model is most effectively presented in diagrammatic form as a group of interlocking circles in the following form.

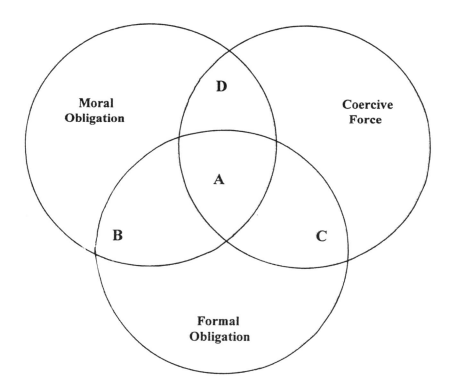

In this diagram, the central zone, marked 'A', is that of maximum interaction in which a norm satisfying formal criteria of identification is purposively appropriate and backed by the potential for coercive enforcement, thus being a focus for all three categories of 'obligation'. This is the ideal situation approximating to a Thomist complete law. The remaining zones represent norms which are to a greater or lesser degree defective in their obligatory character. Zone 'B' represents a norm imposing formal and moral obligations but which is either unenforceable or deliberately not enforced. An example of this might be found in antique legal provisions which criminalize conduct which continues to be seen as immoral but not of sufficient importance to merit institutional repression and which have therefore fallen into actual, but not technical, desuetude.

Zone 'C' comprises those provisions which satisfy formal criteria of identification and are supported by potential coercive enforcement but which are not concordant with moral obligation.   Such laws would include those which are strongly objectionable or abominable from a moral viewpoint, the classic 'bad' laws of naturalist theory.   They might also include particular 'immoral' applications of provisions which are otherwise unobjectionable. A case might be made out also for the inclusion of laws which are morally neutral or value-free.   However, such laws may be perceived to be supported by the Thomist consideration of social stability as a morally desirable end, in which case they would fall within zone 'A'.

Zone 'D' may appear to be somewhat anomalous in a modern western context, representing moral obligation backed by coercive force but not carrying formal obligation.   Examples may readily be found in the past, for example under the medieval doctrine of the Two Powers[15] under which the spiritual power might call upon the support of the secular power even in matters not necessarily having a positive 'legal' dimension.   Some more recent ideological systems might be cited but these, as in the former Soviet Union, must be considered doubtful upon a variety of grounds.   It should be added that the practice of Islamic states does not fall into this category in that where *Shari'at* law is strictly applied the 'western' division between 'moral' and 'legal' norms is not recognized since the law itself is taken as a moral and religious provision.   The situation described in zone 'D' might be argued to be seen in societies in which there is no formal 'legal' infrastructure, accepting for this purpose very dubious criteria of anthropological analysis, in which accepted norms of social conduct are supported by varieties of community pressure including, ultimately, ostracism or expulsion which might in practice actually be fatal.

Outside the zones of interaction the various forms of obligation appear to exist as 'naked' phenomena without contact with other categories.   In the instances of moral obligation and coercive force this presents no conceptual difficulty.   Both relate by their nature to a much wider field of action than that of positive law.   A 'naked' formal obligation may seem much more problematic, but this is not necessarily the case.   It has been argued above that formal and moral obligations are by no means necessarily coincident.   Coercive force is an institutional tool but it need not necessarily be used.   It may be in the light of this that many provisions, such as the Wills Act 1837, which may be considered essentially facilitative represent just such 'naked' formal obligations, at least in so far as they set up procedures, e.g., for the act of testamentation.   Such an analysis would avoid the distortions associated with the attempt by Austin to force such provisions into the mould of a sanctions-based 'command' theory.   In case it be objected that the idea of a facilitative provision imposing 'obligation' at all is itself distorting, it may be pointed out that such provisions are clearly not suggestive in their operation.   They represent, rather, voluntarily assumed 'obligations', e.g. by those undertaking testamentation, but which are nonetheless obligatory once so assumed.   It might also be argued that in the particular case of will-making there is a moral duty to endeavour to make fair and effective provision for the distribution of property upon death, but this must be considered a separate issue from the formalities of testamentation per se.

The diagram as it is presented upon page 211 is clearly over-simplified. The zones of interaction are not defined by neatly drawn boundaries but shade one into the next across 'fuzzy' borders marked by some degree of uncertainty.   One such area of uncertainty has been explored in some detail in the preceding chapters.   Between formal and moral obligations there exists a region of uncertainty in which a formal obligation is admitted to exist but which is finely balanced on the edge of moral turpitude.   The decision as to which of the zones it falls into will depend upon the levels of morality involved, the *prima facie* claims of social order as such and, possibly, the weight to be accorded to the proportion between the immorality invited and any coercive pressure which may be being applied. Equivalent regions exist between other zones.

If the interactive borders in the diagram set out on p.211 are thus treated as 'fuzzy' it may be seen that each of the zones, 'A', 'B', 'C' and 'D' will bounded by three regions of uncertainty.   These mark the borders in the case of the zone of perfect obligation, 'A', with each of the neighbouring zones of lesser interaction, 'B', 'C' and 'D' and represent areas in which the bordering form of obligation is in question.   In the case of the zones of lesser interaction, 'B', 'C', and 'D', the regions of uncertainty mark the boundaries with the zone of perfect obligation, 'A', and with those of the two 'naked' obligations whose interaction it represents.   The zones of 'naked' obligation, including that of coercive force, are in each case bounded by two regions of uncertainty, marking the boundaries with the zones of lesser interaction in which it combines with one of the other two categories.

An analysis in this form may be suggested to relieve the theoretical treatment of legal obligation of many of the infelicities with which it has come to be burdened. The point may be illustrated by the placement of some of the major theories within the scheme. Classical positivism falls into interactive zone 'C'. H.L.A. Hart's revised positivism falls primarily into the zone of 'naked' formal obligation, with some extensions into interactive zones 'B' and 'C'. Dworkin's argument largely addresses issues in the region of uncertainty between the zone of 'naked' formal obligation and interactive zone 'B'. There is, of course, a perfectly genuine disagreement between Hart's and Dworkin's approaches to the nature of positive legal norms, whether simply 'rule' or mixes of 'rules' and 'non-rules'. Mainstream naturalism in its various forms embraces the whole circle of moral obligation, including the interactive zones 'B' and 'D' and the zone of perfect obligation, 'A'. There are some areas for debate here, e.g. in relation to the work of Lon L. Fuller who may not be a 'naturalist' *stricto sensu* at all. His accurate placement might be closer to that of Hart but with more emphasis upon interactive zone 'B'. Classical Marxist legal theory lies almost wholly in the zone of 'naked' coercive force with, so far as 'law' after a 'proletarian' revolution is concerned, an extension into interactive zones 'B' and 'C'. American Realism is largely concerned with interactive zone 'C'. Scandinavian Realism, on the other hand, is concerned with the psychology relating to the zone of 'naked' formal obligation. The demythologizing endeavours of the Critical Legal Studies movement are similarly centred upon the zone of 'naked' formal obligation - with a view largely to its deconstruction.

It is suggested that this scheme of concordance provides the framework for a modern theory of legal obligation. This is not a 'new' substantive theory of obligation, nor is it being suggested that the doors are closed to new understandings or appreciations. It is, rather, intended to present a context in which existing and future theoretical insights can be considered as part of a framework which accepts the diversity of the factors which in combination make up the perceived obligatory characteristic of law. Using such a framework, the combination of factors leading to the 'perfectly obligatory' law, one carrying formal and moral obligation and having the potential for coercive enforcement in appropriate circumstances, can clearly be seen. This, of course, is the situation represented by zone 'A' in the diagrammatic representation.

The Importance of a Contextual Theory of Obligation

There remains to be made out the larger claim advanced in Chapter 1, that a modern theory of legal obligation provides a key to jurisprudence. In parallel with the linguistically and jurisprudentially inappropriate quest for some simple and singular explanation for the obligatory characteristic of law, there has been conducted the search for some simple and singular definition of 'law'. It may now be suggested that the complexity of the perceived obligatory characteristic of law mirrors the nature of the law itself. Upon this logic the search for any simple 'definition' of law is doomed to failure. The example of the 'command' theory formulation of the command of a sovereign backed by a sanction makes the point, although this choice is a little unfair granted that Bentham himself objected to this formula as misleading.[16] It has, however, become a part of jurisprudential discourse and adequately illustrates the dangers here in question. In his reworking of positivist theory H.L.A. Hart sought to define law as a combination of 'primary' and 'secondary' rules, which may have much to commend it in its particular context but is, again, far from adequate as a comprehensive 'definition'.

The search for a comprehensive 'definition' of law may be mistaken but it does not follow that it is unreasonable to seek a general theoretical understanding of the phenomenon of 'law'. The starting point for the present discussion was H.L.A. Hart's statement of the obligatory characteristic of positive law. The question of legal obligation has indeed been an issue not only of importance in itself, but one of central significance in the development of general legal theory. However it may be viewed, law comprises a body of norms intended in some degree to regulate the lives of human beings in a given society. This is not a useful definition because it begs far too many basic questions about the generation of law and its linkages with other elements of human life and social organization. The proper task of general legal theory may then be suggested to be the analysis of these linkages at all levels and not merely those that fall within some restrictively defined 'province of jurisprudence'.

As in the case of the obligation to obey law it is extremely unlikely that any single theory could take account of all the relevant factors.   The need, again in parallel with the theory of legal obligation, is not for new theories with inappropriate pretensions to comprehensiveness, but for acceptance of a framework of theories dealing with the broad factors contributing to the operation of 'law' as a moral, social, political and economic phenomenon.

Within any such framework of general legal theory, or rather theories, the obligatory character of law would clearly be an important issue, indeed, it could and should play a central role.   Positive law is inevitably normative, even when particular provisions perform an essentially facilitatory function, and it can hardly be controversial to suggest that this general obligatory characteristic goes to the root of the nature of law.   If this is indeed accepted, the multipartite nature of legal obligation may be suggested to provide a key to the understanding of the combination of factors that together shape the phenomenon of 'law'.   The study of law is not, of course, synonymous with the study of legal obligation.   To make such a claim would do no more that assert yet another blinkered and distorted perspective in an area already over-endowed with these.   It is instead contended that the combinations of obligations lie at the root of the operation of law and are central to its comprehension as a social and political phenomenon.   Traditional legal analysis inevitably centres upon the generation, application, interpretation and prediction of formal obligations and this in turn generates a technical mode of discourse which is largely limited to this principal focus of concern.   From the viewpoint of the professional lawyer such issues may appear to be not only the dominant but even the only proper focus of legal studies.   The claims to comprehensiveness of the positivist analyses rest upon precisely such foundations. A jurisprudence founded upon the viewpoint of Holmes' 'bad man', or, to put it less pejoratively, upon that of the lawyer and his or her client is, however, subject to severe limitations. To questions such as 'will I be held liable?' or 'Is this a valid contract?' a clear answer may in most cases be given within the parameters of professional legal discourse.   To treat such questions and the answers to them as the totality of the 'province of jurisprudence' would, however, be to adopt an extraordinarily myopic perspective which tends ultimately to the 'heresy' of legal autonomy. This has been attacked from a number of viewpoints, including those of classical Marxism and the Critical Legal Studies movement.   This is not a modern insight.   Any of the historic mainstream naturalists would have been astonished by any idea that law might be an autonomous phenomenon. The modern response is perhaps more a reaction to the relatively modern problem of a narrowly conceived and limiting form of legal discourse.

Even from a 'professional' viewpoint, a completely autonomous model of law is not maintainable upon closer examination. Law operates by its nature in a social context and professional advisers have to take account of such matters as assessment of loss or sentencing policy which are by no means simply defined by 'black letter' law in its narrow technical significance. Such marginal erosions of the model of legal autonomy may not in themselves be vastly significant, but they serve to emphasize that law as a social phenomenon cannot ultimately be understood in isolation. Law is generated as a formal and, in some respects, minimum expression of the basic normative perceptions of the society in which it operates. This is hardly a matter of theoretical speculation: observation of the legislative process sufficiently confirms the proposition. The observation of that process also confirms the great many factors that go into making the law and from which it cannot be distanced or 'autonomous'. This admission opens the gates of jurisprudence to the whole body of moral-purposive analysis as well as to the variety of other perspectives bearing upon the nature and operation of law. All of these, not only a limited choice amongst them, constitute the whole 'province of jurisprudence' although this does not mean that any given theory should or even could address the whole of that 'province'.

If the 'science' or art of jurisprudence comprises, as it surely must, the study of the whole phenomenon of law, one returns inevitably to the concept of the 'complete' law as a focus of jurisprudence. Bentham may be suggested to have been correct in his opinion that a 'complete law' consists not of individual provisions, but of the combination of provisions and decisions by reference to which a given question is decided.[17] This is certainly true from the viewpoint of Holmes' 'bad man' or, indeed, the more general figure of the 'lawyer's client'. From a wider perspective, perhaps that of the 'informed citizen', Bentham's 'complete law' becomes rather limited. A closer approach may be found, by reason of its wider remit of inquiry, in the Thomist identification of 'law' as simply *rationis ordinatio pro bonum commune ab eio qui curam communitatis habet, promulgata*,[18] a rational ordinance made for the good of the community by those who have the charge of it and promulgated. The combination of 'naturalist' and 'positivist' elements in this model has already been remarked upon above[19] and while this too leaves much open and cannot in itself be considered 'complete' it does draw attention to the range of factors involved more effectively than do most such formulations. A fully adequate statement of the linkages involved in the operation of law would be so voluminous as to have little practical or even theoretical value. The important point is not the seeking of brief formulae, but an understanding of the scope of the phenomenon which is being investigated and the place of each theoretical insight in the broader corpus of jurisprudence.

Law may thus, in conclusion, be seen as the institutional expression of social norms considered to be of basic importance in a given society in accordance with its broader spectrum of values, including the relation of such values and their expression to universal aspirations, potentially capable of enforcement against those who refuse in whole or part to accept the normative structure imposed. It is important to emphasise that this is in no way intended as a 'definition' but simply as a description of broad categories of elements associated with the phenomenon of 'law'. All of them to some degree relate to questions of obligation and whilst much of the detail of law may properly be analysed without reference to it, obligation and its attachment remains central to the legal enterprise. In this sense the understanding of the association of obligation(s) with law is a core element of jurisprudential study and, thus, a case may be made out that the development of a modern theory of legal obligation may also be the key to a modern treatment of general legal theory.

Notes

1 H.L.A. Hart, *The Concept of Law*, 2 ed., with Postscript by P.A. Bulloch and J. Raz (Clarendon, Oxford, 1994). p.82.
2 See Chapter 2.
3 See Chapter 3.
4 See Chapter 1.
5 See K.N. Llewellyn, 'The Normative, the Legal and the Law Jobs: The Problem of Juristic Method' (1939-40) *Yale Law Journal*, 1355.
6 See S. Roberts, *Order and Dispute* (Penguin, 1979), also M. Gluckman, *Politics, Law and Ritual in Tribal Society* (Blackwell, 1977).
7 H.L.A. Hart, op.cit., Ch.II.
8 See Chapter 3.

9   See Chapter 2.
10 See Chapter 7.
11 See Chapter 5.
12 See Chapter 2.
13 See in particular Chapters 2 and 3.
14 See Chapter 6.
15 See Chapter 3.
16 Ibid.
17 Ibid.
18 St. Thomas Aquinas, *Summa Theologica*, 1a2ae.90,4.
19 See Chapter 3.

Select Bibliography

Books

Aquinas, St. Thomas, *De Regimine Principum.*
  Summa Theologica (Dominican edn., Eyre and
  Spottiswoods, 1964, sub. nom. *Summa Theologiae*).
Atwooll, E. (ed.), *Perspectives in Jurisprudence* (University of Glasgow Press,
  1977).
Augustine of Hippo, St., *De Civitate Dei, De Libero Arbitrio.*
Austin, J., *The Province of Jurisprudence Determined* (1832; Weidenfeld and
  Nicholson, 1954).
Bentham, J., *A Fragment on Government* (Blackwell, 1967).
  An Introduction to the Principles of Morals and Legislation
  (Blackwell, 1967).
  Of Laws in General (Athlone, London, 1970).
  The Works of Jeremy Bentham (Athlone, London and
  Oxford/Clarendon, 1968 et seq.).
Berman, H.J., *Justice in the USSR*, 2 ed. (Harvard, 1988).
Beyleveld, D., and Brownsword, R., *Law as a Moral Judgment* (Sweet and
  Maxwell, 1986).
The Holy Bible.
Bigongiari, D., *The Political ideas of St. Thomas Aquinas* (Hafner Press, 1953).
Bodde, D. and Morris, C., *Law in Imperial China* (Harvard/Pennsylvania, 1973).
Brady, J.P., *Justice in People's China* (Harcourt Brace Jovanovich, 1982).
Butler, W.E., *Soviet Law*, 2 ed. (Butterworths, 1988).
Campbell, Lord, *Lives of the Lord Chancellors*, Vol. III (John Murray, London,
  1846).
Collins, H., *Marxism and Law* (Oxford, 1982).
Confucius, *The Analects*, trans. A.Waley (Unwin Hyman, 1988).
Contamine, P., *War in the Middle Ages*, trans., M. Jones (Blackwell, 1986).
Copleston, F.C., *Aquinas* (Penguin, 1955, 1982 edn.).
Cotterrell, R., *The Politics of Jurisprudence* (Butterworths, 1989).
Coulson, M.J., *Conflicts and Tensions in Islamic Jurisprudence* (University of
  Chicago Press, 1969).
D'Entreves, A.P., *Natural Law*, 2 ed. (Hutchinson, 1970).
Devlin, Lord, *The Enforcement of Morals* (Oxford, 1959).
Dias, R.W.M., *Jurisprudence*, 5 ed. (Butterworths, 1985).

Dinstein, Y., *The Defence of 'Superior Orders' in International Law* (A.W. Sijthoff, 1965).

Abdur Rahman I. Doi, *Shari'ah: The Islamic Law* (Ta Ha Publishers, 1984).

Dworkin, R., *A Matter of Principle* (Oxford, Clarendon, 1986).
Law's Empire (Fontana, 1986).
Taking Rights Seriously (Duckworth, 1977).

Finnis, J., *Natural Law and Natural Rights* (Oxford, Clarendon, 1980).

Fitzjames Stephen, J., *Liberty, Equality, Fraternity* (1872; Cambridge, 1967).

Fitzpatrick, P. and Hunt, A. (eds.), *Critical Legal Studies* (Butterworths, 1987).

Frank, J.M., *Courts on Trial* (Princeton, 1040).
Law and the Modern Mind (Stevens, 1949).

Freeman, M.D.A., *Lloyd's Introduction to Jurisprudence*, 6 ed. (Sweet and Maxwell, 1984).

Friedman, L., *The Laws of War: A Documentary History* (Random House, 1972).

Fuller, L.L., *The Morality of Law* (Yale, 1964).

Gluckman, M., *Politics, Law and Ritual in Tribal Society* (Blackwell, 1977).

Goodrich, P., *Legal Discourse* (Macmillan, 1987).

Hagerstrom, A., *Inquiries into the Nature of Law and Morals*, trans. Broad (Almqvist and Wiksell, 1953).

Haines, C.G., *The Revival of Natural Law Concepts* (Harvard, 1930; republished by Russell and Russell, 1965).

Harris, J.W., *Law and Legal Science* (Oxford, 1977).
Legal Philosophies (Butterworths, 1984 edn.).

Harrison, J., *Hume's Theory of Justice* (Oxford, 1981).

Hart, H.L.A., *Essays on Bentham* (Oxford, 1982).
Law, Liberty and Morality (Oxford, 1968).
The Concept of Law, 2 ed., with postscript ed. by P.A. Bulloch and J. Raz (Oxford, Clarendon, 1994).

Hobbes, T., *Leviathan* (1651; Penguin, 1977).

Hume, D., *A Treatise on Human Nature* (1740; Oxford, 1983).

Kant, I., *Groundwork of the Metyaphysic of Morals*, trans. Paton (Hutchinson, 1978 edn.).

Kenny, A., *Wittgenstein* (Pelican, 1975).

Kelsen, H., *General Theory of Law and State*, trans. Wedberg (Harvard, 1949).

Koch, H.W., *In the Name of the Volk: Political Justice in Hitler's Germany* (I.B. Tauris & Co., 1989).

Llewellyn, K.N., *The Common Law Tradition: Deciding Appeals* (Little, Brown and Co., 1960).

Llewellyn, K.N., and Hoebel. E.A., *The Cheyenne Way* (University of Oklahoma Press, 1941).

Locke, J., *Two Treatises of Government* (1690; Dent/Dutton edn., 1977).

Lundstedt, A.V., *Legal Thinking Revised* (Almqvist and Wiksell, 1956).

MacCormick, N., *H.L.A. Hart* (Edward Arnold, 1981).

MacCormick, N. and Weinberger, O., *An Institutional Theory of Law* (D. Reidel-Kluwer, 1986).

McCoubrey, H., *International Humanitarian Law* (Dartmouth, 1990).
  The Development of Naturalist Legal Theory (Croom-Helm, 1987).

McCoubrey, H. and White, N.D., *International Law and Armed Conflict* (Dartmouth, 1992).
  Textbook on Jurisprudence (Blackstone Press, 1993).

McNeill, J.T., *Calvin on God and Political Duty* (Bobbs-Merril, 1977).

Mill, J.S., *On Liberty* (1859; Pelican, 1974).

Moles, R.N., *Definition and Rule in Legal Theory* (Blackwell, 1987).

Morrison, W.L., *John Austin* (Edward Arnold, 1982).

O'Connor, D.J., *Aquinas and Natural Law* (Macmillan, 1967).

Olivecrona, K., *Law as Fact*, 2 ed. (Stevens, 1971).

Pashukanis, E.B., *Law and Marxism: A General Theory*, trans. B. Einhorn, ed. C. Arthur (Ink Links, 1978).

Petrazycki, L., *Law and Morality*, trans. H.W. Babb (Harvard, 1956).

Plato, *The Last Days of Socrates*, trans. H. Tredennick (Penguin, 1969).

Rawls, J., *A Theory of Justice* (Oxford, 1972).

Raz, J., *The Concept of a Legal System* (Oxford, 1970).

Renner, K., *Institutions of Private Law and their Social Functions*, trans. Schwarzchild (Routledge and Kegan Paul, 1949).

Roberts. A. and Guelff, R., *Documents on the Law of War*, 2 ed. (Oxford, 1989).

Roberts, S., *Order and Dispute: An Introduction to Legal Anthropology* (Penguin, 1979).

Ross, A., *Towards a Realistic Jurisprudence* (Einer Munksgaard, 1946).

Rousseau, J.J., *Du Contrat Social* (1762; Garnier-Flammarion edn., 1966).

Schwarzenberger, G., *International Law, Vol. II, Armed Conflict* (Stevens, 1968).

Sheppard, Rt. Revd. D., *Built as a City* (Hodder and Stoughton, 1985).

Shirer, W.L., *The Rise and Fall of the Third Reich* (Pan, 1964).

Simpson, A.W.B., ed., *Oxford Essays on Jurisprudence*, 2nd series (Oxford 1973).

Stone, J., *Human Law and Human Justice* (Stevens, 1965).

Summers, R.S., *Lon L. Fuller* (Edward Arnold, 1984).

Walzer, M., *Just and Unjust Wars* (Allen Lane, 1978).

Articles

Allen, R.E., 'Law and Justice in Plato's Crito' (1972) 69 *Journal of Philosophy*, 562.

Allen, T.R.S., 'A Right to Pornography ?' (1983) 3 *Oxford Journal of Legal Studies*, 376.

Blackett, J., 'Superior Orders - The Military Dilemma', February 1994 *Royal United Services Institute Journal*, 12.

Clarke, C.E. and Trubeck, D.M., 'Restraint and Freedom and the Common Law' (1961-2) 71 *Yale Law Journal* 255.

Davitt, T.E., 'Law as a Means to an End - Thomas Aquinas' (1960-61), 14 *Vanderbilt Law Review*, 65.

Del Vecchio, G., 'Divine Justice and Human Justice: Lecture to the XIIIth Course of Christian Studies at Assissi, 1 September 1955', trans. H. McN. Henderson (1956) *Juridical Review*, 147.

Dias, R.W.M., 'Temporal Approach towards a New Natural Law' (1970) 28 *Cambridge Law Journal*, 75.

Dworkin, R.M., 'Is there a Right to Pornography ?' (1981), 1 *Oxford Journal of Legal Studies*, 177.

Edgeworth, B., 'Legal Positivism and the Philosophy of Language: A Critique of H.L.A. Hart's "Descriptive Sociology"' (1986) 6 *Legal Studies*, 115.

Engels, F., 'The Condition of the Working Class in England' in *Marx and Engels, Collected Works* (Lawrence and Wishart, 1975).

Frank, J.M., 'Cardozo and the Upper Court Myth' (1948) 17 *Law and Contemporary Problems*, 169.

Fuller, L.L., 'Positivism and Fidelity to Law' (1958) 71 *Modern Law Review*, 630.

Goodrich, P., 'The Antimonies of Legal Theory: An Introductory Survey' (1983) 3 *Legal Studies*, 1.
'The Rise of Legal Formalism or the Defence of Legal Faith' (1983) 3 *Legal Studies*, 248.

Harris, P., 'The Moral Obligation to Obey the Law' in Harris, ed., *On Political Obligation* (Routledge, 1990).

Hill, R.E., 'Legal Validity and Legal Obligation' (1970) 80 *Yale Law Review*, 47.

Holmes, O.W., 'The Path of the Law' (1897) 10 *Harvard Law Review*, 457.

Hunt, A., 'The Theory of Critical Legal Studies' 6 *Oxford Journal of Legal Studies*, 1.

Kelsen, H., 'The Concept of the Legal Order' (1982) 27 *American Journal of Jurisprudence*, 64.

Klare, H., 'Law Making as Praxis' (1977) 40 *Telos*, 123.

Lewis, J.U., 'Blackstone's Definition of Law and Doctrine of Legal Obligation as a Link between Early Modern and Contemporary Theories of Law' (1968) *Irish Jurist*, 736.

Llewellyn, K.N., 'The Normative, the Legal and the Law Jobs: The Problem of Juristic Method' (1959-60) *Yale Law Journal*, 1355.

MacCormick, N., 'Law, Morality and Positivism' (1981) 1 *Legal Studies*, 131.

Nielsen, K., 'An Examination of the Thomistic Theory of Natural Law' (1959) 4 *Natural Law Forum*, 44.

Pappe, H.O., 'On the Validity of Judicial Decisions in the Nazi Era' 23 *Modern Law Review*, 260.

Parks, W.H., 'Command Responsibility for War Crimes' 62 *Military Law Review*, 1963.

Rawls, J., 'Justice as Fairness' (1958) LXVII *Philosophical Review*, 164.

Reaume, D., 'Is Integrity a Virtue? Dworkin's Theory of Legal Obligation' (1989) XXXIX *University of Toronto Law Journal*, 380.

Roberts, A., 'Obeying the Laws of War' *The Independent* (London), 29 April 1988.

Semple, J., 'No Slops for Bentham', *The Independent* (London), 7 May, 1990.

Simmonds, N., 'Practice and Validity' (1979) *Cambridge Law Journal*, 361.
'Rights, Socialism and Liberalism' (1985) 5 *Legal Studies*, 1.

Smith, M.B.E., 'Is there a *Prima Facie* Obligation to Obey the Law?' (1973) 82 *Yale Law Journal*, 950.

Stone J., 'Theories of Law and Justice in Fascist Italy' (1937-8) 1 *Modern Law Review*, 177.

Tur, R.H.S., 'What is Jurisprudence?' (1978) *Philosophical Quarterly*, 149.

Unger, R., 'The Critical Legal Studies Movement' 96 *Harvard Law Review*, 563.

Wade, F.C., 'In Defence of Socrates' (1971) 25 *Review of Metaphysics*, 311.

Waluchow, W.I., 'Herculean Positivism' (1985) 5 *Oxford Journal of Legal Studies*, 187.

Index

Alexander II, Tsar 133
Alexander III, Tsar 133
Allan, T.R.S. 106
American Civil War 163
American Realism 28, 40, 150-1
Anastasius 78
Aquinas, St. Thomas 6, 53, 55-
    6, 83, 118, 139, 147, 175-6,
    196, 206, 217
    Bad Government and 78-80
    Theory of 71-9
    Tyrannical Law, upon 75-8
Aristotle 53, 157, 206
Augustine of Hippo, St. 4, 51,
    55, 68-70, 97, 100, 139, 175-
    76, 193, 203-4, 206
Austin, J. 3, 18, 27, 30, 32, 69,
    84, 130, 143, 164-5, 172, 203

Bartlett, K.T. 155
Beilis case 133
Bentham, J. 3, 15 ff., 52, 63-4,
    66, 84, 130, 140, 164, 165,
    203, 215
Berman, H.J. 136
Beyleveld, D. 54, 83-5
Bigongiari, D. 73
Blackett, J. 173
Bolshevik 1817 Revolution 133
British Manual of Military Law
    170
Brownsword, R. 54, 83-5
Butler, W.E. 136

Calley, W.L., Court Martial of
    110, 170-1

Calvin, J. 79
Charles I, King, trial and
    execution of 163-5
Charles II, King, 163-4
Charles the Bold, Duke of
    Burgundy 166
Chechnya 177
Cheyenne, Law of 38
Chin Dynasty, See Legalism
China
    Legal Theory in 60, 137-9
Chudleigh, L. 154
Cicero 204
Collins, H. 132, 136, 141
Command Theory 15-25
Conaghan, J. 154
Confucius 60, 137
Contamine, P. 176
Contextual Theory, obligation
    and 215-18
Critical Legal Studies 8, 151-7
Crito, See Socrates
Cromwell, R. 165
Cultural Revolution (China) 139

Davitt, T.E. 75, 77
D'Entreves, A.P. 79
Dias, R.W.M 120, 165
Domitian 77
Donoghue v *Stevenson* 196
Dover Castle case 168
Dworkin, R.M. 51, 81, 122, 163,
    195-6
    Pornography, debate on 105
    Rights theory of 99-115
    Vietnam, debate on 107-11

Edgeworth, B. 40
Engels, F. 132

Falklands Conflict (1982) 174-5
Fascism 93
Felicific Calculus 26
Feminist Legal Theory 154-6
    See Critical Legal Studies
Finnis, J. 10, 57, 68, 84, 118,
    206
    Theory of 80-83
Fitzjames-Stephen, J. 105
Frank, J. 150
French Military Law 172-3
Friesler, R. 187
Fuller, Lon L. 10, 122, 197-8
    Grudge Informer cases,
        views upon 194-5
    Theory of 94-9

Gang of Four trial 138
Gelasius I, Pope 78
Geneva Conventions (1949) 175,
    198
Gluckman, M. 38
Gorbachev era 136, 184-5
Gregory the Great, St. 74
Griswold, E. 108
Grudge Informer cases 97,
    189-91
    Hart/Fuller debate 194-5

Hacker, P.M.S. 23
Hagenbach, P. von, trial of 166-7
Hagerstrom, A. 142-3, 144
Hague Conventions (1899 and 1907)
    198
Hale, Sir Matthew 165
Hammurabi, Code of 58-9

Harris, J.W. 2, 122-3
    Theory of 120-1
Harris, P. 2
Harrison, J. 3, 17
Hart, H.L.A. 1-2, 5, 21-3, 28, 30,
    70, 93, 97, 99, 104, 106, 116,
    135, 146, 151, 163, 172, 188,
    197, 201, 203-5, 207, 209, 210,
    215
    Authority and 35-6
    Forms of Obligation and 34
    Fuller, Lon L. and 96, 194-5
    Grudge Informer cases, views
        upon 194-5
    Legal Anthropology 38-9
    Officials, role of 39-41
    Rule of Recognition 36-7
    Theory of 33-44
    Validity, view of 41-2
High Command case 169
Hill, R.E. 184, 195
Himmler, H. 187
Hitler, A. 93, 177
Hobbes, T. 66
Holmes, O.W. 9, 82
Hume, D. 7, 17, 52
Hunt, A. 152-4

Isidore of Seville, St. 74

Jaluit Atoll case 173
Jewish Law 59-60
Johannes Teutonicus 175
Johnson, President L.B. 109
Judicial Review of Legislation
    29-30
July Plot 177

Kant, I. 81, 102-3, 106-7
Kelsen, H. 149, 171, 206

Kerensky, A. 133
Knox, J. 79

Laconia Order 169
Legalism, in China 60, 137
Leidmann v *Reisenthal* 191-2,
    194
Lenin, V.I. 133
Llandovery Castle case 168
Llewellyn, K.N. 38, 150, 203
Locke, J. 66-7
Louis XIV, King 28
Lundstedt, V. 146-8

MacCormick, N. 43, 45, 121
    Theory of 115-19
    See also Weinberger, O.
Madzimbamuto v *Lardner-Burke*
    165
Mao Xse Dong 137
Marx, K. 132
Marxism 8, 152
    Dialectic 131-2
    Legal Theory in 131-41
Marxism-Leninism 93, 133-7
Mary II, Queen 140
Mary, Queen of Scots 79
Mencius 60
Menshevik 1917 Revolution 133
Mill, J.S. 105-6
Monk, General 165
Mussolini, B. 93, 185

Naturalism 50-86
    Methodology and 52-5
Nazism 93, 185, 197
Nicholas II, Tsar 133
Niemoller, Pastor 187
Nothmann v *Cooper* 192
Nuremberg Tribunal 170-1

Olivecrona, K. 115, 144-5,
    148
Oppenheimer v *Cattermole*
    192-4, 197

Pashukanis, E.B. 134-5,
    139-40
Peleus case 169, 174
Pentateuch 59
Petrazycki, L. 143-4, 148
Plato 61-6, 108, 114, 161, 177
Political Courts
    in Third Reich 186-7
Positivism 15-48, 184
Post-Positivism 92-124
Potestas Coactiva 4, 136-7

Rawls, J. 57, 102
Raymond of Penaforte, St. 175
Raz, J. 28
Reaume, D. 111-2
Riggs v *State* 167
Roberts, S. 38
Ross, A. 145-6, 147
Rousseau, J-J 67-8

Sanctions, See Command Theory
Scandinavian Realism 9, 115,
    142-50
Sceptical Analyses 129-160
Shar'ia 59
Sheppard, Rt. Revd. D. 123
Shirer, W.L. 187
Smith, R v 167
Smith, H.A. 162
Social Contractarianism
    Later forms of 66-8, 206
Socrates, Plato's view of 61-6
Speer, A. 177
Spycatcher case 111

Stalin, J. 66, 93, 135-6
Stauffenberg, Count von 177
Stoicism 68
Stuchka, P.I. 134
Summers, R.S. 95
Superior Orders and Obligation 161-83

Tarquinius Superbus 77
Third Reich 9, 65, 95, 96-7, 177, 185-8, 198
See also Political Courts
Thomas, R v 167
Thomism, See Aquinas
Trendtex v *Central Bank of Nigeria* 193
Two Powers, Doctrine of 78-9

Unger, R. 153
USSR 66, 93
Law in 133-7, 139
Utility, Principle of 25

Validity, Obligation and 184-9
Vane, Sir Harry 164
Vecchio, G. Del. 74
Vietnam War 107-11
Vyshinski, A. Ia 135-6

Weimar Republic 186, 188
Weinberger, O. 121
Theory of 115-9
See also MacCormick, N.
Weisstub, D.N. 56
Wilhelm II, Kaiser 168
William III, King 140
Wittgenstein, L. 11, 24, 152
Woozley, A.D. 61, 63

Zasulich case 133
Zones of Obligation, proposed 210-14
Zyklon B case 173, 210-14